KT-147-636

Until Choice Do Us Part

KA 0384112 X

UNIVERSITY OF WINCHESTER
LIBRARY

Until Choice Do Us Part

Marriage Reform in the Progressive Era

CLARE VIRGINIA EBY

The University of Chicago Press

CHICAGO AND LONDON

CLARE VIRGINIA EBY is professor of English at the University of Connecticut. She is the author of *Dreiser and Veblen, Saboteurs of the Status Quo* and an editor of *The Cambridge History of the American Novel*.

The University of Chicago Press, Chicago 60637
The University of Chicago Press, Ltd., London
© 2014 by The University of Chicago
All rights reserved. Published 2014.
Printed in the United States of America

23 22 21 20 19 18 17 16 15 14   1 2 3 4 5

ISBN-13: 978-0-226-08566-1 (cloth)
ISBN-13: 978-0-226-08583-8 (paper)
ISBN-13: 978-0-226-08597-5 (e-book)
DOI: 10.7208/chicago/9780226085975.001.0001 (e-book)

Library of Congress Cataloging-in-Publication Data

Eby, Clare Virginia, author.
    Until choice do us part : marriage reform in the Progressive era /
Clare Virginia Eby.
        pages cm
    Includes bibliographical references and index.
    ISBN 978-0-226-08566-1 (cloth : alkaline paper) — ISBN 978-0-226-08583-8
(paperback : alkaline paper) — ISBN 978-0-226-08597-5 (e-book)   1. Marriage—
History.   2. Progressivism in literature.   I. Title.
    HQ518.E19 2014
    306.8109—dc23
                                                                      2013019831

♾ This paper meets the requirements of ANSI/NISO Z39.48-1992
(Permanence of Paper).

UNIVERSITY OF WINCHESTER

For John

Contents

Illustrations

Preface

For centuries, people have been thinking, dreaming, writing—and also fighting—about marriage. But in the Progressive era, the conversation took a distinct turn. A new ideal was taking shape which was changing what people expected, as well as what they would endure, from marriage. As an enthusiast summed up in 1909, "the basis of modern marriage . . . is shifting from necessity to free choice, from the formal to the ethical, from a relation preserved by external pressure to one maintained by internal attraction."[1]

Snapshots of three marriages provide indications of how ideal could collide with reality.

Feminist writer Charlotte Perkins Gilman's marital misery is legendary. In her short story "The Yellow Wallpaper" (1892), the unnamed female narrator struggles against her husband (who, as a super-patriarch, is also her doctor) and the rest cure which he, with all good intentions, has prescribed. Locked in an ominous room with a nailed-down bed, systematically infantilized, and forbidden to write or exercise her mind, the narrator fixates on the wallpaper. She believes she discovers a female figure creeping beneath it, a figure with which she comes to identify powerfully. The story concludes with the narrator's apparent descent into madness as her identity blurs with that of the woman in the wallpaper. But the ending makes it difficult to be certain if the narrator has lost her mind: when the doctor-husband finds his wife, *he* faints like a frail Victorian wife while she crawls over him, declaring she is free at last. Moreover, Gilman's use of a first person narrator—who, in the very act of writing, defies her doctor-husband's orders—suggests some degree of autonomy. The ending thus implies at least a moment's respite from the husband's tyrannical benevolence.

The autobiographical roots of "The Yellow Wallpaper" are almost as well known as the plot. Several years before publishing the story and within the first year of her marriage to painter Charles Walter Stetson, Gilman gave birth to a daughter. Her postpartum depression seemed to confirm something she had warned Stetson about during their courtship: "Much as I love you I love WORK better, & I cannot make the two compatible." They called upon famous nerve specialist S. Weir Mitchell, who mistook Gilman's illness for her cure. Diagnosing her with neurasthenia (nerve prostration), Mitchell prescribed total bed rest and overfeeding, particularly with cream. After she finished the rest cure, he cautioned, "Live as domestic a life as possible. . . . And never touch pen, brush or pencil as long as you live." Gilman, however, dropped her husband and took up her pen. She later explained that the period she lived as Mrs. Stetson had left her "perilously near to losing [her] mind." Boiled spinach, was how she later described her mental state as a young wife and mother.[2]

"The Yellow Wallpaper" has become a landmark feminist text, taught in high schools and colleges all over the country. But an important fact tends to get neglected in its transmission. Gilman was not opposed to marriage per se—only a particular (albeit common) type of it that, for the sake of simplicity, we can call traditional and proprietary. Nor did Gilman think she had landed a bad husband. Years later she declared of Stetson, in fact, "A lover more tender, a husband more devoted, woman could not ask."[3]

In addition to her famous story, Gilman wrote considerable nonfiction that, while criticizing proprietary marriage, also rhapsodizes that there could be no greater happiness than the *right* marriage, one between, in her fine phrase, "class equals."[4] Such a union would allow women the productive work they need to be happy, Gilman believed, while the economic independence of wives would make marriage an affair of the heart, not the wallet. Putting theory into practice, Gilman herself remarried, and the second time was better able to combine work and love. Her outspoken critique of marriage, combined with equal dedication to preserving and reforming the institution, in both theory and practice, exemplifies what this book describes as progressive marital reform.

Around 1900, Elsie Clews Parsons became the first woman to swim in Newport without stockings on. Such alarming behavior for a respectable, newly married woman! The iconoclastic Parsons went on to pioneer in more substantial arenas: she taught sociology at Barnard through two pregnancies and was the first woman elected president of the American Anthropological Association. She certainly did not inherit such trailblazing from her mother, a consummate socialite who annually, it was said, would budget "$10,000 for mistakes in clothes." Lucy Worthington Clews could afford such costly sartorial errors because her husband was a stunningly successful financier. Henry Clews also wrote books, and his *Fifty Years in Wall Street* (1908) remains an important source for shady transactions of old as well as the personalities of the robber barons who engaged in them. The Clews marriage followed the traditional pattern that Gilman excoriated, and which Thorstein Veblen satirized as the gendered spectacle that he called "conspicuous consumption": Henry Clews brought in the money and Lucy Clews spent it. Perhaps Elsie Clews Parsons was thinking of her own parents when she wrote that upon marriage, a woman became isolated, "forced either into idleness or into fictitious jobs by the pride of her family or by the nature of our economic organization. . . . Her wedding ring is a token of inadequacy as well as of 'respectability.'"[5]

Determined not to follow in her mother's footsteps, Elsie Clews grew up with no intention of ever marrying. But then she fell in love with an up-and-coming attorney and politician. Before accepting Herbert Parsons's proposal, she told him, "I would like to be married for a while just to show people how." The wording is fascinating. "For a while" suggests Elsie's belief that a relationship need not last forever and "to show people how" that she was already thinking like a teacher, with marriage as her lesson plan. Six years after their meeting—and only after completing her doctoral dissertation—Elsie Clews married Herbert Parsons in September 1900, the same month her first article appeared in print. According to biographer Desley Deacon, with Elsie Clews's marriage, she "was consciously embarking on an experimental life." Six years later, Parsons would famously make this experimental idea a centerpiece in her textbook *The Family*, in which she advocated "trial marriage."[6] Most people found that idea even more outrageous than when she had shown her legs on the Newport beach.

Like most experiments, the Parsons's own marriage required various adjustments. Herbert Parsons was baffled by what he considered his wife's "new ways" (she later joined the radical feminist group Heterodoxy), while she termed his love of domestic routine a comfortable but stultifying "emotional easy chair." She read with excitement books by sexologist Havelock Ellis and others promoting freer ideas of marriage and sexuality. The greatest crisis in the Parsons marriage occurred around 1909, when Herbert fell in love with the wife of a colleague in the State Department.

FIGURE 1. Elsie Clews Parsons in bathing suit—this time, with stockings on. Courtesy of Elsie Clews Parsons Papers, American Philosophical Society.

He and Lucy Wilson were open about their friendship, and it probably was never consummated, but Parsons was jealous—and angry with herself for her jealousy, because she opposed on principle the idea of marriage constituting what she called a "monopoly" on another human being. Knowing that Herbert got from Lucy Wilson the sort of easy-chair companionship that he would never get from her, Parsons encouraged the relationship, even while venting her feelings in a remarkable unpublished fictionalization, "The Imaginary Mistress." She also had her own affairs, including with University of Chicago English professor Robert Herrick, who later fictionalized Parsons in novels such as *Wanderings* (1925) and *The End of Desire* (1932). But Elsie and Herbert Parsons never divorced, and it wasn't for lack of backbone. While it is impossible ever to know the myriad of reasons why one couple stays together and another parts, a letter that she wrote her husband at the height of her jealousy speaks volumes: "Our relation is still the chief thing in the world."[7] The experiment was not perfect, but it lasted until Herbert died in 1925.

"Oh, if only I were free—free—free!" Edith Wharton wrote her lover in 1911, "Isn't it awful to have a chain snaffled around one's neck for all time." Wharton was nearing fifty and having an affair with Morton Fullerton, a younger, charming, and bisexual journalist and author. The "Love Diary" Wharton left about their affair establishes that she understood from the start it would never last. But it intoxicated Wharton while it was going on. "This must be what happy women feel," reads one of the most heartrending entries in her diary.[8] Fullerton proved something of a cad; he became engaged to his first cousin, who was also his stepsister, right before launching the affair with Wharton. But he also provided Wharton with an intimacy spiritual, intellectual, and sexual.[9] That intimacy could not contrast more sharply with the "chain" she refers to in her letter: her husband, Teddy, to whom Wharton had been yoked for over two decades when she met Fullerton.

Edith Newbold Jones was twenty-three when she married in 1885, dangerously old for a woman who had come out at eighteen. Her parents were pleased with the match, and Teddy Wharton should have been a good catch: Harvard educated, he was said to have been the best-looking man in the class of 1873. But the marriage was such a catastrophe that Wharton's dear friend Henry James could only call it that "inconceivable thing." While the Whartons were incompatible in many ways, it is particularly clear that their sex life was, as a biographer puts it, "a disaster." Wharton later explained one reason why. Several days before the wedding, the bride-to-be approached her mother, admitted her apprehensions, and inquired what to expect on her wedding night. The imperious Lucretia Jones had only this to say: "You've seen enough pictures and statues in your life. Haven't you noticed that men are . . . made differently from women?" Yes, the daughter replied, but what was she to make of that difference? Lucretia abruptly ended the conversation; she would have no more "silly questions. You can't be as stupid as you pretend," she declared. Recent biographers and critics have tended to agree—a well-read twenty-three year-old couldn't have been *that* stupid—and emphasized that this tale sounds as carefully crafted as any of Wharton's fictions. The shape of the anecdote supports Wharton's consistent portrayal of her mother as superficial and distant. It also suggests a pervasive conspiracy of silence surrounding sexuality. According to Wharton, in fact, her mother's refusal to talk about sex "did more to falsify and misdirect my whole life" than anything else.[10] While historians have dismantled the old straw man of Victorians as uniformly sexually repressed, Wharton's portrayal of her mother's belligerent silence—and perhaps her crafting of the tale of her woe for consumption by others—suggests that the sexual problem she had with Teddy was more than an instance of individual compatibility.

Other highlights of the Wharton marriage form a tale too vulgar to be found in her novels. While to the manner born and raised, Teddy (thirty-three and still residing with mum when Wharton met him) was content to live on an allowance from his parents. Until he started living on his wife, that is. Teddy had, according to his wife's biographer R. W. B. Lewis, "no vocation, nor any intention of seeking one." In 1888, three years after they wed, Edith inherited a substantial legacy which Teddy, as her husband, managed (along with her brothers). Once Wharton's writing career took off, she earned substantial amounts by her pen. *The House of Mirth* (1905), for instance, a novel about a beautiful young society woman who refuses marriage as her "vocation," was Charles Scribner's fastest selling book to date. Wharton felt that her husband's interest in her literary career was "purely mercantile." Even if he liked her money, Teddy was rotten at managing it. In 1909 he confessed to having speculated with $50,000 of her funds, losing much of it and using the rest to set up a mistress in a Boston apartment. Teddy also suffered from severe mental problems—an "affliction of the brain," according to his doctor, though today he would probably be diagnosed as bipolar. As one of Wharton's friends described her marital nightmare, she was "tied to a crazy person, who is only just sane enough not to be locked up, but too crazy to be out." No wonder that, in the words of biographer Hermione Lee, "marital bondage" would become one of Wharton's key literary themes.[11]

In April 1913, after twenty-eight years of marriage, Wharton finally cut the tie. In order to avoid publicity, she chose Paris as the venue for her divorce. In January of the same year, *Scribner's Magazine* began serializing her brilliant divorce novel, *The Custom of the Country* (1913). Wharton's protagonist, Undine Spragg, goes through husbands almost as quickly as the latest fashions. Undine is shallow and often repellent—but if we hold our noses as if she is some stinking aberration, we miss the novel's trenchant social criticism. For Undine Spragg, we learn in a crucial scene, is "a monstrously perfect result of the system." That "system" is marriage, American style—making the protagonist's initials, U. S., a wonderful touch. The "custom of the country," it turns out, is that American husbands look down on their wives, and for that very reason throw money at them. The real "passion" of these husbands is making money, and they "bribe" their wives so they can indulge that love. Unlike Undine, Wharton did not remarry, nor is there evidence of another romance after Fullerton. Instead she surrounded herself with a circle of male friends from whom she made, in the words of literary critic Gloria C. Ehrlich, a "composite husband."[12]

Gilman, Parsons, and Wharton are very different writers who would find much to disagree about. Were I to chart their gender politics, Parsons would occupy the position furthest to the left, with Gilman at the center, while Wharton held views that, given her experiences, could be surprisingly conservative. Yet taken together, these snapshots demonstrate how fundamentally attitudes toward marriage were changing during the Progressive era, sometimes even independent of a person's express politics. Increasingly, one could choose to leave a spouse—or imagine alternatives to *coverture*, the doctrine which dictated that wives' legal identities be "covered over" by their husbands'. The Progressive era witnessed, accordingly, an outpouring of writings about marriage—government reports, sociological studies, tracts, novels, legal decisions, plays, memoirs, and reams upon reams of journalism. Writers in different media were all trying to figure out exactly why marriage was changing, and what those changes signified for women, men, children, and indeed, for society at large.

Until Choice Do Us Part argues that in order to understand the Progressive era, we must examine this contested conversation about marriage. I focus specifically on the era's concerted and sustained effort to reform marital norms. Best-selling social scientific and tract writers from both sides of the Atlantic articulated a new ideal. These writers did not speak in a single voice, but a consistent message emerged from Parsons, Gilman, Ellis, Veblen, and also South African-born New Woman Olive Schreiner, popular lecturer (and wife of Havelock) Edith Ellis, Swedish feminist Ellen Key, mystic socialist Edward Carpenter, and the first US author of a history of marriage, George Elliott Howard. They were the primary intellectual architects of what I call the progressive marital ideal; I refer to them collectively as the marriage reformers, the marital theorists, and the experts. Not all of their writings were "progressive" in the layperson's sense of the term, to be sure, and in the next chapter I examine the loaded word *progressive* as the descriptor of a historical era.

The experts' reform message goes like this: the economic basis of traditional marriage distorts relationships that would be healthier and happier between financially independent partners who chose to work—as well as to remain together. Mutual affection, not the sanction of a priest or justice of the peace, defined and justified true marriage. Reforming the law to make divorce a matter of mutual consent—rather than defining it through narrowly written statute—would elevate marriage, not erode civilization, as scaremongers warned. Once marriage and divorce became truly free, the experts maintained, voluntary monogamy would replace compulsory monogamy, further improving the institution. And finally, the experts affirmed female sexuality. Casting themselves as crusaders against a Victorian conspiracy of silence, the marriage reformers insisted that mutually satisfying sex cemented and indeed validated marriage. If most of these ideals now sound commonsensical (at least when stripped of the utopian glow), then that is a measure of how influential and enduring the reformers' message proved to be.

But these tenets of Progressive era marital reform do not alone differentiate the message from efforts to rethink marriage in other periods. The experts also boldly proclaimed that reforming marriage would be instrumental in advancing society more broadly. That is because they believed (as Havelock Ellis puts it) that marriage comprised "the figure in miniature" of social life. One of Gilman's books captures the logic of this surprising notion: "The progress of the mind," she argues in *The Home: Its Work and Influence* (1903), "requires a commensurate progress of the home," which she defines as "a human institution," and as such, subject to change. Gilman objects to the traditional marital model which allows husbands to be "progressive"—a key word—as they interact meaningfully with the world while keeping wives "stationary" in their isolation. She cites the folly of isolating one half of humanity from the progress that, she maintained, occurred only outside of the home.[13] Achieving this "commensurate progress of the home" required, Gilman maintained, reforming marriage so that wives could become public workers and thus socially productive citizens. She believed this domestic transformation would, in turn, advance human progress.

But looking at all the reform theories in the world will tell us only so much about the past. We must also seek out concrete lived experience. Many of the reformers used their own personal relationships as laboratories for testing theoretical premises. And so did many of their readers, as this book will show. I will trace differences of emphasis, even disagreement, in the writings of the experts, and even sharper disagreements in the experiences of some famous couples who read their work and wrote additional accounts of marriage. Disagreements occur because the translation from theory to practice is always tricky, of course, and also because two spouses never experience their marriage identically. A husband delighted with his home life may be shocked to find his wife packing her bags one day. To the extent that surviving documents permit, I juxtapose ideals with lived experience, and also juxtapose husbands' and wives' accounts of marriage—in theory, and also in practice.[14]

The relation of theory to practice is important also because Progressive era marriage reform was a very bookish enterprise. We find a repeated compulsion to textualize marriage—not only in treatises but also in creative writing: thus Gilman's "The Yellow Wallpaper," Parsons's "The Imaginary Mistress," and Wharton's long stretch of novels about marital entrapment.

In order to capture both the lived experience and this bookish quality of Progressive era marital reform, *Until Choice Do Us Part* examines the lives and writings of three literary couples. Upton and Meta Fuller Sinclair engaged in a kind of literary competition for the title of most progressive spouse, and their 1911 breakup led to a feeding frenzy among journalists. Theodore Dreiser told two different stories about his marriage to Sara White Dreiser in two versions of *The "Genius,"* the autobiographical novel that he considered titling "This Matter of Marriage, Now." And the literary partnership/competition/collaboration of playwright and novelist Neith Boyce with journalist and author Hutchins Hapgood shows how their progressive marriage, precisely because it was a source of conflict, fueled the creativity of both partners.

Despite decades of feminist recovery work, the archives do not represent women equally with men. The husbands of my three couples were well-known—Sinclair and Dreiser were even celebrities—and left extensive, indeed staggering, archives. The wives' presence in the public sphere corresponded to their independent renown as writers, and so their archives range from meager to substantial. While Theodore Dreiser signed some of his early journalism with his wife's initials, Sara White Dreiser never published anything. Her literary role was that of the traditional helpmeet and editor as well as serving as her husband's muse—and, in the case of *The "Genius,"* his subject and at times, his target. Meta Fuller Sinclair wrote poetry, little of it published, left an unfinished novel, was interviewed by the press after she left her husband, and published a revealing article about her marriage. Before Neith Boyce met her future husband, she was already a professional journalist who went on to establish a national reputation as a writer of fiction and drama. Her archive is not surprisingly the most substantial by far.

But silences can be revealing. The legal term *coverture* offers a suggestive parallel. The surviving documents speak to a sort of literary or archival coverture, operating most strongly in the case of the Dreisers, less so for the Sinclairs, and scarcely for Boyce and Hapgood. That disparity is unfortunate but allows me to tell different kinds of stories.[15]

Let us move to them now.

Acknowledgments

The subject of this book has shape-shifted a startling number of times over many years as I completed other projects, putting me in the debt of numerous people and institutions along the way. Some of them will not recognize the form this book has finally taken and none, of course, are responsible for its limitations, but all left their marks on *Until Choice Do Us Part*.

For permission to quote from unpublished Theodore Dreiser papers and to reproduce a photograph of the Dreisers, I thank Nancy Shawcross, Curator of Manuscripts for the Trustees of the University of Pennsylvania (and also for her lightning-fast permissions and assistance). The Lilly Library has allowed me to use the Upton Sinclair Papers, the Stone Manuscripts, and the papers of Theodore Dreiser, and to quote from the papers of Arthur F. Bentley. I am grateful to Cherry Williams, Curator of Manuscripts, and her staff at the Lilly for considerable help both during my visits to Indiana and in fielding requests from a thousand miles away. Closer to home, the staff at the Beinecke Library provided one of the best research environments I have ever enjoyed. I thank the Beinecke and Fred Hapgood for permission to quote from the Hapgood Family Papers and to reproduce photographs of Hutchins Hapgood and Neith Boyce. At the University of Connecticut, the interlibrary loan team literally makes my ongoing research possible.

I am grateful to those who have offered advice and wisdom on, and at times resistance to, this book. Early on, anonymous readers for the National Endowment for the Humanities and American Philosophical Society offered sage counsel. The interest and support of my colleague Dick Brown was key when the book began to assume its final shape, while Bob Gross and Patrick Hogan offered extremely useful suggestions for incorporating, respectively, book history and emotion research as I completed it. Receiving a University of Connecticut Humanities Institute Fellowship right as I was pulling together the first draft was the scholar's version of a windfall. In addition to providing time—the greatest gift possible for a writer—the UCHI also provided exemplary fellowship. I will never forget that wonderful year of conversation, support, and pushback from the other fellows: Janet Pritchard, Glen Macleod, Glenn Stanley, Sherry Isaacson, Jennifer Holley, Naem Murr, and especially Jen Terni, nor the exemplary leadership of Sherry Harris. I am grateful for graduate students Kim Armstrong, Jared Demick, Todd Barry, and Jena Rascoe, who cheerfully discussed arcane texts about Progressive era marital reform with me that year. Richard Wall and an American Studies reading group (Anna Mae Duane, Larry Goodheart, Matt McKenzie) offered great feedback on the Dreiser chapter. So did the consummate Dreiser scholar Tom Riggio, who vigorously disagrees with my conclusions. Nina Dayton's suggestions on the Introduction and other matters have been completely on point. With his typical low-key brilliance, Ben Reiss helped me articulate the stakes of my project and solve a structural problem. Two anonymous readers for the University of Chicago Press offered stunningly useful and detailed suggestions. So did Lenny Cassuto, who has once again proven himself a world-class friend, editor, and critic, reading the entire manuscript, parts of it more than once. Lenny's *always* being right would be insufferable were he not such a generous soul.

Working with fellow five-tenner Robert Devens at the University of Chicago Press has been, well, a writer's dream come true. His intellectual engagement with the manuscript was what every author hopes to find in an editor, and his advice and support always kept me on track. Before Robert's departure from the press, Russell Damian answered countless questions; after it, Russ has ably steered the book through production.

In varying degrees of intimacy, my family has lived with this shape-shifting monster as long as I have. My mother, Patsy Aldridge, always provides incredible support, encouragement, and interest in my career and everything else. I inherited a great deal from my father, Cecil Eby—in addition to long legs, evidently also a penchant for writing outside of my "field." I am increasingly awestruck by the professional accomplishments of my "baby" sister, Lillian Eby, and thrilled we have become such good friends. My stepdaughter, Georgia Lo Presti Meckes, understands me as few people do and I am so lucky to have her in my life. Two of the smartest girls I know, my niece, Turner Pascoe, and standard poodle, Portia, rate as two of the three great loves of my life. As to that third love: a grad-school friend posited years ago that all scholarly writing is invariably a form of autobiography, and my interest in progressive marriage is probably no exception. As I never set out to write a book on marital reform, I also never expected to find myself married. That I have been so for two decades is a tribute to the love, friendship, and especially the patience of John Lo Presti, to whom I dedicate this book. We are together for the long haul, but it's being in the present with John that I treasure. I know choice will never part us.

INTRODUCTION

When Upton Sinclair and Meta Fuller wed in 1900, they were idealistic and astoundingly naive youths convinced that he was destined for literary fame and hopeful that she would also find her calling as a creative writer. Like many couples, they expected marriage to further their personal goals—but the Sinclairs also hoped theirs would provide a model for others to emulate. Inspired by what they had read about a new marital ideal, the couple pledged their union would be egalitarian and nonproprietary. In a front page article for the *San Francisco Examiner*, Sinclair explained, "When my wife and I fell in love with each other, we talked the whole marriage business over very conscientiously. We both of us hated the idea of being tied together by either a religious or a legal ceremony, and we tried to make up our minds to set the right kind of example to the world."[1]

The marriage did provide a public example, but not the sort Sinclair intended. When Meta left her husband in 1911 for a "trial marriage" with his former protégée, "tramp poet" Harry Kemp, journalists seized upon the scandal. Five years after *The Jungle* (1906), the muckraker had just published a best-selling *roman à clef* based on his marriage, but the somber *Love's Pilgrimage* (1911) could not compete with saucy newspaper accounts proclaiming "Famous Author and Socialist Reformer Fails to Find Utopia in Own Home." As Sinclair's publisher remarked, "If people can read about you for one cent, they are not going to pay a dollar and a half to do it."[2] I will later examine those newspaper accounts (there were hundreds), as well as Meta's own unpublished autobiographical novel, which provides an instructively different account of the breakup. This proliferation of Sinclair marriage narratives suggests a great deal was at stake in the new ideas about marriage—and that readers consumed those narratives voraciously.

The "Sinclair Affair," as reporters dubbed it, illustrates how a theoretical commitment to a principled marriage can take unexpected turns in the real world of practice. It also illustrates the public's fascination with a campaign to reform marriage in the Progressive era. This movement set the terms for current debates over marriage—but historians have overlooked it. Ideas that now enjoy broad support, such as that divorce should be available to any couple wishing to sever ties, and that marriage should accommodate the career aspirations of both spouses, migrated from fringe positions to accepted truths during this period. Yet one hundred years have also made a strategic difference: while conservatives at the start of the twenty-first century talk about "defending" or "protecting" marriage from those who would alter it, reformers at the turn into the twentieth century embraced marriage as a tool for social change. *Until Choice Do Us Part* excavates an essential chapter in the history of US attitudes toward marriage while providing a new interpretation of the Progressive era.

This book has two primary objectives, one historical and the other literary.

First, historical. In the following two chapters, I establish a self-consciously reformist theory of marriage that threads through more than twenty years (c. 1893–1915) of sociology, journalism, government studies, academic conferences, legal decisions, and tract writing from both sides of the Atlantic. I argue that this new view of marriage constitutes an important strain of discourse defining the much-debated progressivism of the Progressive era. To make that case, I draw from one of my primary archives, a group of writers of influential nonfiction who were the intellectual architects of the new ideal: Havelock Ellis, Olive Schreiner, Ellen Key, Edith Ellis, Edward Carpenter, Thorstein Veblen, Elsie Clews Parsons, Charlotte Perkins Gilman, and George Elliott Howard. Briefly, here is what they had to say: in a collective critique of the economic basis of traditional marriage, these writers theorized an egalitarian form of union that corresponded to many of the values that were coming to be known as *feminist*.[3] They advocated wives' legal status as autonomous agents, women's erotic agency, and non-reproductive sexuality. These theorists and reformers championed private unions sanctioned by mutual consent and affection, and also divorce by mutual agreement if affection ceased. Above all, the marital theorists believed that reforming marriage would ensure human progress.

In tracking this new marital ideal, I chart a different historiographical path from appraisals of the era's progressivism as defined by communal efforts such as government agencies, labor organizations, political parties, or settlement houses. Uncovering a parallel history in attempts to reform personal relationships, I delineate a neglected driving cause of progressivism. The experts considered their new marital ideal a test case and a laboratory for reform. They saw marriage as a test case because if an institution so central to white middle class existence might be revised, they believed, so might other aspects of society be transformed. Marriage became a laboratory when actual couples put theory into practice. And so the marital reformers believed intimate individual decisions could usher in broad social change.

How, exactly, did they think that would occur? Historians of the Progressive era have long emphasized the veneration of science, professionalization, and experiment-based conclusions. One thinks of bureaucrats, efficiency experts, and technicians. But there is another, less positivistic face to the era. The progressive generation was captivated by knowledge for humanistic as well as bureaucratic ends. In the words of Ellen Fitzpatrick, they believed in "education and knowledge as *methods* of reform."[4] Progressives assumed—sometimes with a naiveté that now seems quaint—that they could discover and transmit new ideas and, through education, change the world.

The marriage reformers were above all educators. Some had academic credentials, others were self-taught, but all shared a faith in the power of the written word to effect change. Parsons, Veblen, and Howard were professional educators. While Veblen seems not to have cared much about his audience, Howard extended his with articles in mass-circulation reform magazines such as *McClure's*, and Parsons hers by publishing in diverse venues from the respectable *Harper's Weekly* to the radical *The Masses*. Havelock Ellis, Key, Carpenter, and Schreiner wrote best sellers—some learned, others rhapsodic—promoting marital reform. Charlotte Perkins Gilman wrote several books, while also single-handedly editing a journal from 1909 through 1916, writing every piece the *Forerunner* published. Edith Ellis supplemented her essays (and novels) with a hugely popular lecture tour in the United States, where she was received as a celebrity. Many of these writers cited each other, at times also providing collegial endorsements in introductions, appreciative essays, or blurbs.

A 1906 article by Parsons illustrates the value the marriage reformers placed on educating readers, as well as how lessons could be delivered to possibly unsuspecting pupils. The ostensible subject of "Penalizing Marriage and Child-Bearing" is the upsurge of married women (such as Parsons herself) in the labor force. But she promptly announces, "we are not undertaking at present to justify women's wish to work"—thereby refusing to extend the polemical discussion about whether married women *should* work. Instead, she takes as given that they *do*: working wives are "a condition, not a theory." That fact can be ignored only by refusing to see past one's nose. Parsons then uses that "condition" to launch her broader claim that open-mindedness is a prerequisite for learning—and so, she says, is persistent learning for social improvement. "Failure to think through the subject of the productive activity of married women," she writes, will have more serious consequences than subjugating half of the species, because "the dead-wood of an outgrown point of view chokes progress" in all areas. Rather than ignore change, people must analyze it, and indeed "progress depends upon a study by the whole community" of all the "new social tendencies." Parsons labels retrograde attitudes "taboos" that inhibit learning and promote superstition. And so opposition to sex education—or to lactating mothers on the labor force—belongs in the dustbin with other antique misconceptions.[5]

A fuller picture of the educational message emerges if the article's venue is taken into consideration. "Penalizing Marriage and Child-Bearing" appeared in the *Independent*, which by 1902 had reoriented itself away from religion and toward "current problems." Target readers, then, would be curious about contested social issues. Paratextual elements over which Parsons presumably had no control help package what is a pretty radical message for the time in such a way as to make its lesson more palatable. Two large hearts enclosed in circles edge both sides of the first page, suggesting the contents will not undermine love. Moreover, the editor's blurb introduces "Mrs. Parsons" as a Barnard lecturer and translator of Gabriel Tarde (her controversial first book *The Family* would not be published until later that year). But the editor gives equal space to familial credentials, identifying Parsons as the daughter of celebrated financier Henry Clews and "wife of Congressman Herbert Parsons."[6] While there is certainly condescension in the cutesy hearts and patriarchal credentials, the paratextual elements also promote a more activist agenda. The imprimatur of respectability, and particularly marital respectability, render Professor Parsons's argument less threatening. If readers had the open minds that her article identifies as necessary for progress, who knows but if they might not learn something new.

Recent research in book history has established the cultural importance of reading in the Progressive era, providing several insights crucial to claims

I advance here. First, there is the matter of how many people read, when, and why. The literacy rate may have been as high as 90% by 1850, but "the high-water mark of American literacy," according to Barbara Sicherman in *Well-Read Lives: How Books Inspired a Generation of American Women* (2010), was the Gilded Age, when reading became central to middle-class identity and aspirations. And so the progressive generation came of age during what Sicherman terms a "culture of reading." She traces in particular the critical role that books played for those women who, dissatisfied with dominant cultural scripts for femininity, sought alternatives. Barbara Hochman makes the broader point that, by the late nineteenth century, reading "was regularly invoked as a key to individual and national progress."[7] Such conclusions speak to the importance that reading played in reconceptualizing gender roles during the Progressive era—and promoting activist interests more broadly—both of which enable marital reform.

There is also the matter of what people do with the books they read. Drawing from reader response literary theory, book historians now reject the once pervasive idea that authors (or texts) transmit some predetermined meaning to passive readers. Rather, reading involves a complex interaction between text and reader—and a reader may quite actively extend a text's message, bend it, or make from it something very different than what the author had in mind.[8] For this reason, it is useful to look at reading as a multi-stage process, as I do here: first, what is the content (and intent) of progressive marital theory, and then, how do readers respond? Thinking in stages will also help tease out the relation of theory to practice.

A rich body of evidence suggesting that Progressive era readers thought carefully about the writings of the marital theorists comes from fiction of the period. While it would be foolhardy to assume that what occurs in novels necessarily occurs outside of them, it is remarkable how often fictional characters read, talk about, and resist or try to implement progressive marital reform. This repeated scenario corroborates literary scholar Gordon Hutner's claim that novels are "social objects" that influence actual readers' perceptions of the world they inhabit. He argues in particular that realistic fiction "shape[s] the public sphere in modern America," sometimes in ways that support dominant values, but as often opposing them. Hutner deals with a slightly later period (1920-1940) than do I, but the point holds for the Progressive era. In fact, Hochman establishes that by the Progressive era, the novel—which for decades had been seen as a morally suspect genre—had become respectable, a genre that readers turned to for ideas about what to think and how to behave.[9]

My interest in readers, and also my interpretation of the Progressive movement as committed to reforming marriage through the written word, underwrites this book's contribution to literary studies. Writers can themselves be exemplary readers, as both Hochman and Sicherman show. And so in addition to theories of marital reform, *Until Choice Do Us Part* takes as its second major archive three literary couples' reactions—publicly in creative writing and privately in their experimental personal relationships—to the new ideas. Marrying in 1898, 1899, and 1900, respectively, Theodore and Sara White Dreiser, Neith Boyce and Hutchins Hapgood, and Upton and Meta Fuller Sinclair believed their relationships illustrated new ways of being married. Readers as well as writers, they heard what the marriage reformers were saying and retooled it—sometimes in private letters addressed to a spouse but often in works intended for the public. In doing so at a time of mounting interest in the private lives of authors, these writers extended the reach of progressive marital reform.[10]

These creative writers worked in many genres, including biography, drama, music and art criticism, and journalism. But the type of writing I find most revealing is the hybrid literary text that ranges from autobiographical fiction to novelized autobiography. As Paul de Man and other theorists stress, autobiography eludes generic definition, in part because it bears an intimate yet "undecidable" relationship to the novel. Autobiography also supplies an important if slippery source for the historian. And if Christopher Lasch is correct that autobiography is a characteristic form of writing in the Progressive era, it becomes a particularly useful source for understanding this period. Enthusiasm for the laboratory method popularized by pragmatist philosopher John Dewey (a means of arriving at experiential truths by practice and experience) suggests one reason why: autobiography allows writers to perform experiments on themselves and record the results. That idea accords with my definition of progressivism as an effort at social reform beginning with oneself and one's primary relationships.[11] In line with recent theories of autobiography, my interest is less in seeking out the facts of a particular marriage than the meaning assigned to it. Or, rather, *meanings*, since I am interested in multiple versions and in what readers, particularly those who are themselves also writers, do with texts.

In these ways I use the rubric of progressivism to bring together history and literature. In *Ministers of Reform* (1982), Robert M. Crunden defines progressivism as a "climate of creativity," yet Christopher P. Wilson's *The Labor of Words* (1985) is one of few modern scholarly works to use progressivism as a frame for examining literature.[12] Whereas Wilson defines progressivism in terms of literary professionalism, I do so in terms of efforts to reform personal relationships, as seen in consciously literary and also emphatically didactic texts. I hope that this approach helps to open up the emotional and cultural dynamics of the period.

The Progressive era campaign to change marriage was less transformative than advocates predicted but more successful than historians have realized. Although reformers often ecstatically predicted social transformation, they really sought to *manage* change. Overwhelmingly middle class, white, and supportive of heterosexual monogamy, they kept their ideas about marriage within clearly defined boundaries. For these reasons, the movement to reform marriage provides a new way of understanding the limits as well as the ambitiousness of progressivism.[13]

But those limits do not gainsay the lasting influence of progressive marital reform. Precisely because the goals were modest enough to be embraced by the white middle class, what is technically called "no-fault" divorce (more accurately described as divorce by mutual consent), along with related reform goals, now enjoy broad support. Unlike more radical experimenters such as free-lovers, Greenwich Village bohemians, Mormon polygynists, or hippies, progressives sought to reform—not replace—long-term, monogamous heterosexual pairings. (Some aspects of their heteronormativity may have been rhetorical, particularly since two of the architects of progressive marital theory, as I will discuss in the Epilogue, were homosexual.) Too radical for some, not radical enough for others: the endurance of progressivism as well as its limited efficacy derives from its commitment to limiting change as much as to changing limits.

MARRIAGE AND STASIS, MARRIAGE AND CHANGE: FAMILY HISTORY AND LITERARY HISTORY

Marriage is central to stories that people tell about themselves. *Until Choice Do Us Part* connects two bodies of scholarship informed by that premise: family history and studies of the novel.

The story collectively told by family historians such as Eli Zaretsky, Stephanie Coontz, and Michael Grossberg has a dispiriting conclusion. According to this account, along with the development of capitalism, a new sphere of subjectivity and emotion was constructed and localized within the private home. Marriage and other aspects of family life came to be seen as refuges from the harsh public world of business and politics. At the same time, the family became the locus for reproducing and improving class position. Thus, as people turned inward toward spouses and other relatives for fulfillment, they become increasingly isolated from the external world, and so the structure of the modern family ends up inhibiting social engagement—much less, social reform. For Coontz, this turn inward crystallized in the period immediately preceding the Progressive era, during the Gilded Age. For Zaretsky, the process continues into the present: "increasingly cut off from production, the contemporary family threatens to become a well of subjectivity divorced from any social meaning." In any case, the consensus is that marriage supports the status quo and, as Nancy Cott and Norma Basch among others argue, also underwrites particular ideas of the nation. Historians taking a long view emphasize the inherent conservatism of marriage and the nuclear family, while more specialized studies such as Julian B. Carter's *The Heart of Whiteness: Normal Sexuality and Race in America, 1880–1940* likewise focus on the family as a normalizing institution.[14]

In one respect the progressive reformers agreed with modern historians, for they also saw marriage as a microcosm of society. For Havelock Ellis, marriage was no less than "the figure in miniature" of life; to Ellen Key, "the most complicated and delicate of institutions" and the key to them all.[15] But while recent historical scholarship has established how marriage underwrites social stability, that focus overlooks the relation—which I emphasize—between marriage and social change.

According to Virginia Woolf, "On or about December, 1910, human character changed." Explaining just how she believed historical change occurred, Woolf continues, "All human relations have shifted—those between masters and servants, husbands and wives, parents and children. And when human relations change there is at the same time a change in religion, conduct, politics, and literature."[16] Like Woolf, I believe intimate relationships can disclose a great deal about what are often conceptualized as larger "movements"—religious, political, cultural, and so on. Moreover, Woolf's delicious irony contains an important caution about writing history: change is notoriously hard to fix in time. Was it really "December 1910," or maybe November, when "human character changed"?

History never moves in a simple linear direction, all subpopulations proceeding together in lockstep without looking back. In addition to its enduring influence, Progressive era marital reform is important because it represents a generation in transition. Michael McGerr's reminder that Victorians *became* progressives is invaluable, to which I would add that many progressives became, or were fellow travelers with, more radical groups, including anarchists, socialists, and the sexual rebels of Greenwich Village. Moreover, some of the marital theorists—especially Ellis, Carpenter, and Key—would be reread and re-interpreted by radicals seeking to replace marriage with more avant-garde forms of partnering.[17]

I argue here that the Progressive era generation deserves credit for the wide diffusion and acceptance of modern ideas about marriage and sexuality. Historians typically locate the origins of egalitarian marriage, romantic and sexual intimacy, and divorce by mutual consent with the Greenwich Village bohemians of the 1910s, the 1920s "jazz" standards of freer sexuality, or the companionate marriage movement inspired by Judge Ben Lindsay's popular 1927 book, *Companionate Marriage*.[18] I offer a more capacious understanding of the Progressive era as a time of critical transition between nineteenth- and twentieth-century sexual and marital agendas.

Raymond Williams's analysis of "structures of feeling" provides a supple theory that reinforces several of my claims. The question that Williams sets out to answer is why "no generation speaks quite the same language as its predecessors." Expressive changes differentiating one generation from another manifest in every facet of human life—customs, fashions, music, ways of walking down the street, mores about interacting with potential partners. These distinct behaviors are not, Williams insists, "epiphenomena" of some intangible substructure understood as primary and determining (such as an era's signature beliefs or ideologies). Nor do they constitute "merely secondary evidence" of underlying social or economic conditions. Rather, the tendency to try to abstract "social consciousness" can make it difficult to see what really defines an era: the behaviors of actual people in interaction. As "lived, actively, in real relationships," expressive acts make each era distinct. For Williams, these structures of feeling are primarily "affective" rather than intellectual. They "defin[e] . . . a particular quality of social experience and relationship, historically distinct from other particular qualities, which gives the sense of a generation or of a period."[19] I would add that overlap among generations provides continuity from one to the next.

This theoretical model supports a number of my interests: in lived experience; in the expressive dimensions of progressivism; and of course in the overlooked roles affect and "feeling" play in defining the era. Moreover, Williams's insistence that experience is not secondary to intellect or ideology helps me clarify an important point. I am not suggesting that the new ideas about marriage sprung from the heads of those I call the experts, theorists, and reformers much as Athena sprang from the head of Zeus. The experts were early on the scene and very persuasive in their day, but they were rendering into language structures of feeling that were already emergent. The marital theorists are so useful historically because texts are much easier to trace than behavior, and because the influence of their books is clear. Williams also maintains that new structures of feeling often first appear in literature and art—an idea that reinforces my additional focus on creative writers.[20]

Along with establishing a Progressive era structure of feeling that has had enduring consequences, *Until Choice Do Us Part* advances the broader historical claim that marriage is not a static institution during these or any other times. In my account, rather than having a predictably conservative or liberal function, marriage can be a tool actively used to impede or resist, but also to trigger or promote, wider social change. The proposition that I examine here of marriage as an instrument for reform has fallen between the cracks of two large bodies of historical scholarship: one on marriage, sexuality, and the family; the other on progressivism (which I will examine shortly). Histories of marriage and sexuality either gloss over the Progressive era or, as in the case of John D'Emilio and Estelle B. Freedman's indispensable *Intimate Matters* (1988), gauge its impact only in negative terms.[21]

This book also advances a new interpretation of why marriage is central to the novel. Intimate formal, thematic, and ideological connections between the novel and marriage were established by Ian Watt's *The Rise of the Novel* (1957) and refined by studies such as Nancy Armstrong's *Desire and Domestic Fiction* (1987). Yet Tony Tanner's *Adultery in the Novel* (1979), Joseph Allen Boone's *Tradition Counter Tradition* (1987), and David R. Shumway's *Modern Love: Romance, Intimacy, and the Marriage Crisis* (2003) concur that while novelistic trajectories often culminate in marriage, fiction rarely actually portrays it. Rather, since marriage functions in narrative as a state of achieved happiness, literary scholars find it static and even, as D. A. Miller puts it, "nonnarratable." In a move parallel to historians' view of marriage as a normalizing institution, most literary scholars disparage the bourgeois novel in general—and its treatment of marriage in particular—for enforcing ideological conformity. Thus for Boone, "the very dynamic of narrative, the structure of desire in traditional fiction, has been coerced into upholding a restrictive sexual-marital ideology," while for Tanner, marriage is "the structure that maintains the Structure."[22]

Literary scholars have endorsed another sort of compulsory narrative over the last generation, this one involving the realist/naturalist novel, arguably the defining genre of the Progressive era. Two works that have become indispensable, Amy Kaplan's *The Social Construction of American Re-*

alism (1988) and Walter Benn Michaels's *The Gold Standard and the Logic of Naturalism* (1987), contend that turn-of-the-century American fiction cannot effectively criticize (much less reform) the society it so painstakingly examines because it is a thoroughly bourgeois genre already complicit with the status quo. Kaplan and Michaels have transformed the field, in most respects for the better. But they also exemplify a trend that Gordon Hutner recently identified as an "antibourgeois prejudice" endemic to the literary academy. Looking at which books get taught and written about, Hutner concludes that "novels may be popular for all sorts of reasons, but it seems that they cannot be great unless they assail the middle class."[23] This "prejudice" has come to exercise its own sort of compulsion, making it yet more difficult to consider the realist novel as seriously engaged with reform.

In *The Novel of Purpose: Literature and Social Reform in the Anglo-American World* (2007), however, Amanda Claybaugh argues for structural parallels between reformist writings and literary realism. And for Claybaugh, social reform as it emerged in the mid-nineteenth century "depended on print," an idea that meshes with my focus on progressive reformers as educators who believed that writing could change the world. Following that idea, I pursue an alternative interpretation of American literary realism in line with pioneering works like Donna M. Campbell's *Resisting Regionalism* (1997), Jennifer Fleissner's *Women, Compulsion, Modernity* (2004), and Tom Lutz's *Cosmopolitan Vistas* (2004).[24] These very different books all emphasize efforts to resist supposedly compulsory narratives about gender at the turn into the twentieth century. *Until Choice Do Us Part* continues in that vein by examining how taking marriage reform seriously destabilizes consensus readings, especially the now-standard notion that the marriage plot (as well as the institution of marriage) necessarily promotes ideological conformity.

According to Boone, novels about marriage take one of three forms: courtship, seduction, and domestic or wedlock plots.[25] Portraying the shared lives of married couples, the literary texts I examine have most in common with Boone's third category, but my archive is not the domestic novel per se. The hybrid literary works I consider require a revision of Boone's generalization that wedlock plots invariably hold the individual responsible for marital failings.[26] Rather, as I will show, progressive writers believed the institution had much to answer for.

While *Until Choice Do Us Part* is the first book to focus on marital reform in the Progressive era, some books are fellow travelers in seeing marriage as potentially liberalizing. In particular, Mary S. Hartman's *The Household and the Making of History: A Subversive View of the Western Past* (2004) argues that northwestern Europe became the cradle of modernity precisely because its "anomalous households" granted wives more equitable partnership and greater agency than was true elsewhere. For Hartman, social change originates in households and reflects marital mores. In a project similar to Kelly Hager's *Dickens and the Rise of Divorce* (2010), which challenges critical neglect of marriage plots, I argue that US novelists at the turn into the twentieth century made marriage reform their explicit and extended subject.[27]

Imagining marriage as a laboratory, experiment, and creative process does not guarantee it will become a liberatory institution, but such efforts do unhinge its assumed relationship to social conservatism. Dramatizing evolving, continually negotiated relationships, Progressive era novelists—like their nonfictional counterparts, the marital theorists—infuse marriage with the dynamism it has been said to lack as a narrative subject, ideological structure, or "system." By representing marriage as an evolving social institution, the reformers opened the door for more flexible and relativistic ideas that continue to influence public debate. These efforts comprise a critical but overlooked chapter in the transition toward what Stephanie Coontz terms "the democratization of marriage" and "the love revolution."[28]

One way to locate the dynamic aspects of marriage is by focusing on the emotions it generates. Recent research from various disciplinary bases—including psychology, philosophy, anthropology, and neuroscience—has transformed our understanding of emotion. It was "Descartes' Error," as neurologist Antonio R. Damasio titled his important book (1994), to imagine reason and emotion in opposition. Rather than irrational, solipsistic, and private, emotion is now understood to be rational, ethical, and social. Emotions motivate people to assess complex situations and make difficult decisions, including when no fully rational choice is possible. Emotions also prompt communication so that people can negotiate productively when conflicts arise.[29]

Later chapters will provide ample opportunities to explore these and other ramifications of emotions. For now, two general points about why emotions matter not only to the person experiencing them but also for the broader question of how change happens.

First, strong emotions often precipitate action, according to psychologist Jon Elster. And not simply motor activity; emotions can "communicate the need for cognitive change," says psychologist Keith Oatley. This spur can occur experientially. A woman abandoned by her partner may feel depressed and hopeless. If she is reflective (or therapy successful), she may learn to alleviate her dark thoughts by modifying her mental constructs: perhaps the partner left because he was selfish and shallow, not because she is ugly and stupid. People's ability to change cognitively is amply demonstrated in clinical psychology. Indeed, what stronger motive than painful emotion could there be for changing one's mental construct? For these reasons, in the words of another psychological study, "emotions have principled, systemic effects upon cognitive processes, and . . . lead to reasonable judgments of the world."[30]

An additional way emotions precipitate cognitive change is through reading. Researchers in various disciplines look closely at literary texts which, in addition to representing emotions, also generate them in readers. According to psychologists Oatley, Keltner, and Jenkins, literature provides "common exemplars of action[,] of emotion[,] and of responsibility." Responsibility is an especially interesting concept here, and of all the emotions, empathy in particular is said to be cultivated by reading. Indeed, for literary scholar Patrick Colm Hogan, principled empathy that prompts responsible action is precisely the highest goal of reading: "Literature can have moral consequences only insofar as it alters what we feel about situations and people, what we are motivated to do in our personal and social lives."[31]

Drawing from that insight, a second overarching point about emotions is that they provide a bridge between an individual and the world. For while they take shape within a particular person, emotions are, above all, social. That perhaps counterintuitive point has been richly theorized by emotion researchers. Among them, philosopher Martha C. Nussbaum illustrates the social aspect by tracing an infant's development from solipsistic demands (it's all about me) to appreciation for the independent emotional needs of its parents (oh, it's about other people, too, and if I recognize that, they will love me more). Nussbaum further establishes the social dimension by showing how emotions such as love, grief, and empathy extend the boundaries of the self. (Other emotions, like hate and disgust, contract those same boundaries.) Oatley's account of the social component of emotion is particularly useful for my concerns. He argues that emotions arise at the precise instant where one person's goal meets an obstacle that frustrates its fulfillment. For instance, I become violently angry when my computer crashes and I cannot meet a deadline. More often, however, one person's goal is foiled when it conflicts with another person's. That is why, in one of Oatley's most elegantly simple points, the majority of emotions have to do with other people. Because of this interpersonal quality, he repeatedly references marriage as an especially productive site for analysis: surely in marriage, goals will collide, emotions will explode, and partners will have to renegotiate — or refuse to do so.[32]

Given the role of emotion in precipitating cognitive change and its irreducibly social quality, it is therefore time to bring analysis of emotions to bear on social reform movements. Indeed, according to Oatley, "If voluntary actions are the means by which we change the world, emotions seem to change us."[33]

THE PROBLEM OF "PROGRESSIVISM"

The Progressive era is rarely conceptualized in terms of emotion. Perhaps the closest efforts in that direction are Eric Rauchway's *The Refuge of Affections: Family and American Reform Politics* (2001), Michael McGerr's *A Fierce Discontent: The Rise and Fall of Progressivism in America* (2003), and Leon Fink's *Progressive Intellectuals and the Dilemmas of Democratic Commitment* (1997). Each of these important books focuses, to varying degrees, on interpersonal relationships and hence has some bearing on emotion.[34]

The Progressive era has, however, been approached from many other directions. So many, in fact, that of all historical labels, *progressive* remains one of the messiest. Historians have used the term to describe different, even incompatible agendas and political positions. Richard Hofstadter characterizes progressivism as "the complaint of the unorganized against the consequences of organization," whereas Robert H. Wiebe argues the opposite: that in this period the middle class embraced the bureaucratic revolution. Nor is there agreement on when the period began or ended: influential date markers include 1900–1915 (Hofstadter), 1890–1916 (Martin Sklar), 1877–1919 or 1920 (Nell Irvin Painter and Wiebe, respectively), 1889–1920 (Crunden), and 1870–1920 (McGerr). The definitional problem is exacerbated because the term *progressive* has a healthy life outside of history books, and also because many distinctive phenomena of the era—such as the lynching of African Americans, mounting opposition to immigration, and hostility to organized labor—do not appear at all "progressive." As Robert M. Crunden has observed, considerable irony surrounds the whole notion of a "progressive" era.[35]

Historiography on the period remains vexed and unsettled, but I would hazard two generalizations. First, most accounts define progressivism as characterized by zealous reform. An immediate caveat is necessary: reform efforts do not necessarily lead to substantial change, and when change does occur, it may not be for the better.[36]

A second generalization suggested by existing scholarship is that progressive reformers usually sought macro solutions to problems afflicting large groups of people as a collective. Accordingly, historians of the period have targeted problems in such public arenas as cities, schools, business, governments, political parties—problems that were answered by "movements" of all stripes. As Nancy Cohen puts it, historians focus on the "rise, legitimation, and political institutionalization of corporate capitalism, the articulation of a theory and practice of bureaucratic state activism, and the material and ideological shift from producerism to consumerism as defining . . . features of the Progressive Era."[37]

Those who focus on gender conceptualize the era and its distinctive reform activities somewhat differently. Since Nancy Cott's 1989 call for systematic analysis of gender in the Progressive era, women's agency has become increasingly visible. Robyn Muncy finds no less than an entire "female dominion in American reform" developing out of settlement houses and shaping public policy well into the New Deal. Accordingly, the Progressive era is now seen, in the words of Nancy S. Dye, as the "high-water point of women's engagement in American politics." Yet even with this substantial shift in emphasis, the concentration remains on large-scale movements (such as for women's suffrage or child labor laws; against alcohol or food contaminants). In addition, progressivism is still understood as tied up with, in Muncy's words, "enthusiasm for governmental solutions to social problems."[38]

Until Choice Do Us Part defines progressivism in terms of gender and reform, but in a new way. Progressives, as I demonstrate, also sought *private* solutions to social problems. Marriage, of course, affected huge segments of the population then, as it always has. In that respect, marriage is very much a social and public institution. (In fact, the progressives were the first generation to insist marriage must be understood as a social institution that changes over time.) However, marital reformers believed that change could occur on an intimate scale, couple by couple. In fact, as I will show, most sought to end governmental jurisdiction over marriage, which they believed should be a purely private affair. We have learned to be suspicious of talk about a "private" realm—particularly given the influential argument of Jürgen Habermas that it only distracts from public affairs—and doubtful that the "private" could be kept cordoned off from the "public," in any case. But the progressives had a different idea: that "private acts," in the words of John Dewey, "may be socially valuable."[39] This feedback loop is precisely as the reformers intended, and so, in my account, the social and the private cross over and influence each other. *Until Choice Do Us Part* emphasizes, therefore, how progressivism structured an important strand of public discourse by focusing on the private. It also impacted the most intimate moments in many reformers' private lives.

Given the definitional problems with *progressive*, why not, then, throw the term in the dustbin? Despite the messiness of the term, I find it remains useful precisely because it captures the generation's fundamental belief in progress. A historian at the time and a founder of the New School for Social Research, James Harvey Robinson proclaimed this secular faith as the "vital principle of betterment." This optimism was fueled by the sense of living in a time of dramatic and rapid change. Historian Martin J. Sklar describes the progressive mindset as a "widespread and highly charged sense of the emergence of a new era in American history [,] . . . a sense of an evolutionary outcome that marked a distinct break with the past, comparable to that of the Revolution and Civil War eras." And so when I refer to *progressives*, I have in mind the social liberals who believed in progress and thought it could be realized, one marriage at a time. Let me be clear: I do not use the word as a term of endorsement but rather as a historical descriptor.[40]

Because their optimism was shattered by World War I, the progressives' sunny predictions can appear, in retrospect, naïve—even foolish. There is much to criticize in this generation of reformers, but retrospective judgments upon any era tend to reflect the assumption (generally unacknowledged, and for that reason the more pernicious) that the present is more enlightened. That attitude makes it harder to understand the past and can breed arrogance in the present. I follow the lead of historians such as Nell Irvin Painter who acknowledge the progressives' limitations while believing they instigated many changes in American society—some even for the better.[41]

Let us move, now, to the "general discussion of marriage and divorce" that, according to a 1910 journalist, was just then "looming large."[42] To set the stage, a brief history of marriage will introduce the Progressive era debate.

CHAPTER ONE

A Telescoped History of Marriage and the Progressive Era Debate

The United States has a distinct and complex history of marriage. But the story must begin centuries before Columbus, with the church, which has cast a long shadow on all Western conceptions of matrimony. St. Paul provides a useful starting point, for his distrust of sexuality imprinted a legacy of deep ambivalence. On one hand, Paul thought celibacy a more exalted state than matrimony; on the other, that it was better to marry than to "burn," for Hell was the destiny for those having sex out of wedlock. From the start, then, Christianity identified marriage as a compromise with humanity's lower nature. Paul also believed (perhaps begrudgingly) that marriage, if entered into, should be permanent. That view became church doctrine in AD 314, when the Council of Arles proclaimed the indissolubility of marriage. The twelfth century, when the church endorsed the doctrine of marriage as a sacrament, marks another milestone. The church's authority extended further when the 1563 Council of Trent placed marriage completely under religious (rather than civil) jurisdiction.[1]

According to most accounts, modern conceptions of marriage begin with the Reformation. Luther declared marriage a "temporal, worldly thing" which "does not concern the church." Protestants denied the sacramental nature of marriage, while still seeing it as divinely sanctioned. According to family historian Lawrence Stone, the notion of "holy matrimony" embraced by Protestant reformers elevated marriage from the necessary evil it had seemed to St. Paul to a positive good. This redefinition also laid the groundwork for rethinking marriage's worldly purpose: a union was more likely to be "holy" if harmonious—and harmony more likely if spouses were compatible. For that reason, according to Stone, the Reformation shifted the view of marriage from serving family "interest" (e.g., advancing economic and social power), as it had for centuries, toward fulfilling individual needs for companionship.[2]

From the beginning, the American colonies emphasized the civil over the ecclesiastical foundation of marriage, a fact that may be surprising given how much religion dominates current discussions of marriage. The legal foundation of marriage in the United States, rooted in English common law, has its own intricate history. That history has had, from the start, negative consequences for women.

Sir William Blackstone established the legal ground for the subordination of wives, a doctrine that generations of reformers, among them the progressives, would challenge. His *Commentaries on the Laws of England* (1766), which became foundational legal doctrine in the United States, synthesized the common law that had evolved over the centuries while extending its authority by aligning it with natural law. The key concept here is *coverture*, which means that, when married, spouses become "one person in law." Blackwood identifies that "one person" as neither androgynous nor sexless; rather, "the very being or legal existence of the woman is suspended during the marriage, or is at least incorporated and consolidated into that of the husband; under whose wing, protection and cover, she performs everything." The wife's legal identity is covered over by her husband's. Coverture underwrites what historian Hendrik Hartog calls the "legal fiction" of marital unity, "a set of imaginary 'facts' created to achieve a legal result." While a *feme sole* (or single woman) had, at least theoretically, legal autonomy, a *feme covert* had none: she lost any personal property to her husband, had almost no agency in the matter of contracts or wills, and could neither sue nor be sued. Marital unity provides the basis for the still-familiar provision that spouses cannot testify against each other in legal proceedings. And since the law reads the identity of each marital unit as male, the result was, in the words of Norma Basch, "legal invisibility" for the wife.[3]

The Reformation weakened coverture and marital unity by encouraging wives to seek salvation independent of their husbands. Common law, however, proved resilient, surviving the Middle Ages, the emergence of capitalism, the more companionate nuclear family of the eighteenth century, and flourishing after transplantation onto US soil. The conclusion of *History of Woman Suffrage* (1888–1922), edited by Susan B. Anthony and Elizabeth Cady Stanton, that the common law was always "unjust to women" is borne out in the case of marriage.[4]

Two US legal writers, Tapping Reeve in *The Law of Baron and Femme* (1816) and James Kent in *Commentaries on American Law* (1826 and 1830), reinforced Blackstone's conclusions. The result, explains Basch, was that state laws upheld marital unity (and thus also women's subordination within marriage) in a manner both "more subtle" than in English common law and "more ominous."[5]

At first glance the antebellum wave of married women's property laws makes it seem as if marital unity were losing hold. In 1839, Mississippi became the first state to pass a statute allowing married women to own property; by the end of the Civil War, twenty-nine states had similar provisions. (England would not enact its first Married Women's Property Act until 1870.) These theoretical improvements, however, did not translate into much practical consequence: *de facto* coverture persisted long after the beginnings of its *de jure* dismantling. One reason for that persistence, Nancy F. Cott explains, is that judicial interpretation can vitiate the letter of a law—and judges continued to uphold common law principles favoring husbands, in effect nullifying married women's property rights. Another reason, according to Linda K. Kerber, is the tenacity of supposedly "common sense" views about husbands' sexual rights—as reflected, for instance, in the absence of any legal definition of marital rape until the 1970s. Kerber declares that coverture, "as a living legal principle, died" only in 1992, when the Supreme Court decided in *Planned Parenthood v. Casey* that husbands do not have power over their wives' bodies.[6]

A controversy over whether marriage constitutes a legal contract or status has considerable ramifications for the story of progressive marital reform. The law differentiates between *status* (a permanent condition) and *contract* (a voluntary agreement that can be broken). In 1861, Henry Sumner Maine explained the consequences for family law: if family were understood to be a status, then the unit would assume primacy over its members. But if the family were a contract, the individual would prevail. Positing the family as a legal contract, then, renders it a less powerful, even less coercive, institution. Maine believed the long view of legal history demonstrated just such a shift away from the family and toward the individual.[7] Cott clarifies an important consequence of this legal distinction: if marriage is a status, then it is a "public institution"; if a contract, marriage is a "private arrangement." Wanting to have it both ways, the United States has evolved the distinct view, according to Cott, of understanding marriage as both "a private relationship" and "a public value"—both of which remain "enshrined in legal doctrine."[8]

While the history of marriage in the United States follows patterns established in Europe, particularly England, from the outset signs of national distinctness are evident. Blackstone defined marriage as a curious amalgam of contract and status, with status ultimately prevailing.[9] But the American colonists, drawing from Calvinism, Anglicanism, and English ecclesiastical law, tipped the balance toward contract, a view that intensified after the American Revolution. Women's rights advocates seized on the distinction; Elizabeth Cady Stanton was among those finding "the grossest absurdities and contradictions" in calling marriage a contract while limiting spouses' right to terminate their contract by divorcing. By 1910 a former supreme court justice voiced an increasingly common position when he asserted the legal equivalence of marriage and commercial partnerships since both are contracts. Because a commercial arrangement could be terminated by mutual agreement, marriage could not, in his view, be "indissoluble."[10]

So-called "common law" marriage, initially an extralegal arrangement, also plays an important role in marital reform. Defined as cohabitation leading to the presumption of an enduring relationship—but without any legal seal of approval—common law marriage was widespread in the United States by the early nineteenth century. In the last quarter of that century, however, common law marriage entered legal doctrine. In *Commentaries on American Law*, James Kent provided the rationale, asserting "the consent of the parties is all that is required." As Michael Grossberg summarizes the significance of the legal recognition of common law marriage, courts were shifting to value "practice over form." Positing marriage as an experiential and personal relationship rather than a formal, official one will become, as I will show in the next chapter, central to progressive marital reform.[11]

A peculiarity of US marriage law derives from the "full faith and credit" doctrine, which obliges each state to accept the laws and provisions of the others. In 1776 the states assumed jurisdiction over matrimonial and divorce law, which lay the groundwork for what would evolve into chaotic inconsistencies. States established contradictory laws—for instance, regarding the age of consent and rules restricting marriageability (such as restrictions due to race or degrees of consanguinity). As a result, a couple might meet legal requirements for marriage in, say, Indiana but not in South Carolina. One landmark Progressive era case, *Haddock v. Haddock* (1906), provides a glimpse of the resulting confusions. In 1881 a man divorced his wife in Connecticut on the ground that she had deserted him. But eighteen years later, the wife petitioned the New York court for a divorce of her own. She claimed the earlier divorce was invalid since their residence as a married couple had been New York, not Connecticut. The New York court ruled in favor of Harriet Haddock, in effect nullifying the Connecticut decision. More to the point, New York granted Mrs. Haddock alimony—which Connecticut had not. The New York decision was subsequently upheld by the Supreme Court. Such messy situations illustrate why Basch concludes that US marital law is "an incoherent amalgam of inconsistent moral precepts based on competing ideological foundations."[12]

Marriage assumed a distinct cast in the United States also because of nineteenth-century experiments by communitarian utopian movements. Shakers and Rappites favored celibacy, but other utopians put sexual activity at the center of reform projects that challenged existing marital mores. Robert Owen's New Harmony colonists, for instance, rejected the notion of pledging oneself to another for life; they believed that when love fades, spouses should part. Owen's Fourth of July "Declaration of Mental Independence" (1826) renounced, in addition to private property and established religion, "marriage founded on individual property"—that is, a man's ownership of his wife. While that anti-proprietary ideal would have a huge bearing on other reform movements, including in the Progressive era, Owen also helped import another utopian movement into the United States. Owen urged French novelist and politician Etienne Cabet, founder of the Icarian movement, to purchase land in Texas. The Icarians, who saw celibacy as unnatural and declared marriage obligatory, believed all marriages would become happy once society embraced true equality and fraternity. Robert Owen's marital experiments were continued by his son Robert Dale Owen, author of the widely read birth control text *Moral Physiology* (1830). The younger Owen considered coverture and marital unity "barbarous relics of a feudal, despotic system" and repudiated all legal powers over his own wife.[13]

Led by John Humphrey Noyes, the Oneidan experiment lasted thirty years, longer than most utopian movements. Oneidans practiced what they called "complex marriage," whereby each member was understood as married to every other community member of the opposite sex. Believing that monogamy bred many evils (such as encouraging adultery and prohibiting people from communing with kindred souls to whom they happened not to be married), Oneidans saw their own "pantagamous" marriage as superior. Their attitudes are notable also for the emphasis placed on women's sexual satisfaction and birth control. Believing that men could climax without ejaculating, Oneidans encouraged what they called male continence to reduce unwanted pregnancies.

Andrew Jackson Davis placed marital reform at the center of an important mid-century religious movement, Harmonialism, which later evolved into Spiritualism. Drawing from the Fourierist idea of "passional attraction," Davis encouraged followers to seek their "spiritual affinities." Believing that each person had one true mate—whether encountered in this world or the next—Harmonialists affirmed a sort of super-monogamy. Davis was also a Perfectionist, which, translated into marital beliefs, meant that while marriage ties were holy, divorce remained necessary until society progressed to the higher, harmonial stage. At that point, unions between spiritual affinities would last into the next world. Davis saw divorces, therefore, as "good steps to better things" and sanctioned sexual experimentation in the interim.[14]

Roderick Phillips concludes that the lasting impact of these intriguing marital experimenters was minimal. Not surprisingly, they provoked more opposition than support.[15] The utopians in fact never sought to change society at large, intending their marital reforms only for the elect. Yet many of their ideas resurface in forms that would prove more widely acceptable during the Progressive era.

Due to their nonconformity with prevailing marital norms, these various dissenters were branded "free lovers" by their opponents. As a term, "free love" was a call to arms, but as a practice it was nebulous. Historian Ann Braude explains that free love is difficult to define precisely because the term was usually invoked as an insult.[16] But two broad tenets can be discerned: on the ground of their commitment to women's emancipation, mid-century free lovers rejected marriage based on coverture; they also held individual sovereignty as the highest principle.

The free love controversy raged most famously in two series of *New York Tribune* articles. The first debate began with Henry James (Senior)'s review of a free love text in November 1852. Since James considered only unions based on love to be valid, he concurred that marriage would be improved by allowing unhappy couples to divorce. This mild position was enough to persuade *Tribune* editor Horace Greeley that James himself practiced free love. In articles that ran through February 1853, Greeley defended marriage from what he saw as attacks by James as well as by anarchist-abolitionist Stephen Pearl Andrews. The latter (who unlike James was in fact a free lover) took a more radical position, denying the state any jurisdiction over matrimony whatsoever. In 1860 Greeley repeated the performance in a series of debates with Robert Dale Owen, whom he accused of promoting free love in Indiana. Owen fired back that New York was the real den of free love (due to its stringent laws permitting divorce only when adultery could be proven which, according to Owen, thereby encouraged infidelity).[17] The flamboyant Victoria Woodhull—publisher, stockbroker, and 1870 presidential candidate—was one of the most visible free love advocates. She campaigned for the abolition of marriage because under coverture, wives were treated as property. In an 1872 essay outing the affair of popular minister Henry Ward Beecher with one of his parishioners, Woodhull (who objected not to the affair but to the secrecy surrounding it) claimed she was "conducting a social revolution on the marriage question."[18] Often married themselves, the vast majority of nineteenth-century free lovers were misty idealists rather than lustful decadents: they believed mistaken ideas of marriage corrupted true love.

The Church of Latter Day Saints (better known as the Mormons) provided the most significant nineteenth-century challenge to US marital norms. In 1843 founder Joseph Smith claimed to have received a revelation from God sanctioning polygyny, a practice the church initially limited to its leaders. Nine years later Brigham Young made polygyny official doctrine for all the faithful. A centerpiece of Mormonism became "celestial marriage"; while believers saw monogamous earthly marriage as contracted only for "time" (the duration of mortal life), polygynous celestial marriages were understood as contracted for "time and eternity." The national controversy over Mormonism spawned sensational novels and tracts such as the piquantly titled *Polygamy or, the Mysteries and Crimes of Mormonism, Being a Full and Authentic History of this Strange Sect From its Origin to the Present Time With a Thrilling Account of the Inner Life and Teachings of the Mormons and an Exposé of the Secret Rites and Ceremonies of the Deluded Followers of Brigham Young* (1904). Dedicated "to the Women of America, Whose Sympathies are ever active in behalf of their Suffering and Oppressed Sisters," this tract features vaguely salacious illustrations, one of them depicting an anthropomorphic "Mormon Octopus enslaving the Women of Utah"[19]

A protracted struggle between the Mormons and the federal government included several congressional bills to outlaw polygamy, which the church resisted by invoking the First Amendment. Playing its trump card, the government denied Utah (at that time a territory) the status of state, and only after the Mormons renounced polygyny in 1890 was Utah so recognized. As various scholars have shown, the national outrage over Mormonism and the federal government's intervention in what amounts to legislating monogamy demonstrates the importance of particular notions of marriage to national identity.[20]

THE MORMON OCTOPUS ENSLAVING THE WOMEN OF UTAH

FIGURE 2. This illustration from J.H. Beadle's *Polygamy or, the Mysteries and Crimes of Mormonism, Being a Full and Authentic History of this Strange Sect From its Origin to the Present Time With a Thrilling Account of the Inner Life and Teachings of the Mormons and an Exposé of the Secret Rites and Ceremonies of the Deluded followers of Brigham Young* (1882) registers the scandal over Mormon "celestial marriages."

I can do no more than glance here at the nineteenth-century women's movement's complex relationship with marital reform. Mary Wollstonecraft's indictment of marriage as legal slavery for women in *A Vindication of the Rights of Woman* (1792) was a commonplace in reform circles by the 1850s. Antebellum women's rights advocates concentrated on reforming married women's property law; after the Civil War, suffrage became their primary cause. Thereafter, women's rights advocates remained sharply divided over marriage and divorce. As Basch explains, "many women were reluctant to undermine the institution that sustained and defined them," while others were more interested in reforming men than in changing marriage or divorce. Marriage was a central topic at the first public women's rights conference in Seneca Falls, New York, in 1848. Reflecting the more radical wing within the movement, the Seneca Falls "Declaration of Sentiments" charged marriage law with the "civil death" of women. In protest against that legal death, when Lucy Stone and Henry Blackwell married in 1855, presiding minister Thomas Wentworth Higginson read a prepared statement explaining the couple's rejection of matrimonial law for "refus[ing] to recognize the wife as an independent, rational being, while . . . confer[ing] upon the husband an injurious and unnatural superiority." Elizabeth Cady Stanton minced no words: "the right idea of marriage is the foundation of all reforms." John Stuart Mill provided further ammunition, arguing in *The Subjection of Women* (1869) that anything less than "ideal" egalitarian marriage was the "relic[] of primitive barbarism." Mill believed that marriage rightly reconstructed could bring about "moral regeneration."[21] The progressives would champion many of these ideas, particularly the linking of marital reform with personal, social, and moral regeneration.

DIVORCE, AMERICAN STYLE

While marriage is a dearly held US institution, so is divorce.[22] Alexis de Tocqueville found "no country in the world where the tie of marriage is so much respected as in America"—but also noted a "restless disposition" and "excessive love of independence" that worked against permanent unions.[23] The history of divorce law in the United States diverges more sharply from the British legal tradition than is the case with marital law.

English divorce law was for centuries enmeshed in ecclesiastical law. Canon law allowed for *divortium a vinculo* (divorce from bonds of matrimony) and *divortium a mensa et thoro* (divorce from bed and board, or judicial separation) only on very restricted grounds. Moreover, in neither case could either spouse remarry. The church recognized only three grounds for divorce: adultery, "spiritual adultery" (such as heresy or apostasy), and cruelty. Annulment—which did permit remarriage—necessitated proving some prohibited relationship between the parties (such as incest) or some precontract voiding the marriage (such as if one party had previously agreed to wed another).

None of those options sufficed for Henry VIII, the single most important individual in this history after St. Paul and Luther. Henry VIII sought what would later come to be known as an absolute divorce, allowing him to remarry. Since the option did not then exist, he petitioned for a private act to dissolve his marriage, and so began the process of Parliamentary divorce. Time-consuming, cumbersome, and expensive, Parliamentary divorce evolved as a practice available only to the wealthiest and most powerful— and thus by definition almost never to women. One scholar proposes £1,000 as a conservative estimate of the cost of divorce before 1857, when Parliament passed the Divorce Act, which shifted jurisdiction from the church to the courts. (In today's figures, that would be nearly £72,000, or well over $100,000.)[24] Even then, the law remained extremely restrictive, recognizing only adultery as a statutory ground for ending a union.

The United States inherited the canon law provisions for annulment and separation along with England's Parliamentary divorce procedure. (The colonies, lacking a parliament, simply transferred jurisdiction to the legislature.[25]) Yet while British colonies were forbidden from enacting laws opposed to what prevailed in England, beginning in the seventeenth and eighteenth centuries, Massachusetts and Connecticut passed laws permitting absolute divorce. Other states followed suit after independence. The Puritan scheme provided an enduring framework for American divorce, with many states accepting as statutory grounds adultery, desertion, and/ or cruelty. More liberal states included an "omnibus" clause granting the legislature discretion in expanding the grounds for divorce.[26] In sum, divorce was easier to get in America than in England, practically from the beginning.

The American Revolution extended the shift away from British attitudes toward divorce. As soon as "Americans create[d] a rationale for dissolving the bonds of empire," Basch writes, "they set about creating rules for dissolving the bonds of matrimony." US citizens were soon claiming divorce as a right.[27] During the half century after independence, many states liberalized divorce laws further, for instance by admitting additional statutory grounds (such as insanity, felony conviction, or alcoholism). While the grounds varied from state to state, by 1800 the American legal formula for divorce—predicated on the guilt of one spouse and innocence of the other—was in place. That formula would remain in place until California led the "no-fault" legal revolution beginning in the 1970s. New York was (along with South Carolina) the state with the most restrictive laws, a point to which I will return, in discussing Upton and Meta Sinclair's divorce in Chapter 3.

Divorce made headlines internationally in the nineteenth century, but the US chapter again tells a unique story. As early as the 1830s, a French visitor remarked on how marriages were much more "easily dissolved" in the United States than in Europe. By mid-century, states like Indiana, with their relatively lax requirements, were seen as "divorce meccas" or "divorce mills," laying the groundwork for what would become, according to historian Glenda Riley, a "national scandal." Divorce accelerated after the Civil

War: in 1860, over 7,000 American couples divorced (1.2 per 1,000 marriages), a number growing to nearly 11,000 by 1870, and then nearly doubling by 1880 and tripling by 1890. In 1900, over 55,000 American couples divorced (4.0 per 1,000 marriages). The trend is clear, but historians differ in how to interpret it. Basch, Riley, and Carl N. Degler see feminist implications in women's ability to divorce their husbands—suggesting what Basch terms the "radical possibility" of women's independence, a position with which I agree. William O'Neill and Roderick Phillips, however, see the divorce boom as a way of extending traditional gender expectations, the patriarchal family, and the reach of capitalism.[28]

THE PROGRESSIVE ERA DEBATE

Contrary to popular perception, the nineteenth-century trend throughout Europe as well as America up to midcentury was to make divorce easier, not harder, to acquire. Over the nineteenth century divorce became legal in many states, while others extended statutory grounds. But then things changed in the Progressive era.

In an effort to understand the sharp increase in divorce, the Department of Labor published two landmark documents. The first, *A Report on Marriage and Divorce in the United States, 1867 to 1886*, appeared in 1889. It was compiled by the founding US Commissioner of Labor Carroll D. Wright, who had achieved a considerable reputation as a labor statistician. After much agitation for an updated investigation, in January 1905 President Theodore Roosevelt urged Congress to authorize the collection of statistics for the twenty-year period just concluded. The president explained, "the institution of marriage is, of course, at the very foundation of our social organization, and all influences that affect that institution are of vital concern to the people of the whole country." Roosevelt was alarmed by the escalating divorce rate, which he believed, in reasoning that still sounds familiar, "result[ed] in a diminishing regard for the sanctity" of marriage. In February 1905, Congress approved a resolution directing the census division to collect and publish additional statistics; the result was *Marriage and Divorce 1867–1906* (Volume One, 1909; Volume Two, 1908). Both volumes include dozens of statistical tables exemplifying what Robert H. Wiebe famously called the Progressive era's "search for order."[29]

If statistics are themselves value-neutral, the same cannot be said of the conclusions drawn from them in *Marriage and Divorce 1867–1906*. Notwithstanding the report's title, fewer than forty pages actually consider mar-

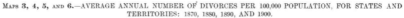

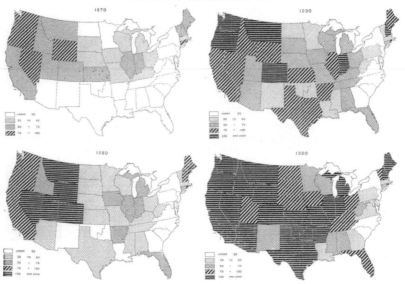

FIGURE 3. This graphic depiction of the escalating divorce rate as dark passages appears in the somber government report *Marriage and Divorce 1867–1906*. Reading from top left down, the years depicted are 1870, 1880, 1890, and 1900. The editors gloss this image as demonstrating a "dark cloud" is sweeping the United States.

riage. Nearly eight hundred track divorce, broken down by many variables such as cause, libellant, duration of marriage, and state of residence. More remarkable is the editorializing within the discursive section of the report. Finding the rate of divorce "markedly higher" than that of the population increase, *Marriage and Divorce 1867–1906* declares it "startling and difficult of belief" that one in twelve unions end in divorce. There was no doubt: a "dark cloud" was passing over the United States. The report made clear that divorce had become, in the words of a modern historian, an "American tradition."[30]

As divorce became more common, opposition mounted. The antidivorce movement gained in force as well as sanctimoniousness after the Civil War, peaking in the Progressive era. In reaction to the swelling numbers of divorces, a "legal counterrevolution" developed. Between 1889 and 1906, more than a hundred pieces of restrictive legislation were enacted by state legislatures, particularly in the East, seeking to curtail divorce.[31]

Civic organizations also played a significant role in trying to restrict divorce, most notably the New England Divorce Reform League. The league found its champion in a Vermont minister who had been defrocked when he refused to officiate at the second marriage of a divorced congregant. From 1884 to 1913 Samuel W. Dike served as secretary of the league. Broadening its reach, it was reorganized in 1885 as the National Divorce Reform League before assuming in 1897 a more ideologically charged name: National League for the Protection of the Family. (The rhetoric of "protection" anticipates a piece of legislation passed one hundred years later, the 1996 Defense of Marriage Act.) Dike was skeptical that legislation, however, could slow the divorce boom, which he saw as a social "evil," not a legal problem. He believed the indissolubility of marriage rested not on human but natural and divine laws. While Dike did not believe Christ intended to impose his teachings on state laws, he maintained that His ideas would be "work[ed] out in the historic progress of Christianity." Not surprisingly, Dike rejected the interpretation of marriage as a legal contract, countering that contracts "generally transfer things" and allow for no "personal relations" such as he understood to lie at the center of marriage.[32]

The reaction against divorce generated an additional movement, this one promoting uniform national laws. Organized by Pennsylvania Governor Samuel L. Pennypacker, the 1906 National Divorce Conference hosted representatives of forty-two states. The aim was to draft consistent legislation that states could voluntarily adopt to curb the "special evils and scandals" caused by variation among state laws. With the failure of states to voluntarily adopt these provisions (only New Jersey, Delaware, and Wisconsin did so), interest mounted in a constitutional amendment that would give Congress exclusive jurisdiction over matrimonial and divorce law. TR himself liked the idea.[33] While this effort to nationalize marriage law failed, it had a belated triumph in different form in 1996, when President Clinton signed the Defense of Marriage Act, which denies federal recognition of same-sex marriage. (In a 5-4 decision on *United States v. Windsor* [opinion issued June 26, 2013], the Supreme Court struck down the Defense of Marriage Act as violating the Fifth Amendment.) Even if citizens in the Progressive era could not agree as to who might divorce, they could agree a century later on who might not marry.

As Herbert Croly noted in his classic articulation of progressivism, *The Promise of American Life* (1909), his generation was divided over whether divorce was an "abuse" or a "fulfillment" of marriage.[34] Thus while TR, Dike, and the National Divorce Conference participants interpreted the government reports as documenting a mounting "evil," others examining the same statistics drew more hopeful conclusions.

Particularly notable, Walter F. Willcox's response to the first (1889) report in "The Divorce Problem—A Study in Statistics" (1891) provides an early and influential statement of what will become the progressive position on marriage reform. A Cornell economist and statistician, Willcox experienced what he intriguingly described as a "conversion" while studying *A Report on Marriage and Divorce in the United States, 1867 to 1886*. The Cornell professor had previously considered marriage an indissoluble sacrament, but reading the Wright report had the unexpected consequence of convincing Willcox that legal measures could not restrain divorce. Even more significantly, it convinced him that marriage should, but currently did not, support the emancipation of women. Instead of marriage based on "the despotic authority of a single head," Willcox called for a "democratic" model of marriage determined by "the consenting and harmonious wills of two equals."[35]

Willcox's "The Divorce Problem" exemplifies an interpretation that would become increasingly common among liberals: the rising divorce rate demonstrated that Americans were expecting more, not less, from marriage. As one example of this new interpretation, Hutchins Hapgood challenged the claim that the divorce statistics proved marriage to be "passing away." To the contrary, he wrote, those numbers indicate "the vitality of marriage" and even the persistence of "a marriage ideal that is hard to attain." But that ideal must still be pursued: "We again demand spiritual marriage," Hapgood insisted, "and to attain it are restlessly striving to work out deeper social and more human bases than those of the past."[36]

The new cohort of professional social scientists such as Willcox established an influential conception of marriage not as sacrament, status, or contract but rather an evolving social institution. One of the foundational texts for this view, Herbert Spencer's *Principles of Sociology* (1876), asserts "the marital relations[,] like the political relations, have gradually evolved" and that "progress towards higher social types is joined with progress towards higher types of domestic institutions." In the wake of Spencer, comparative evolutionary studies of marriage began appearing in the late nineteenth century. Landmarks include Edward Westermarck's ethnographic *The History of Human Marriage* (1891) and the first historical study by an American, George Elliott Howard's *A History of Matrimonial Institutions* (1904)—of which considerably more will be said in the next chapter.[37]

At the American Sociological Association's 1908 conference, which fo-

cused on the topic of the family, most discussants embraced the new insti-
tutional/evolutionary view. ASA President William Graham Sumner set the
tone: "the family has to a great extent lost its position as a conservative institution and has become a field for social change." Several naysayers spoke
at the conference, for instance Rabbi Joseph Krauskopf of Philadelphia,
who reaffirmed the spiritual view of marriage and that "the tendencies of
human nature implanted by the Creator" could never change. But the conservatives were outnumbered by the voices embracing progressive marital
reform, such as Howard, Charlotte Perkins Gilman, and Elsie Clews Parsons. Howard, for instance, proclaimed that the divorce numbers signified
"the mighty progress of spiritual liberation which is radically changing the
relative positions of man and woman in the family and in society."[38]

Rather than try to reform marriage or divorce, a significant cohort of
activist women preferred to opt out altogether. Most notably, the white,
college-educated women who ran settlement houses were, in the words of
Allen F. Davis, "progressives with a vengeance." The most famous of these,
Jane Addams founded Hull House in Chicago in September 1889 along with
her close friend Ellen Gates Starr. Addams described Hull House as "an experimental effort to aid in the solution of the social and industrial problems"
of the city. Resident workers in Hull House and other settlements immersed
themselves in crafting solutions — setting up nurseries and kindergartens
for immigrant children, campaigning to end child labor, inspecting facto-
ries. Merging public activities and private life, the settlement house was also
a domestic space, easily identified as the "only house with flower boxes" on
a grimy block, often with neighborhood children running in and out.[39]

The settlement house was decidedly an *alternative* domestic space. While
men participated, women so dominated that Robyn Muncy calls the settlement house an "institution of separatist feminism." One male reformer at
the time snidely called the residents "sexually unemployed," echoing the
pervasive view that they were spinsters. But historians now emphasize that
settlement workers formed intense, intimate, and sometimes passionate relationships with each other. According to Muncy, these women did not have
to make the difficult choice between marriage and career; they had "rich,
emotional partnerships," and they had deeply satisfying work. The often
imperious Addams, for instance, found a life partner in the mild-mannered
heiress Mary Rozet Smith. A poem Addams wrote for Smith describes their
nonproprietary union as superior to "The 'mine' and 'thine' of wedded
folk." The couple enjoyed, according to Addams biographer Victoria Bissell
Brown, a life of "tenderness and affection, the root of mutual admiration

and devotion that typifies any strong marriage," while another historian calls Smith the only person to know the "private" Addams. The two women spoke of themselves as a couple, and Addams cherished the "healing domesticity" of her life with Smith. We know that the two slept in the same bed (common for women friends at the time), but will never know if this Boston marriage was sexual—and despite prurient curiosity (in which I share), that is not really the point. The Smith-Addams relationship was a permanent union, the most important one in either of their lives, and a successful alternative to heterosexual marriage. As Brown puts it, just as Addams did in social reform, she also "innovated in the intimate, domestic, and material arrangements of her life."[40]

Another notable resident, Florence Kelley appeared at the door of Hull House in December 1891, three young children in hand. A Cornell graduate who had also studied in Zurich and was a translator of Engels, Kelley had just left an abusive husband in New York. She picked Illinois as her destination precisely because of its more lenient divorce laws. Within her first few years at Hull House, Kelley divorced her husband, won a custody battle, took back her maiden name, went to law school, and also set up a labor bureau for immigrant women. She developed, according to her biographer Kathryn Kish Sklar, "a radical view of marriage" and believed women would not be free until they discarded the outmoded roles of "wife, spinster, and prostitute" and made their own reproductive decisions freely, independent of such labels. According to Sklar and other historians, the settlement house movement, so important in the history of American reform, was predicated on a group of educated, activist women's principled rejection of marriage.[41]

INDIVIDUALISM, FEMINISM, AND MARITAL REFORM

The Progressive era debate over marriage and divorce comprises an important aspect of what historians have identified as a "crisis" in gender roles at the turn into the twentieth century. A volatile economy and the rise of corporate culture, among other dislocations, caused considerable anxiety in white middle class men. Many responded by embracing an ideal of hypermasculinity as embodied in TR's "big stick." According to historian Peter Gabriel Filene, during this period, "regulation, co-operation, 'feminization'" all forced men to "compromise" their gender identity. Another way of interpreting this crisis comes from the so-called "father" of American sociology, evolutionist Lester Frank Ward. He advanced what he termed a "gynaecocentric" theory that "life begins as female" and that males, evolving later, are "a mere afterthought of nature." Ward thus considered "female superiority . . . a perfectly natural condition" and the current patriarchal structure illegitimate — even "make-believe." Whether or not they read Ward, anxious men found additional cause for alarm in New Women who married later than their predecessors (if at all) and tended to favor education and work for pay over the nineteenth-century feminine ideal of the stay-at-home wife.[42]

Both liberals and conservatives identified the new trends with women. Walter F. Willcox, the Cornell statistician who challenged the dire conclusions of the first government report on marriage, found a strong correlation between women's ability to earn a living and the divorce rate. A woman could not possibly *choose* to divorce, Willcox reasoned, when the economy offered scant means to support herself. Likewise for George Elliott Howard, the movement for freer divorce reflected women's increasing independence.[43]

The conservative alignment of women with change could be misogynistic, even hysterical. And women indulged in it almost as often as men. For instance Anna A. Rogers's screed *Why American Marriages Fail* (1909) blames "the scandalous slackening of marriage ties" on the "devouring ego in the 'new woman.'" Neglecting their eternal obligations — foremost among them, marriage — unruly modern women ruined themselves, their marriages, and society. University of Chicago English professor Robert Herrick, in his novel *Together* (1908), a panoramic look at changing views of marriage through the lens of eight different couples, captures another aspect of the conservative lament. In answer to the question explicitly raised by one character, "What is marriage?" Herrick's narrative arc condemns modern experiments, doomed by the foolishness and excessive independence of wives. As the most individualistic wife in *Together* puts it, in a remark intended to sound self-pitying, "marriage is an awful problem for a woman, — any woman who has individuality."[44] Ironically, Herrick would himself go on to have an adulterous affair with a woman who had considerable "individuality" and promoted the new views: Elsie Clews Parsons.

In addition to discussing changing gender roles, commentators on marriage from the left to the right debated the era's mounting individualism. Broadly speaking, proponents of marital reform championed the interests of free individuals whereas opponents defended the ideal of social cohesion. Such a generalization requires immediate qualification. Progressivism as a movement challenged the possessive individualism of classic liberalism in favor of a sense of solidarity and the common good. However in doing so, it put forward an alternate sense of a reconstructed individual. In *The Ethics of Democracy* (1888), John Dewey captures this idea by advocating "an individualism of freedom, of responsibility, of initiatives to and for the ethical ideal, not an individualism of lawlessness"—nor individualism defined in economic terms. Thus, as James T. Kloppenberg concludes, "Securing the independence of the individual seemed to these [Progressive era] thinkers the central challenge of the twentieth century."[45]

The conflicting axes of interest—personal freedom and group cohesion—have been negotiated by many societies, and Herbert Spencer provided the progressive generation with a particular understanding of how to do this. The popular philosopher maintained that while evolution privileged the survival of the species over that of the individual, in the nineteenth century the individual no longer needed to be sacrificed to the group. That was because, in an advanced stage of society such as the progressives believed they enjoyed, social and individual interests became harmonious, at least in theory. Thus Havelock Ellis, for example, could affirm "civilization means the differentiation of individuals." And for muckraking novelist David Graham Phillips, individualism marks the "object and aim of civilization—to encourage and to compel each individual to be frankly himself—herself." Marital reformers believed they lived in a transformational era in which each spouse could claim a right to happiness—and in doing so promote the broader social good. In this respect they differed sharply from mid-nineteenth century utopian reformers such as the Oneidans, for whom the individual and private family posed the greatest threat to reform.[46]

Social conservatives, generally advocating the earlier ideal of possessive individualism, did not find harmony between individual and social interests. Anti-divorce crusader Samuel Dike, for instance, believed so many marriages were ending precisely because people looked "solely from the individual point of view" and thus forgot about their higher responsibility as social beings. Likewise, in "The Change in the Feminine Ideal" (1910), novelist Margaret Deland claims to be hopeful about the New Woman—but then finds the Victorian mother's "*selflessness*" superior to the unfortunate new cult of "feminine individualism." As to divorce, Deland believed it signifies "supreme individualism," fretting that "divorce, the most intensely social question in the world, is almost invariably treated as an individual question." Because marriage, after all, "is civilization's method of remaining civilized," it must be protected against rampant individualists who promoted divorce.[47] TR's fears of "race suicide" provide one of the more

panic-stricken variants of the conservative partiality for the interests of society—often figured as civilization itself—over the individual.

In his invaluable study of divorce in the Progressive era, William O'Neill
points out an interesting shift in this debate over individualism that has occurred across a wide swath of American history. Whereas Progressive era
conservatives opposed individualism, modern conservatives position themselves as champions of the individual.[48] The intense debates over marriage
and divorce at the turn into the twentieth century continue into the present,
although terms and positions have the most curious way of changing sides.

Let us now look at a transatlantic group of writers who articulated a new
vision of marriage in the Progressive era.

CHAPTER TWO

The Architects of the Progressive Marital Ideal

Frank Norris's over-the-top novel *McTeague* (1899) condenses many Progressive era concerns about marriage into one memorable scene. Immediately after Trina Sieppe marries her bumbling dentist, the narrator focuses on the bride's thoughts:

> She—perhaps McTeague as well—felt there was a certain inadequateness about the ceremony. Was that all there was to it? Did just those few muttered phrases make them man and wife? It had been over in a few moments, but it had bound them for life. Had not something been left out? Was not the whole affair cursory, superficial?[1]

A binding decision, marriage was strangely insubstantial. Sealed by ceremonies authorized by church and state, marriage rested on the notion that a particular set of words—some abracadabra—exerted magical power that bound people together for life. Were there not, as the bride wonders, all sorts of vital things "left out" by this idea of marriage?

This chapter examines writers of influential nonfiction who articulated exactly what had been left out—as well as what they felt should be added in to marriage. America's foremost feminist theorist in the Progressive era, Charlotte Perkins Gilman (1860–1935) wrote, in addition to the fiction for which she is now best known, influential treatises such as *Women and Economics* (1898). As an index of her prominence as a thinker on social problems, Gilman delivered a paper at the American Sociological Association's 1908 conference, which focused on the family. She shared the podium with George Elliott Howard (1849–1928), who had recently published *A History of Matrimonial Institutions* (1904), the first such history written by an American.[2] Also speaking at that 1908 conference, sociologist Elsie Clews Parsons (1875-1941) wrote extensively about the new ideas, most notably in her controversial *The Family* (1906). On the other side of the Atlantic, Swedish reformer Ellen Key (1849-1926) showcased her curious variety of essentialist feminism in the wildly popular *Love and Marriage*, translated into English in 1911. (Key has recently reentered the public eye as a character in Nancy Horan's bestselling historical novel *Loving Frank* [2007]).[3] Romantic socialist Edward Carpenter (1844-1928) published *Love's Coming of Age* in 1896; by 1918 it had appeared in seven US editions. Havelock Ellis (1859-1939), after weathering an obscenity trial in England over the first of his seven-volume *Studies in the Psychology of Sex* (1896-1910, 1928), found a more hospitable home for the series with Philadelphia publisher Davis. His wife, novelist and essayist Edith (Lees) Ellis (1861-1916), achieved fame in the United States during her popular lecture tour through twenty-four states in 1914. America, she wrote her husband while on that tour, "understand[s] what you and I stand for."[4] South African–born Olive Schreiner (1855-1920) had a huge US readership beginning with her novel *The Story of an African Farm* (1883), in which the protagonist rejects marriage and chooses unwed motherhood. I focus here on Schreiner's treatise *Woman and Labour* (1911), which, like *The Theory of the Leisure Class* (1899) by political economist Thorstein Veblen (1857-1929), concentrates on the destructive division of labor within marriage. These writers were the foremost intellectual architects of progressive marital reform. I will refer to them collectively as the marriage reformers, the marital theorists, and the experts. Their books inspired and in some cases were directly cited by the couples I examine in later chapters.

Progressive marital reform boils down to five basic premises. First, the economic arrangement of wage-earning husband and dependent wife corrupted marriage. The reformers sought to make spouses, in Gilman's pithy term, "class equals."[5] Second, the marital theorists denied that marriage gained legitimacy from external arbiters such as law or religion. Championing what they considered a higher and emotion-based morality, they maintained that only the couple could validate a marriage. A third goal was to replace what the reformers saw as compulsory monogamy with voluntary monogamy. Fourth, they believed no marriage was valid unless it could be dissolved at the will of either spouse. Accordingly, they championed what would later become known as "no fault" divorce, which would sweep the United States, beginning in the 1970s. And finally, the reformers affirmed

UNIVERSITY OF WINCHESTER
LIBRARY

female sexuality, arguing that mutually satisfying sex cemented and indeed validated marriage.

Although this chapter synthesizes these writers' ideas, I do so with the caveat that they did not mount some monolithic front. They represent more a convergence of thought than a deliberate program. There are differences of opinion and emphasis among the marital theorists—sometimes even sharp disagreement. Those variances do not, however, gainsay that the reformers agreed on much, nor that their collective message provided a theoretical rationale for a shift in marital mores. Theirs is not a grand theory of sexuality such as Foucault's or Freud's; rather, what I might call the small-t theory of progressive marital reform was oriented toward changing expectations and behavior, and through that, transforming social arrangements. A different sort of caveat is also in order: the reformers' egalitarian views coexisted with some ideas that now appear regressive. While committed to gender equity, they believed men and women were intrinsically different in ways that now appear suspicious. They romanticized "nature," posited a Golden Age, and, most distressingly, trafficked in eugenics. I will discuss these suspect positions at the end of the chapter; for now I repeat my disclaimer regarding the word *progressive*, which I use as an historical descriptor of an era, not an evaluation nor an endorsement.

These reform ideas, the appealing and unsavory alike, result from the Darwinian paradigm shift. Evolutionary theory made it possible to conceive of marriage as an institution that inevitably changed over time. "All human institutions are open to improvement," Gilman writes, adding that marriage had, of yet, "not fully evolved." Carl Degler usefully differentiates reform Darwinism from its better-known conservative cousin: "Social Darwinists might rephrase Darwinism to suit their defense of the present, but reformers could not help but find Darwinian evolution congenial since it clearly proclaimed the ubiquity and persistence of change." Two quotations capture the tone of the marital theorists' reform Darwinism. First, Key explains how Darwin made it possible to conceptualize a better sort of marriage: "It was evolutionism that first gave man courage to ask . . . whether . . . marriage did not exist for mankind, and not mankind for marriage." Second, like the other reformers committed to preserving marriage, Gilman insists that there was no danger of its "passing," as conservatives warned, because the "true spirit of marriage" would flourish through the evolutionary process of critique and reform.[6] This paradox of change and stability structures progressive marital reform. The challenge was how to align marriage rhetorically with evolutionary progress.

REFORM 101: MARRIAGE AND ECONOMICS

The root of the contemporary problem, the theorists maintained, lay in women's economic dependence. They called the prevailing middle class model of marriage "mercenary" and "proprietary"—and also "coercive," because the economic differential inevitably also became a power differential. Since the reformers believed "the problems of marriage and the family can be solved only by grasping their relations to the economic system" (in Howard's words), that is the place to begin examining progressive marital theory.[7] Gilman, Schreiner, and Veblen provide the supplest critiques of what Gilman termed "The Business Side of Matrimony." While their ideas do not map perfectly onto twenty-first century concerns (such as over married women's conflicts balancing home and work, or the impact on

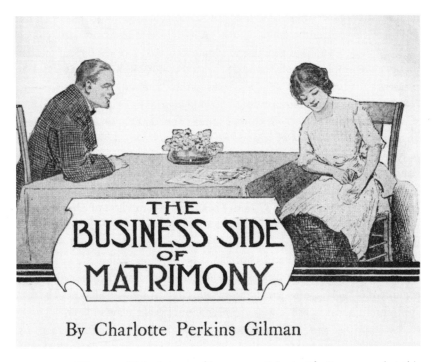

FIGURE 4. Gilman published many of her own articles in *The Forerunner*, but this article appeared in the January 1914 issue of *Physical Culture*, edited by fitness guru Bernarr Macfadden.

marriage when a wife is the primary breadwinner), their focus on economic problems within marriage remains instructive.

In an estimation that may surprise her readers today, Gilman considered *Human Work* (1904) her most important book. The title identifies one of her essential ideas: that labor is a defining attribute of humanity—not just of masculinity. For Gilman, work serves deep personal and social needs: allowing a person to assert her humanity, work also connects her with society. Moreover, Gilman understood worker and work as generating a cycle of creative evolution: "in the act of working the individual is modified, and by the work accomplished humanity is modified." Productive work, therefore, helps evolution along.[8]

The problem Gilman identifies is that while women had been exemplary workers in early history (as she extrapolated from the demands of motherhood), proprietary marriage defines work as male. She addresses the ensuing crisis especially well in *Women and Economics*. That treatise, hailed by Jane Addams as a "Masterpiece," went through eight American editions (as well as numerous translations) by 1915.[9] Gilman argues that the only work consistently available to middle- and upper-class white women was marriage—and that the job candidate had only her sex appeal to offer prospective employers. Or, rather, prospective buyers, for the wife became property, a man's "most precious possession." Gilman believed marriage consequently turned into a twisted "sexuo-economic relation" in which a husband constitutes his wife's "food supply," even her entire "economic environment." Woman could achieve "wealth, power, social distinction, fame" only one way: "through a small gold ring." Gilman sums up the perverse result: "we are the only animal species in which the female depends on the male for food, the only animal species in which the sex-relation is also an economic relation. With us an entire sex lives in a relation of economic dependence upon the other sex, and the economic relation is combined with the sex-relation."[10]

Through this fusion (and confusion) of the sexual and the economic, the wife, then, becomes functionally identical to the prostitute. Gilman's argument of marriage-as-prostitution, inherited from Marx and Engels, was common in her day, reflecting anxieties about "white slavery" and sexually transmitted diseases.[11] Gilman makes the argument her own by focusing on the result of women's needing to compete for husbands: "Here may be given an economic reason for the oft-noted bitterness with which the virtuous women regard the vicious." That is, the "virtuous" wife-to-be "refus[es] to part with herself—her only economic goods—until she is assured of legal marriage," whereas the "vicious" prostitute offers a man "the same goods—though of inferior quality, to be sure—for a far less price." In one of her best lines, Gilman terms the wife's revulsion at the prostitute "the hatred of the trade-unionist for 'scab labor.'" There is a strong class bias here, as throughout Gilman; the prostitute is one of few working-class women to appear in her writing. And women of color remain invisible to her, except for when they appear as a nebulous threat. To her credit, however, Gilman does challenge her intended reader's class loyalties. By framing marriage as the selling of sexual "goods" for a sizable fee, and wives therefore as members of a trade union, Gilman forces readers to see wives and prostitutes as varieties of the same species: women in the sex trade. She argues as well that sexuo-economics undermines morality more generally. When we see sex exchanged for money "in the open market of vice"—that is, in prostitution—"we are sick with horror." Yet "when we see the same economic relation made permanent, established by law, sanctioned and sanctified by religion, covered with flowers and incense and all accumulated sentiment"—that is, in marriage—"we think it innocent, lovely, and right." As she sums up the prevalent hypocrisy, "The transient trade we think evil. The bargain for life we think good."[12]

Gilman uses science as well as class loyalty to advance her argument. Following Darwin, she believed that evolution unfolds by the dual processes of natural and sexual selection. Usually those processes balance each other, with natural selection modifying the individual to its environment, while sexual selection "modifi[es] it to its mate." However, the critical point for Gilman is that in a state of nature, females select males, whereas under sexuo-economics, men select women, and "the balance of [evolutionary] forces is altered." Men continue to work and progress while unworking women remain stationary, finding themselves "left behind, outside, below, having no social relation whatever, merely the sex-relation."[13] For Gilman, then, the circumscribed position of the wife impedes the evolution of society at large.

Unlike Gilman, when Olive Schreiner married in 1894, she kept her own name—while her husband assumed hers. Like Gilman's *Women and Economics*, Schreiner's similarly titled *Woman and Labour* was hailed as a breakthrough feminist text, in this case the "Bible of the Woman's Movement." The two books share a focus on the inadequate opportunities middle- and upper-class women find for work and an assumption of a Golden Age in which women's labor had been integral to society. Schreiner defines women's work, however, in different terms. For centuries, child-bearing had been woman's "highest duty," according to Schreiner, a type of work valued as highly as hunting. Thus, rather than Gilman's emphasis on women's sexual attractiveness in *Women and Economics*, Schreiner focuses on reproduction.[14]

At a time when socialism was more respectable in the United States than at any time since, Schreiner emphasizes the conditions of production and formation of classes.[15] Throughout history, she maintains, whenever a separate group is isolated to perform unpleasant work, class hierarchy emerges. She traces the pattern back to ancient Greece but believes the Industrial Revolution intensified the class schism, since machines generate greater profits, but for fewer people.

The Industrial Revolution is crucial also to Schreiner's analysis of gender. She contends, counterintuitively, that industry rendered men's work more exacting and stimulating even while eroding the social value of reproduction. This downgrading of women's traditional work occurred because the increasing use of machines called for fewer laborers to run them. Since the Industrial Revolution also led to improved food and medicine, more children survived to become adult workers, exacerbating the problem of excess labor. And so mothers, for centuries valued because they reproduced and nurtured children who eventually entered the workforce, found themselves reclassified—as social burdens. Schreiner warns that "the time is now rapidly approaching when child-bearing will be regarded . . . as a lofty privilege." What follows sounds rather like a threat: "millions" of contemporary women will "go through life not merely childless, but without sex relationship in any form whatever."[16] Should that trend continue, heterosexual men might find themselves lonely indeed—to say nothing of sexually frustrated.

Schreiner sounds her loudest alarm for the elite: the society lady has become a freak. Schreiner's skill as a novelist serves her well here, for the creature she delineates is plausible and, in its repulsiveness, fascinating. When an affluent woman has offspring, Schreiner says, servants do the work of raising the children, and so the mother degenerates into "'the fine lady,' the human female parasite." The absence of work makes the lady a Dorian Gray-like creature who initially attracts but ultimately repulses. Contrasting robust working women of the past with their debased sisters of the present, Schreiner writes, "in place of the active laboring woman, upholding society by her toil, has come the effete wife, concubine, or prostitute, clad in fine raiment, the work of others' fingers, fed on luxurious viands, the result of others' toil." Epitomizing the "debilitating effect of wealth," this privileged parasite claims riches as her due while herself making no social contribution.[17] While Gilman's trade unionist wife is hypocritical in her scorn for the prostitute, Schreiner's parasitic wife is abhorrent.

Schreiner sought to convince men that the diminished social status of reproduction was not some remote "women's" issue but rather vital to their own interests. She therefore addresses the parasite wife's wider social impact. In doing so Schreiner constructs a fable of disastrous maternal influence by fusing graphic gynecological language with the belief of natural scientist Lamarck that acquired characteristics could be inherited. Schreiner grounds her fable in the birth process: "With each generation the entire race passes through the body of its womanhood as through a mould, reappearing with the indelible marks of that mould upon it." One might assume that description to be metaphoric, but Schreiner intends the molding process to be taken quite literally, for she then says, "the os cervix of woman, through which the head of the human infant passes at birth, forms a ring, determining forever the size at birth of the human head, a size which could only increase if in the course of ages the os cervix of woman should itself slowly expand."[18] Not particularly persuasive as a logical account, the explicit gynecological details nevertheless support a memorable fable of how a socially constructed limitation—the parasite wife—can end up having disastrous biological consequences. All children of parasitic mothers, boys just as much as girls, would be impaired.

Schreiner extends her alarm call by turning to history, where she finds a consistent pattern. Across the ages, periods of acute female parasitism precede social collapse, she says. For example, she attributes male homosexuality in ancient Greece to the poor company that parasitic wives provided. Ancient Rome, after developing "the most appalling . . . parasite female that earth has produced," likewise disintegrated. And Schreiner claims that if the Progressive era "parasite woman on her couch, loaded with gewgaws, the plaything and amusement of man, be the permanent and final manifestation of female human life on the globe, then that couch is also the deathbed of human evolution."[19] Progress, quite simply, would end.

And so *Woman and Labour* portrays the lost value of reproduction as first women's, but ultimately society's, fall from a state of grace. Schreiner's notion of women's essential work as reproductive, which sounds reactionary today, has made her a difficult pill for modern feminists to swallow. (Her analysis of the depreciation of motherhood may, however, be worth reviewing for light it may shed on the dreadful discourse about "welfare queens.") But while Schreiner's idea now seems constricting, she takes an expansive view of the future, calling for women to "have our share of honoured and socially useful human toil, our full half of the labour of the Children of Woman." She calls for no less than opening all jobs to women—not simply to liberate one half of the species but also to save civilization. Her conflicting notions about the scope of women's labor exemplify Carolyn Burdett's claim that Schreiner's thinking is simultaneously romantic and modern.[20]

More focused on what's wrong with the present than how to redeem the future, Veblen demonstrates the absurd yet integral role of the wife in sustaining capitalism. Like *Women and Economics* and *Woman and Labour*, *The Theory of the Leisure Class* posits women to have been the original workers, not so much because of motherhood as because they innately have more of the productive "instinct of workmanship" that Veblen admires.[21]

Leisure Class focuses, however, on wives' role as consumers, which Veblen believes alienates them from their own nature as workers. That superimposed role causes a universal mystification. The general population, conditioned to idealize the stay-at-home, money-spending wife, mistakes an absurd social construct of feminine uselessness as an unchanging principle. For this misunderstanding alone, "it grates painfully on our nerves to contemplate the necessity of any well-bred woman's earning a living by useful work," Veblen says dryly; "it is not 'woman's sphere.'" His analysis unmasks as humbug the ideology of separate spheres, a rationalization for excluding women from the labor force by enshrining them in the private home. Veblen exposes the supposedly private wife as actually having a very public role as the most conspicuous of all consumers. In doing so, the wife leads only a "vicarious" existence; her life is but an "expression of the man's life at the second remove."[22] For Veblen, there is no private sphere over which the wife presides; the entire world is a stage, one where men pull all the strings.[23]

For Veblen, all behaviors, no matter how irrational, have underlying economic causes. He traces the vicarious position of wives (and loss of their one-time role as laborers) back to the origins of the institution of ownership. Like many thinkers in his generation, Veblen identifies private property as originating with the ownership of women. Whereas for Gilman the tipping point occurred when women lost their role as sexual selectors, and for Schreiner when reproduction lost social value, for Veblen it occurred when women became more "useful[] as trophies" than workers. Even the wealthiest wife "still quite unmistakably remains [her husband's] chattel in theory; for the habitual rendering of vicarious leisure and consumption is the abiding mark of the unfree servant."[24] And so Veblen's chattel-wife joins the ranks with Mrs. Parasite and Madame Trade-Unionist. His critique of marriage is more abstract than either Gilman's or Schreiner's, but also funnier, and he takes obvious delight in undermining cultural idols.

In many ways Veblen differs from the other marital reformers. He positioned himself as objective analyst, not engaged reformer. And no one, to my knowledge, has ever accused Veblen of buoyant optimism. However, a string of comments, particularly toward the end of *Leisure Class*, insinuate that *if* reform were ever to happen (not that the cagey Veblen would ever make such a prediction), it would begin with wives overthrowing their vicarious existence as consumers. First, he suggests "woman's temperament includes a larger share of this instinct that approves peace and disapproves futility," making the wife's obligatory nonproductivity alien to her. Second, Veblen tips his hat toward a group more likely than leisure class wives to campaign for change—the "'New Woman' movement." He puts the phrase in scare quotes, presumably, to indicate that movement is not so much new as an effort "to rehabilitate the woman's pre-glacial standing," that is, their standing as purposeful workers lost eons ago. Veblen's support for the women's movement become more evident when he identifies "'Emancipation' and 'Work'" as its keynotes. Work (when productive and not merely "ceremonial," another of Veblen's key words) is one of few things to which he assigns positive value. By linking work with emancipation as the defining qualities of the women's movement, then, he endorses it while also indicating that emancipation itself is predicated on women's autonomous work.[25] Marriage constitutes for Veblen the chief mechanism by which women become alienated from work and from themselves.

NOBODY'S BUSINESS

Once upon a time—or so the reformers believed—marriage had been a natural, healthy, organic relationship between two lovers. But then the Catholic Church took hold and pronounced it a sacrament, making external authority necessary to legitimate marriage. At that precise point, the reformers charged, marriage became artificial. Most (but not all) of the marital theorists maintained that state interference further corrupted it. And so they sought to put external authorities out of the marriage business so as to return it to individual lovers. Marriage should be, as Elsie Clews Parsons concisely put it, "nobody's business."[26]

The reformers made their case for "Privacy in Love Affairs" (Parsons's phrasing again) through a variety of arguments, some scholarly, others mystical. Even the most plausible of these arguments are tied up with the ir-rational assumption of a past Golden Age that I will take up later. I concen-trate here on the use of an interesting assortment of facts (as the reformers defined them) to discredit church and state jurisdiction over marriage. The logic corresponds with what historian Morton G. White identified years ago as a "revolt against formalism." Late nineteenth- and early twentieth-century anti-formalists, according to White, rejected arguments from au-thority and deductive reasoning. They preferred data over dogma.[27] So did the Progressive era marital reformers. Facts, they argued, should take pre-cedence over forms. The source for their facts could vary considerably, with one writer turning to history, others to sex, and still others to experiential knowledge.

George Elliott Howard was an impressive compiler of facts. His 1,400-page *A History of Matrimonial Institutions* (1904), based on two decades of research, remains a superb historical source. Howard was the first lecturer in history at his alma mater, the University of Nebraska, taught for ten years at Stanford (which he left in protest when sociologist Edward Ross was fired for his defense of Chinese laborers), and lectured at Cornell and the University of Chicago before returning to Nebraska, becoming in 1906 the head of its new department of political science and sociology. A memorial tribute describes Howard as one of the "great foundation stones of Ameri-can social science," comparing him to William Graham Sumner and Lester Frank Ward, among others. Tantalizingly few details can be reconstructed about the extent of the collaboration, but Howard's wife, Nebraska class-mate Alice May Frost, helped with the research for the *History*.[28]

A reader could spend days poring over Howard's historical data: persons, dates, statutes, canon laws, variations among states, and court decisions. But the book's most distinctive feature is its reformist trajectory. Howard traces a path of slow but certain improvement as the church loses its grip on marriage and can no longer impose its "sterile" notions. A reactionary institution, the church "retard[s] progress." Milton (who advocated easy di-vorce) and Luther (who said marriage was a worldly thing and no business of the church) make brief appearances in the *History* as heroic figures. The key historical event, of course, is the Reformation. Turning the church's authority against itself, Howard selects his words carefully when he says that overthrowing the sacramental idea of marriage was necessary to end the "evils" of ecclesiastical jurisdiction.[29]

Redefining marriage from religious sacrament to "social institution[]," Howard claims it for the classroom of the progressive social scientist.

Rather than passed down by some unchanging god, marriage is an evolving institution to "stud[y] in connection with actual conditions of modern social life."[30] Those ever-changing conditions define marriage anew for each era.

In the finale of the *History*, Howard's voice as reformist educator becomes most clear. Having identified a trend toward companionate, egalitarian relationships, Howard charges his contemporaries to join the "mighty movement for social liberation which has been gaining in volume and strength ever since the Reformation." The increasingly democratic forms of marriage, he argues, reflect changing social conditions and in that (admittedly curious) sense are natural. Locating multiple reasons why "the reformer may gather new courage," including "a better-educated popular sentiment," Howard agrees with labor historian John R. Commons that marriage and family are becoming less "coercive," more "spiritual and psychic association[s]." Howard even glimpses the family's "future evolution" as it moves toward "a higher and nobler spiritual domestic life." All of the *History* but particularly its concluding chapter demonstrates how Howard saw academic work as a platform for progressive reform. He fits the cohort of emergent social scientists described by Carl Degler, "reformers to a man," who believed "the purpose and point of social science were to hasten and channel" progress.[31]

Because Howard frames US history in exceptionalist terms, the progressive trajectory speeds up on this side of the Atlantic. With evident satisfaction, he notes that colonists understood marriage as a civil, not a sacramental affair. Perhaps this soft spot for US history accounts for his enthusiasm for legislating marriage in the present. Howard embraced the idea of marriage as a civil contract, detested common law marriage because its paralegal status pointed to "anarchy," advocated uniform divorce laws across the states, and wanted to see licensing regularized and strengthened.[32] While most reformers believed the government was as bad an arbiter of marriage as the church, Howard welcomed increased state power.

For another antiformalist, Havelock Ellis, "the facts of human nature are more important than the forms." The sorts of facts he uses to discredit forms, however, differ from Howard's. Ellis's encyclopedic *Studies in the Psychology of Sex* organizes facts about sexuality into seven large volumes. Recent commentators have not been very kind to the sexologist, emphasizing (as with Edward Carpenter) his treatment of homosexuality. In particular, many modern feminists reject Ellis's views of lesbianism and lament his influence on women in his own day, such as lesbian novelist Radclyffe Hall and suffragette and birth control activist Stella Browne. His legacy has also been eclipsed by Freud, causing a blind spot in the historical record since in the short term, and particularly in the United States, Ellis was more influential.[33]

The candor with which Ellis writes about sex is still disarming, and must have been truly shocking a century ago. In his autobiography Ellis agrees with a critic that his writing style was characterized by "a calm and mat-ter-of-fact way of making daring revolutionary statements." For example, in an inspired analogy, he maintains "the artificial support of marriage by State regulation . . . resembles the artificial support of the body by corset-wearing." Hoisting fact over form to discredit both religious and state inter-vention, Ellis argues that "the same act" of sexual intercourse "cannot be-come good or bad as it is performed in or out of marriage. There is no magic efficacy in a few words pronounced by a priest or a government official." Reducing religious and civil authority over marriage to a set of magic words is like saying the emperor has no clothes. Ellis offers only restricted praise for the Reformation because he believes the Protestant conception of mar-riage perpetuates a "fiction" both "glaring and mischievous" that "a legal sex-contract . . . is . . . sanctified by the promise of exclusive and permanent mutual love."[34] He rejects as absurd such efforts to "contract" sex through the supreme artifice of law, seeing the state as no improvement over the church. In denouncing the contract model of marriage, Ellis takes a more radical position than do those legal reformers who sought to define marriage as a contract rather than a status, as discussed in the previous chapter.

Ellis's rebuttal of the "fiction" that law could "sanctif[y]" marriage points to another important strand in his argument. While using the language of sanctification, he unhinges it from religious authority. Ellis maintains that each couple creates its own authority because "love brings its own sanc-tity." Turning received opinion on its head, Ellis claims "it is not the legal or religious formality which sanctifies marriage, it is the reality of the mar-riage which sanctifies the form."[35] Emotion, not dogma or statute, authen-ticates marriage.

Ellen Key sought to put marriage on her own sort of high plane. She extends Ellis's idea about marriage providing its own sanctity, proclaim-ing what she calls a "new morality." Her bestselling *Love and Marriage* was touted by novelist, playwright, and *Masses* editor Floyd Dell as "the Talmud of sexual morality." *Harper's Weekly* editor Norman Hapgood (brother of Hutchins) called *Love and Marriage* the most influential work on the subject since Mill's *Subjection of Women*.[36]

Key is one of several marital theorists to posit experience as the decisive fact that authenticates marriage. Thus she maintains, "only cohabitation can decide the morality of a particular case." No external body can grant or deny "sanction . . . in advance." Rather, "each fresh couple . . . must themselves prove its moral claim." Seeing the couple itself responsible for this demonstration, Key makes experience the arbiter and indeed "the moral ground of sexual relations." Endorsing all this high talk, a 1915 popularizer of progressive marriage perceptively noted that Key and the other "leaders of the modern marriage revolt" could at times prove "the sternest of moralists."[37]

Elsie Clews Parsons also believed experience alone legitimizes marriage. Yet unlike Key, Parsons does not rely on moral justifications, which made her textbook *The Family* (1906) controversial. Seeking a national podium, Parsons developed the book out of a course she had taught at Barnard from 1902 to 1905. At a time when study guides were popular in middle class women's groups, particularly for married women, Parsons used a familiar genre for unsuspected ends. Unlike existing study guides that used cross-cultural comparisons to demonstrate the superiority of the Anglo-American family, *The Family* deploys ethnography to indicate how far that family had to go.

A sociologist (later, she would shift to anthropology), Parsons was an impeccable researcher. But at a time before the ideal of objectivity came to dominate the social sciences (and as with Howard), Parsons's scholarship indulges what friends called her "propagandist" tendencies. According to her great-nephew (and biographer), she admitted to writing "propaganda by the ethnographic method." And so the concluding chapter of *The Family* does not simply describe what Parsons calls "*trial* marriage"; it also advocates the practice. The idea sounds pretty mild today: couples should experiment with living together and be free to part without "public condemnation." Ironically, Parsons herself was publicly condemned for this position, even though *The Family* was not the first book to advocate trial marriage. The *New York Herald*, for one, exaggerated that it was the most "radical" work on marriage ever published and denounced its "morality of the barnyard" and "diabolical" tendencies. Parsons's own husband did not read the book when it appeared, assuming *The Family* would be too extreme for his taste. The Baltimore journalist and wit H.L. Mencken, who made a career of mocking what he saw as American "Puritanism," however, called this brouhaha the sort of "uproar which invariably arises in the United States whenever an attempt is made to seek absolute truth."[38]

Edith Ellis concurred with Key and Parsons that sexual experience should precede marriage. Like Key and her husband Havelock, Edith Ellis uses the rhetoric of the church to undermine its power. She does so by recommending that parents encourage youths to experiment as what she calls "Novitiate[s] for Marriage." Like novitiate nuns before taking vows, young people should enter a clearly demarcated period before marrying. Edith Ellis believes such a practice "would surely minimize the gambling element in modern unions, and pave the way to a true monogamy."[39]

I will return to this idea of "true monogamy" presently. For now, I wish to stress that the claim variously made by both of the Ellises, Parsons, and Key that sexual experimentation justifies marriage—not the other way around—charts a new way to think about ethical as well as social issues. As Parsons puts it, "There is an ethical, as well as an intellectual, obligation in seeing things as they were and are before concluding what they ought to be."[40] In addition, these writers' joint recommendation that couples cohabitate (or at least copulate) before taking any vows suggests that, as in the philosophy of pragmatism, truth is best sought through experimentation.

One of Edith Ellis's favorite books was Carpenter's *Love's Coming of Age* (1896), which she considered nearly as revolutionary as Marx's *Capital*. The comparison is useful, since many women of the day dissatisfied with the treatment of gender and sexuality in what one historian terms "mainstream socialism" embraced *Love's Coming of Age*.[41]

Carpenter's emphasis on organic relationships provides an additional rationale for why marriage was nobody's business. An admirer of Walt Whitman, Carpenter believed authentic marriage unified body and soul, male and female—and had nothing to do with the law. Indeed, for Carpenter, the legal system by definition reflects the mores of the dominant class, and so social progress inevitably entails fighting entrenched laws. Hence he declared all "outer laws," whether of church or state, "dead and lifeless." Instead Carpenter urges people to follow "inner laws." And love, he maintains, constitutes a "law unto itself, probably the deepest and most intimate law of human life."[42]

A very different sort of "intimate law" under construction at the time provides a useful context. In a seminal 1890 article in the *Harvard Law Review*, Samuel D. Warren and Louis D. Brandeis issued the first major call to acknowledge a legal "right to privacy." Although the marital reformers (apart from Howard), as I have shown, had little use for the law, the "right to privacy" legal movement intersects with theirs in important ways. A primary spur for Warren and Brandeis, in fact, was protecting a specifically domestic privacy, which they believed was under siege. Moreover, they posit "emotional life, and the heightening of sensations which came with the advance of civilization" as a treasured characteristic of modern life, just as the marital reformers do. By calling for a right to privacy, Warren and Brandeis explicitly make the extraordinary claim that "emotions" deserve legal protection. While the lawyers' concerns are finally more domestic than romantic, their attempt to shield privacy has much in common with what Parsons terms "Privacy in Love Affairs." Rather than church or state interference, Warren and Brandeis were more concerned with the media intrusion on privacy (a subject to which I return in the chapter on the Sinclairs), but like the marriage reformers sought to end "intrusion upon the domestic circle."[43]

VOLUNTARY MONOGAMY

Consistent with this idea that marriage is a private affair, the reformers considered union valid only for so long as partners chose to remain together. And so they differentiated between two types of monogamy: one dead and entombed in laws demanding that unwilling partners remain bound for life; the other alive, flourishing in the hearts and wills of the spouses. The first version was official and compulsory, the second organic and voluntary. Carpenter thought it best to make no vows, "either for a year or a lifetime." Instead, couples could choose to remain together—and keep renewing that choice, day after day. This idea, which I call voluntary monogamy, is the marital theorists' most distinctive. As Havelock Ellis puts it, "since marriage is not a mere contract but a fact of conduct, and even a sacred fact, the free participation of both parties is needed to maintain it."[44]

The reformers believed traditional marriage, by keeping wives economically dependent and de facto prostitutes, undermined voluntary monogamy. Key is particularly adamant about the moral superiority of voluntary over official monogamy. Challenging the "common but erroneous opinion that monogamy has given rise to love," she claims that official monogamy reflects instead the debasing idea of sexual proprietorship. Under official monogamy, husbands compel wives to remain chaste (so as not to lose sexual property to a rival) while covertly enjoying mistresses or prostitutes. Having broken from the faith at an early age, Key criticizes Christianity for promoting such debased "monogamy . . . [as] indeed the law" while "polygamy is the custom." What Key called "real fidelity can only arise when love and marriage become equivalent terms."[45] Emotion, again, prevails over law.

The ideal of voluntary monogamy was especially useful when critics accused the reformers of sabotaging marriage. Consider, for instance, how Gilman responds to conservative worries about the erosion of marriage. Claiming for herself the moral high ground of marital reform, "we shame our own ideals," Gilman writes, "our deepest instincts, our highest knowledge, by this gross assumption that the noblest race on earth will not mate . . . monogamously, unless bought and bribed through the common animal necessities of food and shelter, and chained by law and custom."[46] Surely marriage could do better than that.

Another way the reformers believed voluntary monogamy would improve marriage was by fostering the independent development of each spouse. According to Ellis, heightened individualism generated greater intimacy, allowing marriage to "reach its highest point of creative spiritual unity." The Ellises practiced this ideal by living most of their life in separate dwellings. Havelock Ellis recalls in his autobiography his wife's conviction that "the beauty and intimacy of our relationship was largely founded on this independence and the frequent separations." Anticipating by a decade Crystal Eastman's "marriage under two roofs," Edith Ellis called the practice "semi-detached marriage" in a lecture she gave on her US tour. Using their own domestic life as Exhibit A for marital reform, Edith Ellis explained they "lived as the man and woman of the future will most certainly live—interdependent with regard to . . . love, and independent in all things concerning money."[47]

To illustrate the superiority of voluntary monogamy, the reformers turned once again to evolutionary theory. Ellis and Howard drew heavily from the evolutionary ethnography of Finnish sociologist Edward Westermarck. In *A History of Human Marriage* (first edition 1891, expanded into three volumes in 1922), Westermarck disputes the prevalent idea that the earliest humans lived in a state of promiscuity. He postulates monogamy as the original, most common, and also the highest form of relationship, with polygamy (or, more commonly, polygyny) a later and aberrant phenomenon. Howard draws from Westermarck to emphasize the crucial role that choice makes in the quality of a marriage, particularly for women. Howard sees free consent defining marriage in the earliest stages of human history until, with the advent of private property, marriage by contract or purchase came to the fore. "But fortunately the victory is not complete," writes the reformist historian; "Just as monogamy is never displaced by polygyny . . . so the consent of woman . . . is never entirely destroyed by wife-purchase." As people embrace altruism and sexual egalitarianism, monogamy and consent would again define marriage. For Howard, therefore, "monogamy and self-betrothal," by which he means the ability to give oneself in marriage rather than being given, "are connected by a psychic bond, and together they constitute the highest type of marriage."[48]

Voluntary monogamy, however, assumes a particular idea of freedom that, when pushed to its logical conclusion, leads into sticky territory. Only free parties can choose to be together, and without freedom, "marriage is a fiction . . . possessing no spiritual or moral meaning." But as Carpenter admits, "liberty bring[s] with it risk." Risk emerges because the freedom each partner grants the other includes the freedom to form what Havelock Ellis calls "new affections."[49] Similar vaguely worded acknowledgments of extramarital relationships appear throughout progressive marital theory. It is often unclear whether the writer intends to approve adultery or simply stress the benefits of platonic friendships.

Carpenter pushes the idea furthest. Describing jealous couples holding the idea of property rights in their spouses, he argues that marriage would be sturdier if neither spouse felt threatened by but instead welcomed ancillary relationships as strengthening the marital bond. (Making a similar point, Ellen Key faults proprietary marriage for encouraging "erotic kleptomania.") Carpenter even speaks hastily of the possibility of a couple's "triune" relationship with a third party.[50]

Whither monogamy in all this discussion of open marriages or even *ménages à trois*? Whether individual writers opposed extramarital relationships (as Gilman certainly did), or flittered ambiguously around the idea (the Ellises, Key) or accepted them (Carpenter), the marital theorists insisted they did not endorse "free love." Thus Edith Ellis claims that her "novitiates for love" would never promote "'free love,' as it is miscalled," but rather monogamy. She proposes the term "'free marriage'" since "'free love,'" she snips, often really means "'free lust.'" Although Key claims for women to right to have sexual relationships outside of marriage, she denounces free lovers as "slaves of eroticism" worse than prostitutes. Even Carpenter, while writing hopefully of spouses who would permit each other secondary relationships, endorses "self-control"—a surprisingly nineteenth-century-sounding virtue.[51]

In negotiating this morass, the marriage reformers made two points. First, because authentic marriage entails a purer commitment than that coerced by official monogamy, couples so joined could not be separated by any outside party. Even adultery would not end the marriage unless the couple so chose. Second (and this may sound like puzzling hairsplitting), the more radical wing of the reformers also advocated an emotional monogamy which need not always correlate with bodily monogamy. Such theories notwithstanding, secondary relationships could wreak havoc on a marriage in practice, as later chapters will explore.

What must be emphasized, however, is the reformers' zeal for long-term committed relationships—in other words, for marriage. Schreiner advocates "a closer, more permanent union, more emotionally and intellectually complete and intimate." Key celebrates "the soul's desire for one single person, among an unlimited selection." Parsons believes "truly monogamous relations seem to be those most conducive to emotional or intellectual development and to health." Carpenter claims that marriage was evolving toward a higher ideal of a "durable and distinct relationship" with one's "permanent mate and equal" which would provide "far more . . . enduring joy and satisfaction . . . than any number of frivolous relationships." He says this ideal union creates an "amalgamated personality"—an androgynous improvement, it would seem, over the patriarchal legal concept of "marital unity." Equally optimistic, Gilman maintains that evolution demonstrates the "gradual orderly development of monogamous marriage, as the form of sex-union best calculated to advance . . . the individual and . . . society." The reformers called monogamy a "fundamental rule," a "natural relation, based on biological law" infinitely superior to matrimony, a mere "social relation based on social law." Havelock Ellis sums up the ideal of voluntary monogamy: the "modern tendency as regards marriage is towards its recognition as a voluntary union entered into by two free, equal, and morally responsible persons, and that that union is rather of the nature of an ethical sacrament than of a contract, so that in its essence as a physical and spiritual bond it is outside the sphere of the State's action."[52]

In many respects, this centerpiece of progressive marital reform anticipated the views of America's premier sex-advice columnist in 2010. Promoter of gay rights and marital enthusiast Dan Savage argues that monogamy simply does not work as the primary gauge of a good marriage. In his weekly column "Savage Love," he says that relationships would be more fulfilling, honest, enduring, and happy if couples granted each other freedom to roam. Savage and his own husband practice what the columnist terms "monogamish," contending that infidelities do not harm a marriage as long as partners are honest about them. As a *New York Times* writer puts it, Savage "embraces the institution of marriage, rather than seeking to overthrow it" while also suggesting the possibility of "transform[ing] marriage from within, creating greater institutional flexibility."[53] Add in the idea that renovating marriage could lead to widespread social transformation, and Savage's recipe sounds a great deal like that for progressive marital reform.

DIVORCE THE REMEDY, NOT THE DISEASE

The accelerating divorce rate in the Progressive era, as I discussed in the previous chapter, was interpreted in various ways. The 1908 Census Bureau report that caused such uproar established that rate to have more than quadrupled during the prior thirty years. By 1906 one in twelve marriages ended in divorce. While conservatives lamented the breakdown of society, the architects of progressive marital reform believed that making it easier for couples to divorce would fortify marriage, a point that today's divorce advocates continue to make. Howard, the leading academic authority on divorce in the United States during the Progressive era, maintained that "the most enlightened judgment of the age heartily approves" of liberalizing divorce. For Howard, the trend toward easier divorce was "part of the mighty movement for social liberation" picking up speed ever since the Reformation.[54]

Free divorce is a necessary component of the progressive marital reform agenda. If a partner cannot exit a marriage, then she cannot *choose* to stay, either. Carpenter places the argument in practical terms. Young lovers, swept up in the "transcendentalism" of their raptures, often wish prematurely "to swear eternal truth" to each other. Yet, Carpenter attests, "there is something quite diabolic and Mephistophelean in the practice of the Laws, . . . clap[ping] its book together with a triumphant bang."[55]

Drawing on comparative ethnography, Parsons locates liberal provisions for divorce in societies uncorrupted by proprietary notions of marriage. Discussing the age-old double standard allowing a man to divorce his wife if she committed adultery—even though the reverse rarely obtained—Parsons concludes, "only in very primitive or in highly advanced communities, where the idea of marital proprietorship has either not arisen or has not appeared," does a man's adultery become legal ground for his wife to divorce him. The implication is clear: a highly evolved society growing away from proprietary ideals will grant women equal access to divorce.[56]

An additional argument ran that it was simply unethical to remain married without love. Key believes "the erotically noble person" would be humiliated to remain with an unloved, or unloving, spouse. An additional reason she offers for why "free divorce" would improve marriage concerns the impact on husbands. Under the proprietary marital regime, a suitor treats a woman better than a husband does, since the suitor "receives by favour what the husband takes as his right." If a man knew that his wife could divorce him, then he would stop treating her as his exclusive sexual property. This ethical improvement on the part of husbands would cause them to behave more chivalrously, producing happier wives, better sex, and more durable marriages.[57]

In these various ways, the reformers argued that the mounting divorce statistics reflected not the breakdown of society but rather its transition to a higher plane. Once marriage became egalitarian, voluntaristic, and cooperative rather than patriarchal, compulsory, and proprietary, the divorce rate would plummet. "Divorce is a remedy and not the disease," Howard sums up, cautioning that "to forbid the use of a remedy does not prove that there is no disease."[58]

REFORMING SEX

The marital theorists sought to bring sex into a public discussion they maintained had been prohibited by a Victorian conspiracy of silence. One casualty of that conspiracy, according to Havelock Ellis, was the frigid woman, a figure that he claimed was a social construct of the nineteenth century—and decidedly a myth. Carpenter thought the "sexual passions . . . essential and decent" but found the Victorian climate "saturated with the notion of the uncleanness of sex." According to Edith Ellis, the emblem for conventional sexual ethics could be "a sneering hag with her fingers on her lips." Even Upton Sinclair, without doubt the most prudish of the figures this book will examine, looked down upon what he called the "avoidance and anxious evasion" of sex, and labeled it "Victorian." [59]

After Foucault, these claims sound rather suspect. The Victorians, as Foucault has made clear, did not ignore sex; "on the contrary, [they] put into operation an entire machinery for producing true discourses concerning it," extending the "discursive explosion" that began in the eighteenth century. Following Foucault, historians have systematically dismantled the notion of Victorians as uniformly sexually repressed, and with it, what Kevin White calls the "repression/liberation dichotomy" once believed to distinguish the nineteenth and twentieth centuries.[60] There is no doubt, then, some exaggeration in the Progressive era reformers' claims that they were dismantling a conspiracy of silence.

Yet there may also be a degree of truth to those claims. Consider Parsons's 1906 article "Sex Morality and the Taboo of Direct Reference." "Perhaps there is too much" discussion about sex, Parsons begins—approaching Foucault's point about the discursive proliferation—but little of it intelligent. That superabundant discourse "is so superficial, so circumvented by traditional silences, that it is inevitably fallacious or unenlightening." White slavery, sexually transmitted disease, the solitary vice: plenty was said about such topics. Yet Parsons found little enlightened discussion of what she considered the fundamental fact that sexual morality was in a state of "rapid transition." As to actual "instruction," sex education was verboten; "the taboo of direct reference is perhaps the sturdiest" of all contemporary taboos. For Parsons this uninformed and expurgated discourse about sex was worse than no discourse at all. Although she does not make the point, the taboo probably operated especially strongly for the white middle class audience that she and the other marital theorists targeted. Too many people (such as Edith Wharton, whom I quoted in the preface, and Upton Sinclair, whom I take up in the next chapter), testified to their abject ignorance of sexuality for the taboo to be mere apocrypha. Reasoned discussion of the facts of sex, its power, its personal and social significance, were excluded from public discourse. And that is precisely where the progressive marital theorists thought it belonged.[61]

Havelock Ellis's *Studies in the Psychology of Sex* plays the leading role in the Progressive era reform of sex. Contemporary reader responses were all over the map. Conservatives warned that reading Ellis was "like breathing a bag of soot," calling the *Studies* a "cesspool." (Such reactions further suggest the accuracy of Parsons's claim about taboos.) But for reformers like his close friend (and, for a time, his romantic partner), birth control activist Margaret Sanger, Ellis, more than anyone, could "clarify the question of sex and free it from the smudginess connected with it from the beginning of Christianity, raise it from the dark cellar, set it on a higher plane."[62]

Studies in the Psychology of Sex focuses on what Ellis strategically terms "normal" sexual behavior. "Histories of gross sexual perversion have often been presented," he explains, nodding toward other sexologists such as Krafft-Ebing, yet ignorance still prevails about "normal sexual development." Ellis's emphasis on the norm is easy to dismiss today as reactionary. Foucault has established how sexology helped institutionalize "the legitimate couple, with its regular sexuality" as the norm, based on which homosexuality and other practices could be defined as "'unnatural'" and even criminalized.[63]

I do not dispute Foucault's contention that Ellis was among those who helped "invent" homosexuality, nor that the "norm" can be a terrible tyrant. Ellis's rhetorical use of the norm, however, charts a very different ideological path from that of other sexologists (and sex police more generally) because there is no intellectual bullying of those who fail to meet it. To the contrary, Ellis conceptualizes the norm in extremely capacious terms, declaring that "the range of variation within fairly normal units is immense."[64]

The case study method is Ellis's primary pedagogical strategy for vastly extending the terrain defined as "normal" sexual behavior. To Foucault, the case study marks another instance of the discursive policing of sex; he mentions "autobiographical narratives" (such as those throughout Ellis's *Studies*) as part of the apparatus. But the formidable Foucauldian account of discipline and surveillance obscures an important point about Ellis, who uses the case study, rather, to stretch the "norm," thereby also expanding what passes as *acceptable* sexual behavior. Ellis does so by delineating a single overarching human sexual theme: tumescence and detumescence (in other words, arousal and release).[65] All sexual practices, according to Ellis, are but variations on that theme. He thus locates practices that earlier writers, some contemporaries, and, alas some commentators still define as perversions—such as masturbation, fetishism, homosexuality, and urolagnia—as mere "exaggerations" of a radically extended sexual norm. Through the case study method, Ellis grants all sex acts legitimacy.

The basic humanity of this legacy has been obscured not so much by Foucault as by generations of commentators who dismiss Ellis, often without reading much beyond the quotations included in other secondary accounts. It is easy to cherry-pick a comment that sounds retrograde; thousands of pages are bound to reveal some howlers. But even today, reading straight through the scores of case studies—uncensored, and in the voices of the individuals who told Ellis their stories—one comes away amazed by the complexity and variety of human sexuality.

One time Ellis strategically uses the concept of abnormality is in addressing female frigidity (which he calls "sexual anesthesia"). Countering the dominant medical wisdom of his day, Ellis charges that what is "unnatural" and indeed "perverted" is female sexual anesthesia, reflecting only "the prejudice and false conventions they [women] have been taught." Frigidity, in other words, is a product of social conditioning unique to so-called advanced civilizations. If a woman experiences no sexual pleasures with some man "or even with a succession of men," that only proves "these men have not been able to arouse" her.[66] Ellis accuses many husbands of inept lovemaking which fails to arouse their wives. He also notes that such husbands declare their wives frigid rather than consider their own inadequacies as lovers.

With logic typical of the progressive marital theorists, Ellis concentrates, therefore, on reforming husbands by educating them. He explains that courtship should not end with marriage but remain "the natural prelude to every act of coitus." In his most influential volume, *Sex in Relation to Society* (1911), Ellis unfolds what he calls "The Art of Love," a detailed account providing the basis for what would shortly become a flourishing trade in marriage (i.e., sex education) manuals.[67] In later chapters I will return to Ellis's advice to husbands (in the context of the Sinclairs) and the "art of love" (in the context of Boyce and Hapgood).

A key part of the reformers' educational program concerned instruction in the importance of erotic pleasure in marriage, particularly for women. Also committed to liberating female sexuality, Key tilts the balance toward women's role in reforming marriage. She believed "only the wife who remains a mistress can be sure of victory" and urges women to assert their "erotic greatness." Key's erotically great woman would "no longer be captured like a fortress or hunted like a quarry; nor will she like a placid lake await the stream that seeks its way to her embrace." Rather, she would be sexually self-directed: "A stream herself, she will go her own way to meet the other stream."[68]

If women were to be so sexually expressive, birth control, naturally, was essential. As in their arguments that women's autonomy would make marriage more satisfying for men and that divorce would improve marriage, the reformers again packaged what was a fairly radical message in its day as a way to elevate marriage to a higher plane. Schreiner proclaimed that "the sexual relations between man and woman have distinct aesthetic, intellectual, and spiritual functions and ends, apart entirely from physical reproduction." Ellis went further: sex provides the "best moral development of the individual," even when reproduction is not the goal. He considered birth control no less than "essential" to a happy marriage and discusses it at length as "The Science of Procreation" (a section that counterpoints "The Art of Love"). Parsons tried to put theory into practice when she urged a group of married women who had themselves used contraceptives to publicly support Sanger's birth control campaign. Most refused, on the ground of not wanting adverse publicity—particularly for their husbands. Rejecting that excuse, Parsons replied, "at times, testimony about the private life takes on a sufficiently public significance to free it from ridicule or the charge of bad taste."[69] Unfortunately, as every teacher knows, logic does not always prevail.

THE FAULT LINES IN PROGRESSIVE MARITAL REFORM

I expect most readers would agree that many of these ideals of progressive marital reform, while occasionally peculiar, were indeed improvements over proprietary marriage. However, other tenets appear regressive, even reactionary.

The first fault line in the reform platform reflects a now discredited view of gender and sexuality. Writing at a time before current distinctions between sex and gender, and biology and culture, became axiomatic, progressive marital reformers believed in innate gender differences. In what now appears incongruous, the reformers strenuously advocated gender equality even while affirming men and women would always be different. Resembling the logic of the contemporaneous—and disastrous—idea of "separate but equal" races enshrined by *Plessy v. Ferguson* (1896), the marriage reformers subscribed to what might be called essentialist egalitarianism.

Individual writers bought in to varying degrees. Gilman, Schreiner, and especially Parsons are less enamored with the notion that women and men have essential differences. As seen above in Havelock Ellis's and Key's discussions of female sexuality, those two tend to celebrate difference, and there is much of the same in Carpenter. But I believe all of the marital theorists—even Veblen, who has the least to say on the subject—would finally agree with Ellis that not just "quantitative" but also "qualitative differences" separate men and women.[70]

For most readers today, this proposition of essential difference undermines the reformers' egalitarian message. More than two decades after theorist Diana Fuss identified the tendency, distrust of and even "paranoia around the perceived threat of essentialism" prevails in twenty-first century discussions of gender. Recent criticism of sexology, indeed, routinely takes its essentialism as a point of departure. Perhaps the idea of Ellis's that has worn the least well is that in the bedroom, men are (and should be) forceful pursuers, women the coy pursued. "Nothing is gained by regarding women as simply men of smaller growth," Ellis asserts; "they have the laws of their own nature." He promotes personal freedom—but "only . . . when it is a freedom to follow the laws of one's own nature." As discussed above, the notion of "inner laws" helped progressives challenge the grip of church and state on marriage. It now becomes clear that "inner laws" also constrained how far marital reform could go in promoting gender equality. As Jeffrey Weeks observes, "Ellis read[s] into 'nature' the social forms of masculine and feminine behaviour that he observed around him," and the same can be said of his contemporaries. But if Fuss is correct that social constructionist accounts of gender always contain essentialist premises, then the marriage reformers' believing that gender roles were socially constructed *and* reflective of essential differences demonstrates a much larger tendency.[71]

A fuzzy thinker, Ellen Key demonstrates especially the fault lines in essentialist egalitarianism. Her claims that men are inherently more promiscuous and women more spiritual in their eroticism are indistinguishable from conservative platitudes in her day (or in ours). Undermining her commitment to women's self-development, Key maintains "a woman's essential ego must be brought out by love before she can do anything great." And because Key is so deeply heteronormative, that means that a woman *still* needs a man to complete her, to fill in her "erotic[] blank." Key proclaims that after woman becomes emancipated "as a human being and a citizen, there remains her emancipation as a *woman*."[72]

Contemporary readers reacted strongly and variously to Key's gender essentialism, although of course they would not have described it in those words. A like-minded writer for *Putnam's Monthly* explained that Key's "ideal of emancipation is an enlargement and enrichment of woman's soul, based upon a larger and deeper understanding of her natural mission." Some US feminists, most notably Gilman, disputed Key on this very point. The American charged the Swede with overestimating sexuality and underestimating work. A journalist summed up their much-discussed public argument as between a "female feminist" (Key) and a (Gilman).[73]

Key's now-puzzling fusion of conservative and radical beliefs culminates in an idea that might be termed vocational motherhood. Herself unmarried and childless, a lecturer for twenty years at the People's Institute in Stockholm, and the author of books translated into many languages, Key wanted other women also to work—but at motherhood. To her credit she does reject the traditional notion of stay-at-home mother dependent on her husband. Vocational motherhood, to the contrary, defines child-rearing as legitimate work deserving a salary. Whether a mother chose to live with the father of her child, alone, or with another man, the state and the child's father would provide her income. Key believed vocational motherhood would allow women to use their brains even while fulfilling their "eternal mission." In a revealing image she warns, "Nothing is more necessary than that woman should be intellectually educated for her new social mission. But if meanwhile she loses her womanly character, then she will come to the social mission like a farmer with a complete set of agricultural implements but no seed."[74] No sexual conservative could have put it better.

Key's legacy is curious and uneven. In 1913, when Floyd Dell included her in *Women as World Builders*, he noted that many American readers considered her "radically 'advanced'" and *Love and Marriage* a "revolutionary document." Yet Dell concludes, and I think indisputably, that she was also "a conservative force." As Nancy Cott remarks, regardless of what readers were looking for, they could find it in Ellen Key.[75] Her essentialist egalitarianism typifies the mixed legacy of progressive marital reform. The reformers sought a transformation, but one that left many traditional ideas intact.

A second fault line in progressive marital reform derives from muddled views about civilization and nature. The reformers sought to excavate a "natural" form of marriage from beneath the detritus of so-called civilization. According to Ellis, for example, "marriage in its narrow sense is a mere social institution," while "in its true biological sense . . . it is no merely human institution but the substance of the process by which all the chief forms of life have persisted on the earth." The reformers hypothesized a natural state of harmony, a marital Golden Age, which had been distorted by social pressures. Having their cake and eating it too, they cast civilization as the problem—but also as the solution. For the marital theorists also believed society was progressing back (the strange phrasing seems necessary to capture an odd concept) to that state of nature. In Gilman's words, humans needed to "grow natural again."[76] Following nature, in other words, becomes the way to reform society.

In this respect, the ideal future would look a great deal like the prelapsarian past. At the end of *Woman and Labour*, for instance, Schreiner prophesies a new Garden of Eden. Rewriting the devastatingly patriarchal message of Genesis, she imagines a garden in which "woman shall eat of the tree of knowledge together with man." Rather than marking a fall, this communal meal would celebrate the embrace of redemptive labor for all. God is not even necessary in Schreiner's account, for the couple, working together, "shall together raise about them an Eden . . . created by their own labour and made beautiful by their own fellowship." Even Veblen indulges his own sort of prelapsarian vision when he reads the New Woman movement as "a reversion to a more generic type of human character."[77]

Edward Carpenter articulated the most influential variant of the back-to-nature marital ideal. A mystical rather than political thinker, he considered civilization a disease. From his study of Whitman and Indian mysticism, Carpenter concluded that when early humans lived harmoniously with nature long ago, they enjoyed a spiritual unity that their descendants had lost.

But Carpenter also believed, in the words of his biographer, that humans could restore a "millennium on earth." Marriage would flourish in this imminent utopia because monogamy was "a natural fact, independent of any laws, just as one might believe in the natural bias of two atoms of certain different chemical substances to form a permanent compound atom or molecule."[78]

These misty ideas about nature have a complex intellectual history. The roots trace back to Herbert Spencer, who juxtaposed legal with "natural" bonds, the latter of which he found superior–and ultimately back to Rousseau, who aligns nature with emotion. Rousseau believed humans had both beneficial, natural emotions and harmful, artificial ones. Anthropologist Catherine A. Lutz elaborates that for Rousseau, "the natural (including emotion) is depicted as synonymous with the uncorrupted, the pure, the honest, the original." While the marital reformers clearly followed Rousseau's lead, their back-to-nature ideal also owes a debt to a movement from which they sought, ironically, to dissociate themselves: the mid-nineteenth-century free lovers. Those earlier (and more radical) reformers wanted, in the words of one historian, "to remove the artificial restraint placed on sexual desire . . . and return it to what they believed to be its natural, benign condition." The progressive reformers' concept of nature also bears the imprint of what T.J. Jackson Lears terms "antimodernism," a late nineteenth- and early twentieth-century mindset which held progress as the "official" doctrine even while rejecting much of modernity. In addition, the back-to-nature ideal participates in the fin-de-siècle romantic revival, which Nancy Glazener says "depended on turning evolutionary discourse on its head to suggest that contemporary social life consisted of an artificial, inauthentic set of constraints cloaking and obstructing people's unchanging instincts."[79]

A third fault line emerges when reformers beat a hasty retreat from their stance of marriage as Nobody's Business. And writer after writer does so immediately upon turning from the couple, whose privacy they staunchly advocate, to consider a likely eventuality: the birth of children. Ellis's quip exemplifies how the reformers believed children change everything: "Not what goes into the womb but what comes out of it concerns society." Only after children are born can the community "interest itself in the sexual acts of its members." Even Parsons, who was probably the furthest to the left politically of all the reformers, believed the state belonged in the parenting business as much as it didn't belong in the marriage business. She recommended a "parent's certificate" as far more constructive than a marriage certificate, and a "parent's registry and a parent's court" to replace the "marriage registry and divorce court."[80] As sexual privacy gives way to public interest, the reformers who campaigned to keep the state out of marriage now cordially invite it to sit at the table with baby.

Most disturbing, this concern with the social consequences of reproduction led most of the marriage reformers to support eugenics. Recent scholarship has emphasized the interrelationship of ideologies of gender and eugenics, and so it is not surprising to find marital reform part of the jumble.[81] Ellen Key, for instance, advocates "freedom for love's selection, under conditions favourable to the race"—a qualification that now sounds terrifying.[82]

The brainchild of Sir Francis Galton, eugenics originated with two articles published in 1865 in *Macmillan's Magazine* and later expanded into *Hereditary Genius* (1869). Galton believed that his cousin Charles Darwin's theory had overturned the Christian idea of the fall: the human species had, according to Galton's interpretation of evolution, ascended. He also maintained that through eugenics—a term he coined from Greek roots to signify good breeding—humanity could help evolution along. In Galton's famous words, "what Nature does blindly, slowly, and ruthlessly, man may do providently, quickly, and kindly."[83] These ideas about human ascent and working with "nature" to ensure progress mesh seamlessly with the marriage reformers' goals.

The United States provided fertile soil for eugenics, which became extremely popular among educated whites, particularly between 1900 and 1929. Two approaches were common. So-called "positive" eugenics involved encouraging favored groups to reproduce. "Negative" eugenics (such as sterilization, prohibiting certain groups from marrying, and immigration restrictions) entailed curtailing births deemed undesirable. Personally in favor of negative eugenics, Teddy Roosevelt found the positive variant more politically expedient and so urged "getting desirable people to breed." He sent a personal congratulation to one couple—apparently of the right type—for having twelve children.[84]

How could liberal marital theorists embrace eugenics as the ultimate reform? Given the anxiety of such prominent figures as Roosevelt and Scott Nearing over "race suicide," to say nothing of the hindsight gained by the later horrors of Nazism, it is hard to fathom. Yet it is important to remember that, as Molly Ladd-Taylor remarks, while eugenics most certainly led to fascism, that trajectory was not inevitable. As historian Frank Dikötter explains, "Far from being a politically conservative and scientifically spurious set of beliefs that remained confined to the Nazi era," as it now appears, "eugenics belonged to the political vocabulary of virtually every significant modernizing force between the two world wars."[85]

A wildly popular didactic utopian novel helps to clarify how progressives a century ago could embrace eugenics as the ultimate tool for reform. Edward Bellamy's *Looking Backward* (1888) opens with a man from the late nineteenth century waking up after a hundred years, finding a society that has perfected marriage (along with everything else). Married women, fully integrated into public life, are financially independent. Because women no longer *need* to wed, marriage has become completely voluntary. Since "there can be no marriages now except those of inclination," Bellamy's spokesman explains, "for the first time in human history . . . sexual selection" operates unhindered. With the unnatural reasons for marriage eliminated, pure sexual selection—which equates seamlessly with pure love in Bellamy's account—determines unions. Women, consequently, select the best men, and only the best men. Apart from this spontaneous and voluntary practice of positive eugenics, people do not reproduce. The resulting "race purification" over several generations has developed not only superior biological types but also a general "mental and moral improvement."[86] The marital utopianism of *Looking Backward* inspired a generation of readers to believe that reforming marriage through voluntary eugenics could perfect human society.

Progressive reformers also looked to eugenics as a way to reposition women as agents, not victims, of sexual selection. If women resumed their role as sexual selectors, Gilman (who adored *Looking Backward*) believed, humanity would improve because the "mother-duty"—in marked contrast to sexuo-economic motivations—"is to choose wisely, that her children may be well fathered." Taking a far-reaching view of "The Race" (she capitalizes), Gilman concludes, "Our Past we cannot help. Our Present slips from us in the making. Only the Future can be molded." Her racism has rightly been scrutinized, and it is entangled with her feminism and ideas about marital reform alike. Gilman's thinking was hardly unique. Using almost the same language, Ellis looked forward to a time when "love" would "mould[] races to the ideal of the female," and Key to when "womanly love's selection" could advance "the race."[87]

Obnoxious as these positions now sound, they mark an advance from those of conservative "mainline" eugenicists, who hoped, in addition, to curtail women's freedom and prohibit birth control.[88] Ellis's view of eugenics diverges from two additional positions of the mainliners. He censures the "foolish and mischievous" notion of "'race suicide,'" characterizing jeremiads about "a falling [Anglo-Saxon] birth-rate mean[ing] degeneration and disaster" as the "wild outcry of many unbalanced persons to-day." (Parsons similarly found that discourse "monopolized as yet by scatterbrains or fossils.") The lunacy over race suicide, Ellis maintains, betrays a misunderstanding of how evolution actually works. "Properly understood," he contends, native-born Americans would not fear their declining fertility, because that is what happens to highly evolved stocks. Ellis counters paranoiac worries with reasoned feminism: "We have been accustomed to say in later days that the State needs children, and that it is the business and the duty of women to supply them. But the State has no more right than the individual to ravish a woman against her will."[89]

Ellis also criticizes the movement to legislate negative eugenics. Between 1896 and 1914, thirty states enacted laws prohibiting or declaring voidable various types of "unfit" marriages (such as among the feebleminded, insane, epileptics, alcoholics, or when either party had venereal disease). Eugenics also figured prominently in anti-miscegenation statutes. Ellis labels such efforts "hopeless[] and even absurd[]." He attributes the legislative craze to the misguided belief that heredity trumps environment. Hoisting the mainline eugenicists by their own petard, Ellis notes, "Those who affirm that heredity is everything and environment nothing seem strangely to forget that it is precisely the lower classes—those who are most subjected to the influence of bad environment—who procreate most copiously." He was equally contemptuous of compulsory sterilization and mandatory prenuptial health certifications. Diagnosing the attempt to secure "social reform by moral legislation," Ellis preferred education to legislation.[90]

Generalization is a risky business, all the more so across historical periods, but I would suggest that these fault lines in Progressive era marital reform retain a strong presence in twenty-first century debates over marriage. But while today's liberal marriage reformers have extended the egalitarian ideals of progressive marital reform, the regressive tendencies have found a new home in conservative discourse on marriage, particularly when grounded in religion, a point to which I will return in the Epilogue.

Although they often sound as if evolution would cease once marital perfection was attained, Progressive era reformers understood that marriage would continue to evolve. "One cannot help wondering . . . what new and fantastic shapes await our marriage system in the future," Ellis reflected, "For man never stands still." At the same time, "the more marriage changes in form the more obviously it will in substance remain the same thing."[91] This paradox of marriage as stable yet malleable captures the curiously divided message of progressive marital reform. Another keynote is the idea that if marriage—that "most complicated, the most delicate, and the most significant of institutions"—could be changed, then the world would follow.[92]

In the following chapters I turn to fiction—which, as novelist Naeem Murr says, "is all about intimacy"—and trace the complexities of trying to mesh theory and practice.[93]

CHAPTER THREE

Sex, Lies, and Media: Upton and Meta Fuller Sinclair's Marital Experiment

Upton Sinclair described his roman à clef *Love's Pilgrimage* (1911) as a marital lesson plan for readers. This "novel about modern marriage," Sinclair said, "would show the possibility of a couple's agreeing to part, and still remaining friends." The lesson was so ambitious, in fact, that he intended to extend it over three volumes. (The second volume, "Love's Progress," exists only in manuscript, and he never made it to the third.) The inspiration was his own first marriage, to Meta Fuller, but their separation just months after *Love's Pilgrimage* appeared caused unforeseen problems when it came to getting Sinclair's message across. An ardent self-dramatizer, he later called the marriage "the great tragedy of my life."[1] Herself an aspiring writer, Meta left an unfinished novel of her own, also inspired by their marriage. Her unpublished version, "Corydon and Thrysis," closely parallels Upton's account, although with strategic shifts of emphasis that this chapter will examine.[2] Both versions trace how a theoretically progressive marriage is tested by poverty, the difficulties of establishing dual writing careers, and emotional and sexual incompatibility, all compounded by the strains of raising a child.

Sinclair also intended *Love's Pilgrimage* to be what might be called a companionate novel. That is, just as companionate marriage provides an egalitarian forum for balancing the needs of both spouses, so Sinclair wanted his novel not only to include his wife's perspective but actually to incorporate her writing. Accordingly, *Love's Pilgrimage* draws liberally from Meta and Upton's letters to each other and also some of her poetry. She did help craft several scenes and took an active hand in revising others.[3] Decades later,

Upton judged his companionate novel a success. Writing Meta's third husband in 1964 after her death, Upton mentioned *Love's Pilgrimage*, recalling how Meta helped revise the manuscript, incorporating some of her own letters to provide her perspective. Nothing, he concluded with satisfaction, could have been more fair.[4]

Meta definitely had a hand in *Love's Pilgrimage*, but she denied that it captured her perspective, much less fairly. While assisting her husband with the unpublished sequel, Meta protested in a letter, "I am having such a hard time to get Upton to write it as I think it ought to be and as I wanted the first volume to be." Consequently, "as there are to be three volumes of *Love's Pilgrimage* from the man's standpoint, I feel it imperative that I should write a fourth."[5]

The differences between *Love's Pilgrimage* and Meta's "Corydon and Thrysis" illuminate several debates at the heart of Progressive era marital reform. The most fundamental concerns the impetus of the progress in "progressivism." Despite the marriage reformers' conviction that they could improve the world, they were neither systematic nor consistent in assessing where reform originates. In terms of the marriage debate: who, exactly, reforms whom? Does the man reform the woman or vice versa? The two Sinclairs answer that question differently in their dual—and often dueling—accounts.

I argue here that *Love's Pilgrimage* plays a crucial role in Upton Sinclair's lifelong career as a reformer, and also that reading it alongside Meta's version reveals their competition for the position of the more progressive spouse. The key differences—concerning sexuality, childbirth, and adultery—also illustrate the transitional nature of the Progressive era, with Upton looking back more to the nineteenth century while Meta peers forward into the twentieth. Eric Rauchway has argued that the varying cultural politics of men and women indicates that there were in fact *two* Progressive eras, with male reformers often opposing the "female agenda."[6] The Sinclair archives suggest that such a division along gender lines informs the marriage debate. But their marriage assumes greater importance because it lived on in the public imagination well after the principals parted. Accordingly, I examine journalists' depictions of the Sinclair marriage that proliferated after their separation. The media obsession sparked, in turn, a flurry of additional publications by Upton (and one by Meta) culminating in *The Brass Check* (1920), his journalistic exposé of journalism itself. These proliferating accounts show one way that Progressive era marital theory became widely disseminated. A marital experiment that initially seemed kooky ended up achieving such cultural resonance as to generate further support for marriage reform.

Both Sinclairs sought to make their experience of marriage into a text about marriage. In later chapters, I will trace that impulse manifesting in additional ways in the Dreiser and the Boyce-Hapgood marriages. For both of the Sinclairs, the imperative to textualize experience is part of a bookishness so intense that it becomes one of their major literary themes. Consider, for instance, the names that both Sinclairs use for their husband and wife characters, Corydon and Thrysis. These odd names come from a poem by Milton, "L'Allegro," in which the two are (of all things) male shepherds. And Sinclair hung on tenaciously to this borrowed literary construct: even after divorcing Meta in 1912, he continued to write about Thrysis and Corydon, who over time became increasingly fused in his mind with the historical actors. That is, while Sinclair had three wives over the course of his long life, he returned to write about the first again and again, routinely referring to himself and Meta as Thrysis and Corydon. The need to turn marriage into an instructive text will haunt his career-long reform efforts, as I will show. Because of Sinclair's deliberate conflation of literature and life, this chapter entails a good deal of shuttling back and forth, not only between fact (Upton and Meta Sinclair) and fiction (the characters of Thrysis and Corydon), but also between the Sinclairs' dual accounts.[7]

REFORM'S PROGRESS

Sinclair, who championed reform causes throughout his life, wanted desperately to be seen as a leader of them all. He identified as a socialist and radical, but marshaling evidence for the more modest claim of reformer proves a sufficient challenge. *The Jungle* (1906), of course, played the leading role in establishing that reputation. Considerably less familiar today, Sinclair's founding of the cooperative community Helicon Hall (November 1906–March 1907), financed largely with royalties from his bestselling novel, consolidated his image as reformer in his own time. (Sinclair said that Helicon Hall was inspired by another book, *Women and Economics*, but Gilman denied he had any basis for that claim.) Sinclair's 1933 campaign for governor of California under the EPIC platform (End Poverty in California) brought his activism back to the center stage of US politics.[8] A neglected but essential aspect of Sinclair's reform platform, as I will show here, is his attempt to establish leadership in the most important cause of all: marriage.

Upton and Meta married in October 1900 with the express intent of putting progressive marital theory into practice. He explained that after "talk[ing] the whole marriage business over very conscientiously," they agreed that they "hated the idea of being tied together by either a religious or a legal ceremony." Rejecting such a formalistic, proprietary union, they sought, in Sinclair's words, "to set the right kind of example to the world."[9]

Love's Pilgrimage and "Corydon and Thrysis" both document the ideas inspiring this marital experiment, often naming specific authors. (While I will draw upon Meta's manuscript, when the two accounts run parallel, I quote from *Love's Pilgrimage* since this published account is available in Google books, whereas "Corydon and Thrysis" requires a trip to Indiana University's Lilly Library.) After the couple discovers socialism, Corydon starts seeing its relevance to women. Accordingly, she reads Gilman's *Women and Economics* in one sitting. Thrysis studies a sociologist who had been a huge influence on Gilman, Lester Frank Ward, in addition to an unnamed volume by Havelock Ellis. These tomes provide Thrysis with a potentially transformative insight: women are not innately superficial but rather trained to be so. He continues his own education by reading *The Theory of the Leisure Class* (1899) and then passes it over to his wife, who recognizes herself in Veblen's leisure class woman—"an exposition which Corydon found almost too painful to be read." These books about marital reform incite the couple to put theory into practice. And so Thrysis lectures on marriage as a "slave-custom," calling it "cowardly" to promise eternal faithfulness, ridiculous to bind oneself to "forms." Corydon concurs: "we shall both of us know that neither would ever dream of wishing to hold the other a moment after love ceased."[10]

But other reform ideas prove difficult for Thrysis to assimilate. Since he hopes to lead the world into the promised land, what is Thrysis to do with the marital theorists' suggestions that women may have an inherent edge? While the reformers wrote extensively about how the role of proprietary wife disabled women, a very different idea simmers beneath the surface: that women possess an inherent progressivism, if only social conditioning could be stripped away. For that reason, the reformers considered the position of women an index to the development of society. Thus, in Ward's influential formulation, "true science teaches that the elevation of woman is the only sure road to the evolution of man." Olive Schreiner likewise predicts that with the advent of more egalitarian relationships, woman, "by reason of those very sexual conditions which in the past have crushed and trammeled her, . . . is bound to lead the way, and man to follow." This notion also informs works popularizing the theorists' tenets, such as William E. Carson's *The Marriage Revolt* (1915), which maintains "the modern, progressive woman is . . . unconsciously developing a new type of man."[11]

However, when it came to sex, Progressive era marital theorists maintained a position that now sounds regressive: the man needed to initiate the woman. Havelock Ellis was particularly influential on this point. Published the same year the Sinclairs separated, Ellis's best-selling *Sex in Relation to Society* provides a virtual instruction manual on how a husband can please his wife sexually. In an often-quoted passage, Ellis maintains that woman is "on the physical side, inevitably the instrument in love; it must be his hand and his bow which evoke the music."[12] I will return to Ellis later; for now I would like to emphasize that in contrast to Ward's and Schreiner's conception of the woman leading the man into the future, in the progressive bedroom, it seems, man leads and woman follows.

The opening scene in *Love's Pilgrimage* stages a related conflict. Young Thrysis discovers his calling as a reformer at the precise moment he internalizes a Manichean view of sexuality. A boy "with delicate and sensitive features," Thrysis appears within a scene of staggering, reeking drunks, one of whom turns out to be his own father. (Sinclair, who was a teetotaler, himself had an alcoholic father.) Quickly concluding "the god of business" has caused this debauchery, Thrysis decides the world contains "great evil"—and that he is the one to redeem it. And so "within him grew a passionate longing to cry aloud to others, to open their eyes to this truth!" (10). Unfortunately for Thrysis, he discovers a temptation of his own in the same scene. Alcohol disgusts him, and so does a prostitute with "wanton black eyes . . . hinting unimaginable things." However, while the thought of sex repels Thrysis, it also entices him. Instinctively he apprehends that sexual "self-indulgence" could ruin him (11). For the rest of the novel, Thrysis stands guard against his own sexuality, the dangers of which a clergyman soon confirms. If stored up and sublimated, "sex-energy," the minister says, can be "transmuted to the gold of intellectual and emotional power" (29). The narrator then provides this proleptic view of the novel's trajectory: "It was in this long and bitter struggle that [Thrysis] won whatever power he had in his future life" (37).[13]

Basically, in order to be a good reformer, Thrysis has to repudiate sex. But he remains committed to romance in a fuzzy way and so convinces himself that abstinence would "not [be] a denial of love, but on the contrary a consecration of love" (29). This notion of "consecration" is no idle metaphor. I have discussed how the marriage theorists coopted religious language, but in order to affirm sex. Sinclair takes religious discourse in another direction. His own first hero was no less than Jesus Christ, and his wife Meta aptly diagnosed Sinclair's "Messianic complex." *Love's Pilgrimage* repeatedly illustrates that grandiose self-image, for instance when Thrysis, tempted to compromise his art for commercial success, recalls Satan's temptation of Christ (368). Sinclair identifies the reformer as one who has conquered temptation; only such a spiritual leader can lead the fallen to purity. As Thrysis believes, "some one must bring America face to face with its soul again" (488). The character epitomizes historian Leon Fink's account of the progressive's "missionary sense of public service."[14]

This conflation of spiritual leadership and sexual abstinence structures Sinclair's portrayal of courtship and marriage. Thrysis, naturally, identifies his first girlfriend, Corydon, as his greatest temptation. He describes himself to her as "weak and struggling" over "a thousand temptations," predicting, "when I marry you, you will be the greatest temptation of all" (96). Although Corydon initially strikes him as pure, two cryptic references to her looking at a dirty word scrawled on a fence lead her husband to conclude "after all she had some taint" (404). As a reformer, he feels superior — yet as a man, "humiliate[ed]" by this new "necessity of the flesh" (205). Within this context, the strangest aspect of *Love's Pilgrimage* begins to make sense: in addition to dedicating their marriage to the Progressive era ideals of voluntary monogamy and divorce by mutual consent, the couple also pledges to remain platonic. The spectacular disaster of that promise comprises much of the narrative interest in *Love's Pilgrimage*.

SEX AND THE MARRIED MAN

First, Upton Sinclair's version. "No human male could have been more pitifully ignorant of the female critter, body, mind, and soul," he confessed, "than I was at the age of 21." He explains in a memoir that his shabby-genteel Southern family went to great lengths to ignore sex, leaving him "bewildered" when he hit puberty. Did Sinclair write *Love's Pilgrimage* as self-censure or as indictment of a conspiracy of silence that rendered young people disastrously unequipped for marriage? Even today, it's hard to tell.[15]

What is clear, however, is that the novel has two trajectories: the upward path of the progressive reformer-in-the-making and the downward path of a progressive marriage-in-the-unraveling. At the intersection lies a dilemma: can a married reformer reunite America with its soul? Or to put the question in different terms, consider the dedication of *Love's Pilgrimage*:

"To those who throughout the world are fighting for the emancipation of woman I dedicate this book." Can the reformer be committed to women in the abstract while fearing them in the flesh?

For several months, the answer seems to be yes. Thrysis and Corydon manage to live together platonically until a doctor informs Thrysis that all women want babies. The phallic response is instantaneous: "His manhood leaped up, and cried aloud for its right. He discovered, almost instantly, that he loved her thus, that he desired her completely" (185–86). As he stumbles from his righteous path, Thrysis degenerates into a naturalistic character blindly seeking sex.

The belated consummation of the marriage is nothing short of a rape. An ugly scene, it is too important to summarize. As Thrysis claims his conjugal right, "the soul of the cave-man awoke":

> But nothing could stop him now. She was his—his to do what he pleased with! And he would bend her to his will! The voice of his manhood shouted aloud to him now. . . .
>
> Then she began to sob—"Oh Thrysis, wait—spare me! I can't bear it! No, Thrysis—no!"
>
> But he answered her, "Be still! I love you! You are mine." . . . Before this they had been strangers; but now he would penetrate to the secret places, to the holy of holies of her being.
>
> Never in all his life had Thrysis known woman. To him woman had been the supreme mystery of life, a creature of awe and sacredness. . . . Now the awful ban was lifted, the barriers were down; what had been hidden was revealed, what had been forbidden was permitted. So all the chained desire of a lifetime drove him on; it was almost more than he could bear. The touch of her warm breasts, the faint perfume of her clothing, the pressure of her soft, white limbs—these things set every nerve of him a-tremble, they turned a madness loose in him. . . .
>
> So with quivering fingers he stripped her before him; and she crouched there, cowering and weeping. He took her in his arms; and in that clasp there was no misunderstanding, for all the mastery of his will was in it. Nor did she try to resist him—she lay still, but shaking like a leaf, and choking with sobs. And so it was that he wreaked his will upon her. (195–96)

In addition to the terrible violence, several notable themes surface. Thrysis achieves a "manhood" that has previously eluded him: "will" and "mastery" emerge as he finally "penetrate[s]" his wife's "secret places." An essentialized conception of gender pervades the scene—the male violent, predatory, insistent; the female passive, submissive, shrinking. Finally, there is the incongruous note of spiritual revelation: even while Thrysis rapes his wife, he approaches with timidity the "forbidden," the "sacred[]," the "holy of holies."

It gets even uglier when Sinclair turns to Corydon's response. While Thrysis feels overcome with shame, he also realizes he has opened a Pandora's box. As if he has flicked a switch, Corydon turns nymphomaniac. Thrysis is shocked by this new "creature of desire—tumultuous and abandoned! She was like some passion-goddess out of the East, shameless and terrible and destroying! She was like a tigress of the jungle" (197). Orientalized and animalized, Corydon suddenly adopts a proprietary view of marriage. "I belong to you now!" she cries, adding the threat, "You can never escape me now!" (197). Corydon's reversion to conventional beliefs—that marriage is permanent, monogamy compulsory, and union entails ownership—imperils the foundation of their once-progressive marriage.

With the wife's descent into possessive nymphomania, Sinclair is able to project the husband's internal sexual conflict outward. That is, while Thrysis will continue to struggle with his own libido, the greater battle now becomes with Corydon's. Her insatiable desire threatens to ruin the reformer. Because Thrysis continues to "fear" that sex is "pollution," with each act of sexual intercourse he must "surrender . . . spiritual autonomy" (204, 472). During the eleven years of their marriage, Thrysis manages to enforce long periods of abstinence, but cannot contain Corydon's sexual demands. The husband's conjugal loathing reaches crisis point when, after years of living apart, or together in tents or dingy rooms, they purchase their first house, in which they sleep together in a bed. The physical proximity erodes Thrysis's will power. Night after night, "a crime was enacted" in their bed, "the vital forces of his being . . . squandered" (604).

This treatment of conjugal sexuality undermines Sinclair's attempt to position Thrysis as a progressive, and even feminist, reformer. Rather than valorize sexuality as cementing marriage as the marital theorists do, Sinclair censors sex and women both. For Thrysis, and I suspect also for his creator, sex remains a guilty and ecstatic vice.

SEX AND THE MARRIED WOMAN

And now for Meta Sinclair's version. She concurs about the fictional couple's spectacular incompatibility, but interprets the root problem differently. In Meta's account Thrysis's own sexual demands, not Corydon's, undermine his calling as a reformer.

Meta's manuscript includes two courtship episodes that do not appear in her husband's account, both depicting Thrysis as overcome with debilitating desire. In the first, his satisfaction in "Corydon's admiring discipleship" fades when he glimpses "a revealing sight of shapely legs" as she gets off a bicycle. Sexual arousal makes it impossible for Thrysis to think well of himself or concentrate on his writing, and so he becomes angry. Then he gets a second look at Corydon's enchanting figure when they take a boat ride. As she bends over to reposition the oars, Thrysis "realized for the first time the outline of her small breasts and the graceful curves of her hips, and suddenly, insistently, he became aware that Corydon was flesh and blood and desirable." While the naïve Corydon has no idea of the turmoil she has inspired, Thrysis feels as though "Eros and Isaiah had come into mortal combat for his soul."[16]

Another strategic difference occurs in how Meta handles the sexual consummation. For one thing, she alters the chronology. In Meta's version, Thrysis has the fateful conversation with the doctor who urges intimacy immediately before the marriage—not months into it. Consequently there is no period of platonic honeymoon; right on the wedding night the couple plunges into the abyss of sexuality. Or more precisely, the husband plunges alone into that abyss. More important than the altered chronology, Meta transforms the tone of the deflowering scene. Like her husband's version, Meta's warrants extended quotation:

At last they could be alone without restraint. Between them hung a breathless sense of waiting, taut and fearful, like the suffocating air before a hurricane.

At first Thrysis approached Corydon slowly, timidly, yet with a suppressed eagerness. To Corydon his eyes looked red and swollen, his aspect almost menacing. She wondered what he would do. She felt tense, frightened, resistant. Suddenly he took her in his arms with crushing certainty. His actions became swift and determined although to Corydon they seemed superfluous, illogical. He removed her dress with hard and clumsy fingers. It seemed to be like the ruthless infraction of a natural law, this mute disregard of her physical identity.

But his will was mighty, dominant, and she submitted herself to him obediently, as to some strange, bitter anaesthesia. She had never known any but Thrysis's embraces, and these she had accepted joyfully with a kind of gratitude. But this—this thing called mating—it seemed to have no true relevance to any feeling she had ever known. She tried not to cry out! He could not know how dreadfully he was hurting her! But wait. Was this not Thrysis, who was having his way with her—Thrysis to whom she had given herself, willingly, unreservedly, and was not this their marriage night?[17]

As in Upton's account, Meta positions male force and female submission as aspects of "natural law" and depicts the husband's sex drive as animalistic. But Thrysis appears in an altered light here because Meta adds the important detail of his clumsiness as a lover. The greatest difference, however, involves Corydon's response. Instead of turning nymphomaniac, Meta's Corydon emerges from the rape feeling her husband's advances are "superfluous" and "illogical," lacking any "relevance" to her life. Meta stresses, that is, the wife's emotional estrangement from her husband rather than the emotional turmoil within the husband himself. The mere physical act that she terms "mating," far from furthering intimacy, precludes it. Whereas Upton associates the husband's assertion of will with a positive assumption of masculinity, Meta, as if literalizing the legal doctrine of coverture, sees the husband's "will" causing complete "disregard of [his wife's] physical identity."

Despite Corydon's negative impressions (to say nothing of the complete absence of any pleasure), she intuits that sexual intimacy could be sublime. Right after Thrysis's assault, Corydon senses a connection with something outside of herself: "before she had been groping, blind. Now she saw herself as a different being in a different world." The sex act which, to her husband, ends with an orgasm seems to her the prelude to what she hopes might become a marriage based on intimacy, passion, and mutual reverence. Such a union would fulfill mind and soul as well as body, and so Corydon hopes that "together they might find what untold regions of the heart's desire."[18] She seeks, that is, what she understands to be a progressive marriage.

But throughout Meta's novel, sexual pleasure and emotional intimacy both elude Corydon. The pattern she traces goes like this: Thrysis represses his libido as long as he can until his desire explodes, at which point he brutally takes his wife. In between these violent outbursts, he abstains completely, emotionally as well as physically. Thrysis even mocks Corydon's desire for a closer relationship. And through it all, Meta writes in a revealing metaphor, "Sex as such was nearly a closed book to [Corydon], love and sex satisfaction never having coalesced in her experience." Their one-sided sexual relationship lacks what Meta calls "mutual expression," "the blending of their respective love-natures," and "ultimate unity." The language derives from Spiritualism, but Meta's source is more likely Edward Carpenter, whose *Love's Coming of Age* later became, she wrote, "a kind of text book" for Corydon and Thrysis.[19]

Much has been written of Upton Sinclair's "Puritanism," a fruitful line of interpretation that assumes added meaning because his first wife was one of those who originated it. Thrysis is so "clums[y]" in the bedroom because, writes Meta, he behaves "like a monk who occasionally threw aside his cassock." He saw sex, she writes, as one of the "unrestrained human emotions along with drunkenness [and] wife-beating." She offers her own suggestive interpretation: "To Thrysis love-making entailed consequences of which he was terrified." Meta's account meshes with the Messianic asceticism that structures Sinclair's portrayal of his own Thrysis. It also corresponds with Sinclair's account in *American Outpost* of his youthful conflict between Messianism and "tormenting . . . sexual desire"—which led him to work fourteen hours a day.[20]

HAVELOCK ELLIS, FEMALE SEXUALITY, AND ABSTINENCE

Since the most substantive differences between the Sinclairs' accounts concern sexuality, Havelock Ellis deserves a seat at the table. Both *Love's Pilgrimage* and "Corydon and Thrysis" mention his name, and indeed an intimate of the Sinclairs called *Studies in the Psychology of Sex* their "Bible." Upton Sinclair, always keen to promote his own work, apparently hoped that Ellis would admire his own tome about marital sexuality, for the novelist mailed the sexologist a copy of *Love's Pilgrimage*. In April 1911 Ellis wrote back that he had only begun to read it but admired its frankness.[21]

Two sections of *Studies in the Psychology of Sex* in particular illuminate the Sinclair marriage: Ellis's discussion of female sexuality and his distinction between chastity and abstinence.[22] As discussed in the previous chapter, Ellis considered female "sexual anesthesia" or frigidity an "abnormal" product of social conditioning. (Notably, as seen above, Meta uses the word "anesthesia" in her account of the wedding night.) For Ellis the epidemic of frigidity exemplifies how "civilization" selects for unnatural conditions which it then pretends to be morally superior. Ellis has no trouble assigning blame: because men dominate society, they create its mores. In fact, "the judgments of men concerning women are very rarely matters of cold scientific observation, but are colored by their own sexual emotions and by their own moral attitude toward the sexual impulse." If the relevance of that statement to *Love's Pilgrimage* needs no comment, consider Ellis's follow-up: "Statements about the sexual impulses of women often tell us less about women than about the persons who make them."[23]

One of the marital theorists' characteristic views, as I have argued, is that individual action could affect social transformation. And so, for Ellis, since patriarchal mores had caused women's frigidity, individual husbands needed to liberate their wives' pent-up sexuality. When a woman seems "indifferen[t]" to sex, Ellis maintains, that was only because the husband lacked "skill or consideration" as a lover. Particularly relevant to the Sinclair marriage, Ellis notes the frequency of a woman's "sexual coldness due to the shock and suffering of the wedding-night."[24] One wonders what Ellis made of the consummation scene in *Love's Pilgrimage*, if he made it that far.

Ellis also contrasts what he terms "the problem of sexual abstinence" with the "virtue" of chastity. He defines chastity not as abstaining from sex but rather "cultivat[ing] . . . the most beautiful, exalted, and effective sexual life." In order to follow Ellis's reasoning here it is necessary to recall how he maps all sexual practices as variations of the shared human pattern of "tumescence" (arousal) and "detumescence" (release). And he considers tumescence "the really essential part of the process." He explains, "tumescence is the piling on of the fuel; detumescence is the leaping out of the devouring flame whence is lighted the torch of life to be handed on from generation to generation." Courtship and foreplay develop tumescence, making sex magnificent. And so, Ellis maintains, does chastity, "charg[ing] the whole organism so . . . that the final climax of gratified love is not the trivial detumescence . . . but the immense consummation of a longing in which the whole soul as well as the whole body has its part." Citing Nietzsche, Ellis suggests that chastity is especially valuable for artists — one point of agreement with *Love's Pilgrimage*.[25] But Thrysis, of course, does not pursue chastity to intensify sexual pleasure; rather, for him, sexual pleasure remains oxymoronic.

While Thrysis's behavior does not fit Ellis's account of chastity, it does correspond with what the sexologist says about abstinence. But whereas chastity supports the highest sexual love, according to Ellis, abstinence promotes only the self. "False" and "artificial," abstinence marks a "deliberate refusal of what is evil in sex" without embracing all that is "good." Interested only in suppressing his own sexuality, the abstainer ignores his partner's emotions and needs, and in doing so neglects "the most important and ennobling half" of sex. To Ellis, the abstainer pursues the futile question, "How can I preserve my empty virtue?" rather than the transcendent one of "How can I bring joy and strength to another?" He urges that the erotic needs of women should be "the determining factor [in a relationship]; for those needs are more various, complex and elusive." The skillful lover-husband "finds a source of endless erotic satisfaction" in pleasing his wife.[26]

Love's Pilgrimage mentions Ellis, but does not say what either spouse gleaned from his books. Meta's "Corydon and Thrysis" does. According to her version, Ellis provided Thrysis an unwelcome education about his own sexual inadequacies. Meta writes that the young man, reading the sexologist ten years into the "quagmire" of their marriage, gets "his first intimation that sex was an inexhaustible field of which he had explored a tiny corner."[27] The tortured sexual logic of *Love's Pilgrimage* suggests that Upton imagined Thrysis clinging to an ideal of chastity. Had Thrysis (or his author) read Ellis more closely, however, he might have learned, as Meta evidently understood, that while chastity might enhance sexual pleasure, abstinence sabotages it.

In another revealing scene, Meta has Thrysis, having just fallen in love with another woman, rush in to tell Corydon about it while brandishing Carpenter's *Love's Coming of Age* and urging her to read it. But in order to appreciate the implications of this additional instance of bookishness, it is necessary to take a brief incursion into legal history.

ADULTERY AND DIVORCE LAW

Divorce in the United States was (and still is) governed by state law. Inconsistency among states could (and still does) cause messy situations, since a couple can be legally divorced in one state and still married in another. The resulting problems, widely discussed in the Progressive era, included the varying statutory grounds themselves as well as how unhappy spouses sought to get around them—by collusion and migratory divorce.

Migratory divorce occurred when a spouse living in a state with restrictive laws brought suit in another with more lenient provisions, by taking up (or fabricating) residence. The practice began in the nineteenth century and increased as transportation improved. There was some discussion between the Sinclairs of seeking a migratory divorce in Reno, known as a divorce mill, but he decided it would cost too much. Although they had been living in Delaware for nearly three years (in a single-tax cooperative community called Arden), Upton sued Meta for divorce in New York in August 1911. He probably chose that location because New York permitted remarriage of the plaintiff within three months, whereas Delaware required a year. But the New York suit was thrown out of court on technicalities twice. With the help of a Dutch friend, Sinclair ended up procuring a divorce in 1912 in Holland, where little paperwork was required if the defendant didn't contest the suit.[28]

Sinclair's changes of venue were necessary because the legal construction of divorce a century ago differed fundamentally from the now-familiar "no-fault" model. No-fault divorce (first enacted by California's Family Law Act in 1970 and sweeping the remaining states thereafter) eliminated the idea that predetermined legal "grounds" must be met before a marriage could be terminated. But before that, during the nineteenth century and much of the twentieth, divorce in America was legally adversarial. (Of course it is often still emotionally adversarial, but I am speaking of the law.) That is to say, one spouse had to charge the other with a fault, and that fault had to conform to one of the statutory grounds for divorce recognized in the state of residence. The grounds most commonly accepted were desertion, cruelty, felony conviction, and alcoholism—but the hands-down winner recognized in the most states was adultery. Progressive era reformers, as I have shown, advocated for "no-fault" divorce decades well before it became law. For instance, George Elliott Howard left the professorial lecture hall for the wider audience of *McClure's* to affirm that every new statutory ground a state acknowledged marked an advance not only in "conjugal rights" but also in "moral fitness" and "social justice."[29]

The crucial difference from today's no-fault divorce is that the party suing had to be innocent. Legal historian Hendrik Hartog explains: "Divorce required guilt, and it required innocence, and it required a public decision that one spouse, and one spouse only, had fundamentally breached his or her obligations." Thus if one spouse sought divorce on the ground of adultery but both were proven to be adulterers, then, in Hartog's wry explanation, "legal policy declared they became thereby 'suitable and proper companions for each other,' locked in permanent matrimony."[30]

Moreover, a mutual decision to divorce could actually ruin the chance of getting one. If a couple collaborated to fabricate a story that would meet statutory grounds (for instance, that one was an adulterer and the other chaste), both would be guilty of the crime of collusion. Thus divorce law recognized only particular narrative trajectories and stock characters. Cases that did not fit a state law's preexisting scripts were not actionable.

Who committed adultery—and who did not—was precisely the focus of many divorce trials in the Progressive era, including the Sinclairs'. In New York, where Sinclair first filed, the only accepted ground since 1787 had been adultery. (Only in 1966 would New York begin to recognize other grounds: cruelty, abandonment, and separation for two years.)[31] And so Sinclair had to convince the court that his marriage conformed to a particular script: Meta was a shameless adulteress and he a spotless cuckold. Auspiciously for Sinclair, he had practiced for decades the role of purist.

When a couple did collude to get a divorce on the ground of adultery, the wife generally took the role of plaintiff. That is because (then as now) wives who have an affair are often judged more harshly than husbands who do the same. Upton Sinclair, however, insisted on being the plaintiff, declaring that moral as well as divine law stood with him (and in case that was not enough, also invoking self-respect and his reputation as a writer). Biographer Anthony Arthur provides an additional reason: casting Meta as a "loose woman" would free Sinclair from having to pay alimony. Although Meta would later regret it, she agreed to play defendant. But as my brief foray into divorce law should make evident, the Sinclairs' role-playing cannot be interpreted as evidence of his innocence nor of her guilt, but rather of their collusion.[32] The last chapter of *Love's Pilgrimage*, in fact, has Thrysis counseling Corydon to perjure herself. If she would "simply . . . admit whatever offense they [state laws] require," Thrysis says, they could "get around" the law and procure a divorce (656).

The differences in the Sinclairs' accounts of how adultery entered their marriage are, therefore, highly consequential. Let me introduce several new *dramatis personae* from the historical record. While both had various flirtations, the first instance of actual adultery seems to have been Upton's, during the Helicon Hall venture. (Ironically, his main impetus in founding that cooperative utopian community had been domestic problems.[33]) In late 1906 or early 1907, Upton had an affair with a married resident, a college-educated journalist Anna G. Noyes who worked as the colony's manager. The next year, Meta had a near-fatal abortion and went to Kellogg's sanitarium in Battle Creek. While there she met Alfred Kuttner, a Harvard graduate who would later write a landmark psychoanalytic interpretation of D.H. Lawrence's *Sons and Lovers* and work with A.A. Brill in translating Freud. Kuttner became Meta's first lover, but the relationship ended disastrously for reasons that remain obscure.[34] In the summer of 1909 she returned to Kellogg's sanitarium, where she met "tramp poet" Harry Kemp, an enthusiast of the fitness entrepreneur Bernarr Macfadden and admirer of Upton Sinclair. After Upton joined Meta at Battle Creek, they met Mary Craig Kimbrough, a Mississippi belle. "Craig," as she was known, decided early on that she intended to marry the famous muckraker. While it is not clear exactly when Craig became Sinclair's lover, it was certainly before his divorce, for she went to England for an abortion in March 1912.

Meanwhile, Sinclair enjoyed a new bookish role—in the words of Harry Kemp's biographer, playing "Emerson to Kemp's Walt Whitman." In the summer of 1911, Sinclair invited the young man to Arden, the single-tax cooperative community where he and Meta were then living. As usual, Sinclair spent most of his time writing, leaving Meta and the handsome young poet to amuse themselves. When Meta and Kemp fell in love, Upton decided to file for divorce.[35]

I turn now to how each of the Sinclairs handles extramarital romance in their novels. In *Love's Pilgrimage*, Corydon has silly schoolgirl crushes, first on a drawing teacher and later a minister. In the second case, Thrysis decides to seize the opportunity to demonstrate his open-mindedness. He lectures his rival about the beauties of voluntary monogamy and divorce by mutual consent. The would-be progressive husband, however, undercuts his principled views by offering to *give* his wife to the minister, as if she were a piece of property. When the minister receives Thrysis's offer letter, he runs off to Switzerland. (Not until the unpublished "Love's Progress" does Sinclair render Corydon's affair with a Kemp figure.)

In Meta's version, Thrysis is the first to commit adultery. His infidelity begins with a Helicon Hall resident (the Anna Noyes figure). Corydon reflects that she "was not unfamiliar with the 'falling in love' process but was unused to seeing it so promptly and practically consummated." At this point, the ever-bookish Thrysis presents a copy of *Love's Coming of Age* to Corydon, adding that Carpenter "would explain the meaning of 'Free Love'" to her.[36]

Through all this, according to Meta, Corydon's crushes have remained platonic, even ethereal. Meta's account of Corydon's first lover is consistent with what can be reconstructed of the historical record. While a patient at Battle Creek, Corydon meets a young socialist and aspiring artist, Erick Steinhart (modeled on Kuttner). Corydon's responds intellectually as much as physically ("her consciousness had been completely revolutionized"). Thrysis belatedly follows Ellis's advice to husbands and "court[s] her as never before." A poem that Meta wrote—and reprints in "Corydon and Thrysis"—captures her conflicted feelings:

> How can I bear thy passion and thy pain?
> When all my soul unto another goes,
> And my torn heart is wrung with mute desire.
> My body like an Indian Wife's who throws
> Herself upon her warrior's funeral pyre.
> And yet I love thee, yes and I would fain
> A penance offer to thy heart's sore stress.
> Wilt thou forgive? Unto my soul again
> I take my body, begging for redress.

Thrysis invites Erick to visit, but still she remains "physically faithful" to her husband. Only when Thrysis demands that Corydon choose between them does she sleep with Erick. After a disastrous affair, when Corydon returns to Thrysis, he confesses that he has meanwhile "made love to his secretary and asked her to marry him."[37]

In Meta's account, the characters' reactions to adultery demonstrate Thrysis's inconsistency and Corydon's continuing commitment to the Progressive era marital ideal. Meta emphasizes the husband's hypocrisy in denying his wife privileges "accorded to the rest of their companions including Thrysis." He soon takes up with a Southern belle (based on Mary "Craig" Kimbrough). Corydon believes they "have a perfect right" to their affair, but their secretiveness annoys her. At this point Andy Webb (the Harry Kemp figure) appears, leading to "the first thoroughly pagan love affair of her life." Thrysis retaliates by tricking them into running off and renting a bungalow together, warning the press is on their heels. Actually Thrysis himself had leaked Corydon's whereabouts to a reporter. In setting up his wife, Thrysis gets not only revenge but, more importantly, evidence of her adultery, giving him grounds for a New York divorce—but only if he can obscure his own adultery. Given this nasty story, it is understandable why Meta concludes, "it was not Corydon that wrecked the genius of Thrysis. He committed suicide as an artist on the day he sued for divorce in New York State."[38]

A TALE OF TWO WRITERS

Companionate egalitarianism itself also becomes problematic in the Sinclair marriage. According to both novels, the couple tried to forge a relationship that would nurture each other's literary careers. But in the Thrysis-Corydon relationship, as rendered by both Sinclairs although with different emphases, the husband undermines the wife's writing.

Throughout *Love's Pilgrimage*, Thrysis has trouble taking his wife seriously. His systematic trivialization proceeds from how Thrysis conceptualizes his mission as a reformer. He sees Corydon as embodying the female reading public that he must reach (53). In addition to objectifying her into a passive audience, Thrysis reduces her to inert subject matter. "You were part of the raw material that I had to use," he tells his wife; "I had mastered you, and was going to make you what you had to be."

Love's Pilgrimage allots only several of its hundreds of pages to Corydon's creative writing, and those reinforce the husband's intellectual authority. Late in the novel, Sinclair shows her channeling resentment at domesticity into composing poetry. Naturally, Corydon wonders what her husband, a published author, will think of her poem. Unimpressed, he offers only platitudes, which thoroughly demoralize Corydon. In a scene that Meta claims to have written, and that may be more revealing than Sinclair realized, Corydon wonders, "But oh, how can I ever get there . . . if nobody gives me any encouragement?" (466).[39]

At one point in *Love's Pilgrimage*, Thrysis acknowledges his wife's literary gifts and simultaneously glimpses the woman-as-reformer that the marital theorists believed still existed beneath the social conditioning. But the scene occurs, ominously enough, when Corydon nearly commits suicide. Holding a revolver to her head but afraid to pull the trigger, she pours out her frustrations. Thrysis is dumbfounded by her eloquence. Unfortunately Sinclair does not record any words Corydon actually said; he provides only second-hand reviews of her "language of great poetry, fervid and passionate, with swift flashes of insight and illumination," even "bursts of prophecy." At this point—nearly five hundred pages into the novel—Thrysis belatedly has an epiphany about "woman [. . . as] an equal" (498). He even senses that Corydon represents a "mighty force that in the end would revolutionize all human ideas and institutions." But after this revelation, the novel promptly takes a new direction, so both Sinclair and Thrysis can forget about it.

An additional description of Corydon's "act of creation" further displaces any literary talent she may have, this time onto her body (284). The creative act in question occurs when Corydon gives birth to their son Cedric (modeled on David Sinclair, born December 1901). As in Upton's version of their sexual initiation, he sets up the birth scene by surrounding Corydon with spiritualistic language. Thrysis abases himself, but in a way that eclipses his wife's personality. She is but "a creature consecrated, made holy by suffering; she was the sacredness of life incarnate," embodying "woman's *fate*!" (277–78). At the same time, the birth threatens Thrysis to his core, for he sees it as a fundamental "reality" that eclipses anything he can write. His reaction to that threat infuses the scene with brutal misogyny:

> The doctor's hands were red with blood now, like a butcher's. . . .
> "You can see the head now," he said once, turning to [Thrysis].
> And Thrysis looked; through the horrible gaping wound showed a little patch, the size of a dollar—purplish black, palpitating, starting forward when the crises shook the mother. . . .
> "But how can it ever get out?" he cried suddenly, with wildness. . . .
> All the while Thrysis had never really believed in the child—it was too strange an idea. He could think only of the woman, and of her endless agony. . . .
> Time and again the girl screamed, in sudden agony; he would toil on, his

lips set. Once it was too much even for him—her cries had become incessant, and he nodded to the nurse. . . .

After a while he rose up. He paced the hall, talking to himself. He could not go on acting in this way—he must be a man. Others had borne this—he would bear it too. . . .

There was an hour more of that . . . Corydon was crying, moaning that she wished to die. There was now in sight a huge, bulging object—black, monstrous—rimmed with a band of bleeding, straining flesh. (279-81)

The infantilized "girl" Corydon is reduced to the spectacle of her pain and "gaping" vagina as observed by two men (or three, if one counts Sinclair). This devastating physical exposure allows Thrysis to regain intellectual superiority over his wife.

By tracing the "tragedy of two artistic temperaments," not just one, Meta creates a very different narrative arc. Emphasizing from early on Corydon's literary aspirations as well as the obstacles to fulfilling them, Meta depicts a talented young woman unable to attend Vassar because her father loses his patrimony. Corydon turns to the local library and normal school to stoke her "ever increasing hunger for knowledge," becoming especially enthralled with Shelley and Keats. When she meets Thrysis, another writer-in-training, he initially seems supportive but ends up as her biggest obstacle. While they pursue "the regeneration of humanity," they also both assume the first step will be Thrysis's writing, and only "afterward . . . Corydon's books, when she had learned to write." Their interactions never allow for the possibility of intellectual parity, which is especially distressing because Thrysis pays lip service to equality and to valuing his wife's opinions. He encourages Corydon to critique his own work, "yet Corydon never dared to hold for long any independent opinions." If she voices any, he turns intellectual bully and "would bend all his energies to persuade her to his way of thinking." Through it all, Thrysis pretends to maintain the ideal of "mak[ing] a religion out of our work together," while being unable to put that ideal into practice.[40]

Meta's conceptualization of what it means to be a progressive reformer differs instructively from her husband's, and not only in terms of gender. Both versions trace the development of an idealist who hopes to reform the world first by setting an example and then by turning it into text. But whereas Upton genders his reformer male and portrays a singular, even reclusive, Messianic genius, Meta genders hers female and depicts a representative figure who embodies a sea change for an entire generation of women. Meta's Corydon is very much a product of her time even while being one step ahead of its mores. She has instincts of the "more highly evolved, complex modern woman" but lacks the requisite financial autonomy to act like one. Corydon craves independence but "had been systematically unfitted for this and in those days the modern woman movement was in its initial stages." In a letter written around 1910, Meta described "the new self I have been trying to bring into being." She envisioned Corydon—as she did herself—as a New Woman, an "artist struggling to be born," and a reformer with a "beautiful even great message to deliver."[41]

This notion that reading and writing could help Corydon find a new way of being a woman does indeed make the character representative of her generation. As Barbara Sicherman establishes, "Women of the Progressive generation were the first to write themselves into history in significant numbers," and they did so quite literally, by picking up their pens. In addition, many contemporary portrayals of the New Woman identified the figure with the books she read. As Edith Ellis explains, works about rebellious women such as Ibsen's *Doll's House* and Schreiner's *The Story of an African Farm* "drove thinking women further towards their emancipation." Critics of the New Woman agreed about the influence of reading, only interpreting the practice negatively. "A world of disorderly notions picked out of books," ran one mocking cartoon of the New Woman as Donna Quixote. Indeed, according to some scholars, the New Woman was very much a product of print culture.[42]

While the New Woman is characteristically single, or else married late in life, Meta's character is a young married woman. Consequently her version of the New Woman takes a shape more like figures such as Edna Pontellier in Kate Chopin's *The Awakening* (1899) who intuit a connection between artistic and sexual expression, even if that expression takes them outside of marriage. In this light I would like to refocus on the contrast between the two Sinclairs' visions of the reformer. Upton Sinclair's singular artist/reformer is emotionally distant (even stunted) and alienated from his body. Meta's representative artist/reformer, to the contrary, imagines visionary literature flowing directly out of sexual experience. Her correspondence makes very clear that Meta intended to shape her romantic disappointments (with her lover Alfred Kuttner as much as with her husband) into inspirational literature.

While she did not finish that ambitious project, Meta did leave behind intriguing literary traces which pursue the transformative potential of sexual passion. Sometimes she doubts herself, as in this segment from one of her poems, probably based on her affair with Kuttner:

> Desire, like a faint winged bird,
> Hovers above my head,
> Perhaps it will lead me to Paradise;
> Or else at my feet, fall dead.

More often, she affirms sexuality as essential to full humanity and creativity, as in her poem "Rivers":

> Forever and forever,
> The little rivers run;
> Rivers of deep Desire,
> Warmed by an endless sun.

In another poem Meta imagines passion as giving birth to a female poet.[43] Unlike Upton Sinclair's notion that the reformer must suppress emotion and sexuality, for Meta, reform would grow out of sexual love—much as marital theorists like Ellen Key and Havelock Ellis maintained.

Meta, in fact, explicitly links women's erotic and romantic fulfillment with progressive reform. Her character Corydon decides "that somebody should be a martyr to the cause, if necessary, and prove that the quest for love or a 'soul mate' . . . was quite as important and justifiable as any other progressive ideal." Meta understood, in other words, sexual expression as central to the progressive—and, for her, clearly also the feminist—project of women's reclaiming themselves. She also understood the idea would threaten others, for she remarked, "You might be radical in any other way you pleased in America, but you must not be radical on the subject of the sacred institution of marriage."[44]

Was Meta a narcissistic nymphomaniac who almost derailed her husband's ascent toward international recognition as a reformer, or was Upton a clumsy lover and cold fish whose theoretical embrace of women's rights did not extend to taking his wife's emotional needs or literary aspirations seriously? While I find the latter interpretation more plausible, I know that the question, however tempting, is the wrong one to ask. I suspect Meta and Upton tried with equal sincerity to distill their marriage into a narrative for their generation.

A question I do think fair is how the Sinclairs' own principled views on marriage—voluntary monogamy, egalitarianism, mutual respect as workers, and divorce by mutual consent—correspond to how they render the marriage of their respective fictional characters. By the Sinclairs' own terms, in other words, which author captures the more progressive spouse? In casting marriage as undermining the reform project, in pathologizing the wife's sexuality, in presenting Thrysis as thinking he can give his wife to another man, Upton Sinclair betrays progressivism. By the very terms that Meta and Upton agreed upon, her Corydon prevails as the better spokesperson for progressive marriage.

EXTRA, EXTRA! READ ALL ABOUT IT!

The Sinclairs' joint project of textualizing their marriage took an unexpected turn when Upton's filing for divorce became national news in the summer of 1911. *Love's Pilgrimage*, which had been selling a thousand copies a week since its publication in March, languished on the shelves, while dozens—perhaps hundreds—of saucy newspaper accounts appeared in August and September 1911 alone. The outraged muckraker believed the media blitz threatened to destroy him financially while also challenging to the core his hard-won credentials as a reformer.[45] As Sinclair lost the ability to control how the public viewed his marriage, readership of that marriage broadened not just in numbers but also in demographic range. By the beginning of the twentieth century, according to one historian, "newspaper reading became an established part of daily life for most Americans." Newspapers, which of all print forms most cut across demographic lines, certainly reached a much broader demographic than novels.[46] The investment of both money and time in reading a brisk column in a five-cent paper was miniscule compared to a novel clocking in at well over six hundred pages and costing a dollar and a half.

Before the media blizzard over the 1911 Sinclair split, there had been two squalls. When Meta went for a second visit to Kellogg's in 1907 by herself, stories spread "rumors . . . that she may never return." In November, Upton issued a statement denying a "virulent editorial" that his marriage was on the rocks and announcing a $50,000 suit against the offending paper. He describes the marriage in surprisingly conventional terms, casting Meta as a housewife and himself as defender of her virtue. Then in 1909 the *San Francisco Examiner* ran a front page article, complete with pictures, titled "Sinclair Sorry He Wed / Says Ceremony is Farce." The story was picked up by papers in New York, Boston, Chicago, Atlanta, Los Angeles—as well as France, Germany, Norway, Sweden, South Africa, Australia, Yokohama, Hong Kong, and Bombay.[47]

This was not how Sinclair had intended to get his ideas across. Especially not because, when the divorce broke in August 1911, many journalists cast him as a kook. "Sinclair Freaky, Papa-in-Law Says," trumpeted the *Morning*

SINCLAIR FREAKY, PAPA-IN-LAW SAYS

Mr. Fuller Believes Author Will Be Great Man if He Will Eat More Meat.

BRAIN IS OVERPOWERING

Adventures in Dieting Cited as Evidence of Mental Unbalance, but Good Turkey Dinner Makes Great Difference.

NEW YORK. Sept. 10.—(Special.)— If Upton Sinclair would recover his balance, eat more meat, stop thinking everlastingly about himself and his diets, he would be a wonder, is the estimate placed on the Socialist author by W. H. Fuller, father of Mrs. Meta Sinclair, who has found that she cannot get along with him—that she loves the Kansas poet, Harry Kemp, better.

FIGURE 5. Like many newspapers, *Morning Oregonian* ridiculed Upton Sinclair after he separated from Meta.

Oregonian, focusing on the muckraker's food faddism. Sinclair's chewing a prune for twenty minutes and his dog's tomato diet made for popular stories. A clever journalist sauced these culinary tales with the by-line, "Adventures in Dieting Cited as Evidence of Mental Unbalance, but Good Turkey Dinner Makes Great Difference" [48]

If national ridicule offended Sinclair, portrayal as a hypocritical reformer must have been torture. "Famous Author and Socialist Reformer Fails to Find Utopia in Own Home," snickered the *Idaho Daily Statesman.* The *Grand Forks Herald* (North Dakota) scoffed, "Mr. Sinclair seems to have devoted himself so assiduously to the problem of reforming society that he had not time to regulate the affairs of his own household" before dismissing him altogether: "incidentally we never did think much of Sinclair as a philosopher." For the *Morning Oregonian,* the saga demonstrated how "bitter personal experience" could undermine "fine-spun theories"; the writer cast

Sinclair as "roar[ing] in jealous rage, just as any untheoretical husband in the universe." *Life* magazine smugly concluded that "our friends who are in the business of reforming society do not seem to have this gift in greater perfection than other people." An anonymous writer for *The Bookman* finishes with a flourish: "sooner or later comes the time when what is sauce for the propagander is no longer sauce for the propagoose — and then the need of new 'soul-mates.'"[49] It is not difficult to imagine readers chuckling.

Another joke the papers loved to repeat, however, pivots on a punch line that performs very different cultural work. During the New York trial, the landlady at the boarding-house where Meta and Kemp were found by the press became a key witness. Journalists loved to quote the testimony of Grace Shanz (always identified with the honorific "Mrs.") that she had remarked to her own husband how Meta and Kemp "'seem to be altogether too loving to be man and wife.'"[50] It is easy to understand why this line got recycled so many times, but its humor derives from the unstated assumption that marriages *should* be companionate, romantic, and sexually fulfilling — even though they usually were not. Repeating this joke is one of several ways in which the press disseminated, even if unintentionally, sympathetic views about progressive marriage reform.

Another characterization of the separating couple helped normalize the reformers' ideas of divorce by mutual consent and tolerance of extramarital loves. In this variant of the narrative, a cheerful Mr. and Mrs. Sinclair agreed politely on the need to part. Co-respondent Kemp even appeared as part of the happy family, joining in the "amiable discussion." The masterpiece in this genre was the *New York Times'* front-page "Sinclair Divorces Wife, But They're Friends."[51] If marriage could be companionate, why not also divorce?

A series of articles appearing the year of the Sinclair breakup explains how mightily newspapers were coming to shape public opinion. Journalist Will Irwin found readers "crav[ing]" news almost like an addiction and society depending on news to function. Irwin particularly emphasizes how newspapers play a critical role in "furnish[ing] the raw material for public opinion." Stories about any "departure from the established order" were, by definition, news. Stories about the Sinclairs certainly emphasized a marital experiment that departed from established norms. However, the very repetition of the story seems to have shaped public opinion toward sympathy for rather than fear of the new ideas.[52] The newspaper coverage, in other words, illustrates the diffusion of Progressive era marital ideals into a broad readership.

The most significant way in which press coverage promoted marriage reform was through its portrayal of Meta. Of course there were self-righteous screeds against her, but they were surprisingly rare, at least as long as she remained with Kemp. As is often the case with a divorce, even disinterested spectators felt compelled to take a side, and most journalists sided with Meta. For starters, she was the source of great copy. The *Hartford Courant* was among the many venues to enumerate respectfully Meta's complaints: "First, he [Sinclair] is not able to devote his time to his wife; second, he is so absorbed in his work that he is not able to keep his wife from being seen with other men, and third, . . . [he is] over-developed intellectually." Another article that quotes Meta directly ends with the insinuating comment that Sinclair "is so overdeveloped intellectually that the rest of his nature suffers in consequence."[53] Ouch.

If such accounts made Sinclair a laughing stock, others had the additional, even if unintended, consequence of making Meta into a popular heroine. Needless to say, her looks didn't hurt. Papers noted her "expressive" eyes and "perfect complexion." Even when appearing with her lover, Meta was often described as a chaste and "girlish figure" in loose-fitting clothing revealing "none of the lines of her figure." Many articles included photographs of Meta in flowing white gowns with flowers woven into her hair like some Greek goddess. In some photos, the dark hair is pulled back and she gazes soulfully out into space. In others, her cascading hair frames a sensuous expression as she gazes unashamedly at the viewer.[54]

Many accounts expressed surprising sympathy for Meta's liaison and public defense of trial marriage. Numerous articles featured side by side photographs of her and Kemp. One enterprising journalist even published the lovebirds' poems side by side under the headline, "These Are Affinity Poems."[55] There was nothing romantic about either poem, but Meta was finally in print.

Other papers took her seriously as an intellectual and reformer, reporting respectfully on what the *Bellingham* (Washington) *Herald* refers to as Meta's "creed." Journalists quoted from a lengthy public statement she had prepared, while others printed its entire text in manifesto form under headlines such as "Sex Independence of Woman, in the Version of Mrs. Sinclair." And so thousands read Meta's criticism of women's dependence ("until woman is on the same economic basis as man there can be no perfect marriage state"), rejection of the fetish of women's chastity, and endorsement of voluntary monogamy. They also read Meta's call to arms: "I am the real radical." When asked if she objected to being charged with adultery, Meta declared she was happy to "sacrifice" herself if doing so inspired other wives

Mrs. Sinclair Braves Opinion

Silent on Affair With Kemp

MRS. UPTON SINCLAIR.

Author Husband, in New York, Shows He Is One
With Her on Question of Marriage Ties.

FIGURE 6. The press treated Meta Sinclair more kindly even while sending mixed messages by focusing on her looks. Here, the white dress and flowers suggest purity, while the scrollwork around the bottom draws attention to her breasts. Courtesy of the Lilly Library, Stone Manuscripts.

FIGURE 7. Meta saved clippings about the separation scandal, including this and the previous illustration. Journalists loved the line about how she and lover Harry Kemp "took husband at his word." Courtesy of the Lilly Library, Stone Manuscripts.

to repudiate their status as "chattel of man." Textualizing her experience in a different way, Meta aligned herself with Ibsen's famous Nora, asserting, "I have permanently come out of the doll's house." Her comments could certainly be grandiose, but the press did not mock her as they did Upton. The Chicago *Examiner* presented her as a principled woman who "will brave conventionality by attempting to solve for herself the proper scope of the relationship of men and women in matters of sex." The *New York Times* continued the lionization by excerpting a letter from Boston suffragette Dr. Antoinette F. Konikow, who praised Meta's "brave stand." Konikow's words to Meta were read by countless readers when the *Times* printed, "'thousands of women down deep in their hearts all bless you.'"[56]

These sympathetic treatments probably reflect the concerted effort of journalists to appeal to a cohort that was increasingly reading newspapers in the Progressive era: women.[57] But regardless of the motivation, newspapers provided an ideal venue for Meta to proselytize. And so when she is quoted defending her affair with Kemp on the ground of seeking her real mate, readers probably felt titillated—but perhaps also inspired.

While Meta longed for renown as a creative writer, not a journalist, she was quoted by the press often enough to merit comparison with the newswomen discussed by historian Alice Fahs in *Out on Assignment: Newspaper Women and the Making of Modern Public Space* (2011). According to Fahs, Progressive era newswomen published articles with appealingly "independent heroines . . . [who] became performative public figures," a description that certainly fits Meta Sinclair. Fahs emphasizes how newspaper work thus helped women redefine their role, putting aside the nineteenth-century ideal of privacy and domesticity in favor of actively shaping the public sphere.[58] Meta was more an object than author of journalism, of course, and "Corydon and Thrysis" never made it into print, but news accounts circulated the very image of her that she courted: representative New Woman and pioneer feminist.

In a study of the social function of sensational news a decade after the Sinclair affair, John D. Stevens posits that readers follow celebrity divorces in order to test and clarify their own values. As Tolstoy also maintained, happy marriage rarely makes for a good story; rather, disruptive or aberrant relationships entice readers. While voyeuristic gossip serves its own needs, the real importance in sensational news, Stevens argues, lies "in forcing society to reconsider its values."[59] While the sheer amount of newsprint about the Sinclairs does suggest voyeuristic interest, the accounts were shaped in such a way as to foster a climate favorable to rethinking marriage.

Harry Kemp also appeared in many newspaper stories, but generally only as an understudy to Meta's starring role. Their trial marriage lasted only for a few months. A decade after she had left him for another man, Kemp belatedly set out to articulate his interpretation of the Sinclairs' marital experiment. (Kemp had since gone on in 1915 to wed actress Mary Pyne, the original for Dreiser's "Esther Norn," and a lover of Hutchins Hapgood.) In *Tramping on Life* (1922), he revisits his fifteen minutes of fame as Meta's lover, and devotes nearly half of the book to "'That Sinclair Affair.'" Kemp explains that Meta initiated him sexually after he told her he was about to visit a prostitute to relieve his frustration. He recalls Meta's explaining that she and Upton "both believe in the theory of free love, though we happen to be married." Unlike anything Upton Sinclair ever wrote, Kemp provides a memorable physical description of Meta as "always moving about leisurely, gracefully, like some strange, pretty animal. . . . She walked about in bloomers, languidly conscious that her legs were graceful and lovely."[60]

The main interest of Kemp's account today lies in how he casts it explicitly in terms of the theory versus practice of a progressive relationship. Upton stands for the empty theory: a brainy hypocrite and "fake radical[]" with the "absurd" penchant for seeing life "through the film of his latest theory." Kemp dispenses with his one-time mentor: "the man who prated glibly of any ready solution, orthodox or heterodox, radical or conventional, of the problem of the relationships between women and men, was worse than a fool, he was a dangerous madman!" Kemp positions himself and Meta, naturally, as representing principled practice. They rejected a formal marriage as beneath them, Kemp explains, thinking a trial marriage would provide a much better "opportunity . . . to put to practical test our theories." He does not mention Parsons by name, who in 1906 had advocated trial marriage. But Kemp does reference "the noble work" of Ellis, Key, and other reformers. He further establishes his credentials as a progressive reader by likening himself and Meta to William Godwin and Mary Wollstonecraft, the eighteenth-century anarchist and feminist (and parents of *Frankenstein* author Mary Shelley). [61] Above and beyond gossipy memories of sexual delight with Meta, *Tramping on Life* insists that of the two Sinclairs, she was the authentic reformer.

The Sinclairs resumed their dueling accounts in their own voices when they published side-by-side articles in the October 1911 issue of *The World To-day; A Monthly Record of Human Progress*. This appropriately named magazine was an ideal venue as lecture podium. The "pride of Chicago journalism for several years" according to historian Frank Luther Mott, *The World To-day* had recently absorbed a University of Chicago journal and regularly published articles by professors who had national name recognition.[62] The two things the Professors Sinclair agreed on in their articles were the need for divorce reform and that their own relationship exemplified progressivism. Beyond that, Upton and Meta competed to reshape the meaning of their marriage according to each one's views of reform.

Meta's "A Plea for Freer Divorce" is one of only two publications of hers that I have been able to locate. In this one, she criticizes traditional marriage as based on "property-right." The "stand-patters" fearing change wrongly consider marriage a "sacred and unchangeable institution which keeps the

pillars of society upright." Citing Ellen Key, Meta calls sex "the great constructive power of the universe." She maintains that people who remain
unhappily married hurt themselves as well as their children—and in doing
so "undermine that very structure of society which they are supposed to be
upholding." The progressive individual who follows his or her heart, then,
contributes to the reform of society. Especially *her* heart, for women are
"more quickly susceptible to the progressive impulse."[63]

Upton's "Marriage and Divorce" portrays women quite differently. He
spins out a Gilmanesque account of the conditioning of middle- and upper-
class women as "sex creatures" raised to see marriage as their only "profes-
sion," while working-class women were forced to satisfy sexual needs in
"hidden ways." Women's limited options, combined with the fact that "the
vast majority" of men seek "casual immoral relationships," causes the epidemic of venereal disease. And then there is that pesky divorce taboo. "Are
you willing to say," Sinclair bluntly confronts any skeptical readers, that a
couple should not be able to divorce if "one of them is a lunatic, or a hopeless drunkard, or an habitual criminal, or a degenerate, or the victim of a
disease which he can communicate to his offspring"? Opponents of divorce,
he says, defend a system of "sex-slavery and degeneracy" typical of "medi-
aeval states"—such as South Carolina and New York, whose divorce laws
were the strictest in the nation. The solution: legalize contraception and
encourage early marriage. These two reforms would allow men to avoid
temptation and women, freed of unwanted children, to support themselves
while also abolishing prostitution and sexually transmitted disease. Not bad
for a day's work.[64]

But Sinclair continued to brood over his failed first marriage and especially its treatment by the press. Two of his most important books—*The
Brass Check* (1920) and *The Book of Life* (1921)—take as inspiration his first
botched marital experiment. These two very different works illustrate how
Sinclair's first marriage continued to shape his understanding of reform.

UPTON SINCLAIR MEETS THE PRESS

Sinclair complained that his words were twisted by the press, but he clearly
also courted it. Late in August 1911 he, along with Meta and Kemp, staged
what can only be called a press conference at the Hotel Imperial in Manhattan, each taking turns at proclaiming his or her views about progressive
marriage. For the finale, Upton publicly served divorce papers on his wife.
But the problem with calling a press conference is that journalists will bring

their own slant to the material. Even such staunch advocates of privacy as legal scholars and justices Samuel D. Warren and Louis D. Brandeis, alarmed by how "instantaneous photographs and newspaper enterprise have invaded the sacred precincts of private and domestic life," would not have sympathized with the predicament which Sinclair created. Warren and Brandeis, who sought legal recognition of a "right to privacy," also maintained that a person lost that right by presenting his views to the public — or, "in other words, publish[ing] it." Even if the nominally fictional status of *Love's Pilgrimage* shielded Sinclair from actually publishing his views, he did exactly that with the press conference.[65]

Sinclair objected to news as entertainment, particularly when he was the butt of it. He lashed back with *The Brass Check*, a muckraking account of journalism that he considered "the most important and most dangerous book I have ever written." While dated in parts, *The Brass Check* remains a "cult classic" among journalists and holds its own with *The Jungle* or any of Sinclair's other ninety-odd books.[66] In *The Brass Check*, Sinclair transmutes the scandal which drew him through the muck of a yellowed press into purifying muckraking which exposes a corrupt press.

When Sinclair wrote *The Brass Check*, journalism was in transition. During the Progressive era, the press achieved some independence from political parties, began to embrace the goal of objectivity, and shifted the emphasis from editorials to news. The heyday of yellow journalism had passed but it left an imprint on the press that endures even today as seen in the human interest story (or personal exposé), sensationalism, and even colorful Sunday supplements. Contemporary concerns focused on how journalism had become big business. As one index, advertising revenues more than tripled between 1892 and 1914. There was, accordingly, much talk about a cleaned-up, wholesome press. The *New York Times,* for instance, reorganized in 1896 under Adolph S. Ochs, was advertised not only under the still-familiar slogan "All the News That's Fit To Print," but also because "It Does Not Soil the Breakfast Cloth." A second landmark in journalism, Mary Baker Eddy's *Christian Science Monitor* was founded in 1908, intended, in the words of one historian, as an "alternative, clean wholesome newspaper with no exploitation of crime and vice."[67]

The Brass Check mounted the most sustained warning of the danger of an increasingly commercial press.[68] Sinclair argued that because the press is controlled by corporate interests, it covers up real news while reporting sensationalistic (and, preferably, salacious) stories — especially accounts that trivialize efforts at reform. The charge still resonates. I would like to focus, however, on how Sinclair's exposé of journalism extends his interest in marital reform and the (for him) ever-pressing issue of his reputation as progressive reformer.

Although describing himself as "by nature impersonal," Sinclair grounds his account of the corruption of journalism in frank talk about the treatment of his divorce. The primal scene that sparked *The Brass Check* occurred when a yellow paper sent a reporter out to interview Sinclair in the late 1900s. She asked for a picture to include with her story; Sinclair obliged with one of himself but didn't care to see his wife blazoned across the papers. After the reporter left, Sinclair realized a picture of Meta was missing. It was printed the following day in the New York *American*—and, an infuriated Sinclair reports, the paper continued to run that photo nine years later, even while misidentifying her as Sinclair's *second* wife.[69]

A chapter called "An Essential Monogamist" identifies the decision to divorce Meta as the moment of an even more heinous violation. After eight years of living in a "maelstrom" of "domestic precariousness," Sinclair made "the greatest blunder in my life." He claims to have agreed to Meta's plea to let her sue him for divorce, so as to protect her reputation. (As I have shown, the suit actually played out with his suing her.) But then Sinclair came upon unspecified "facts" which caused him to telegram his attorney to inquire if he just might himself have grounds for divorce. Three hours later, he received a call from a reporter who had intercepted the telegram. Sinclair sought to control the damage by sending a prepared statement, but it was twisted beyond recognition when published. The exposure caused Sinclair weeks of "horrors" in which "my personality, my affairs, my opinions and my every-day actions became the subject of discourse and speculation." Showing more of a sense of humor than is usual, he sums up: "The generally accepted explanation was that I had married an innocent young girl and taught her 'free love' doctrines, and then, when she practiced these doctrines, I kicked her out of my home."[70]

The lesson Sinclair extracts from this exposure provides the thesis for *The Brass Check*. "The matter at issue," he writes portentously, "is not the character of Upton Sinclair, but the character of the machinery upon which you rely every day of your life for news. . . . If that machinery can be used deliberately and systematically to lie about Upton Sinclair, it can be used to disorganize the people's movement throughout the world, and to set back the coming of Social Justice."[71] In addition to this astounding charge that the press could end progress, *The Brass Check* repeatedly references personal data about Sinclair's first marriage even as its author claims he's not writing about himself; rather, he's denouncing the "machinery," the system, the bias of the press.

Indeed, Sinclair charges, the press systematically uses conventional notions of marriage in order to emasculate radicals. He relays how journalists targeted his friend, the Christian socialist George D. Herron, who was married when he fell in love with the daughter of a wealthy widow in his congregation. There was no adultery, but when Mrs. Herron sued for divorce and Herron remarried, the press pounced: "He was a dangerous man to the 'interests,'" Sinclair explains, "and here was the chance to destroy him." The selective exposure outrages Sinclair: journalists keep quiet when fat capitalists leave their wives to marry stenographers, but "radicals" are "sport for predatory Journalism!" In addition to himself and Herron, Sinclair names Gilman, Veblen, Jack London, George Sterling, Clarence Darrow, Maxim Gorky, and others, all "caught upon the hook of an unhappy marriage, gutted, skinned alive, and laid quivering on the red-hot griddle of Capitalist Journalism."[72]

Sinclair frets about whether readers will discredit *The Brass Check* because it rests on personal experience. "Will the radical movement," he worries, think the book simply "a ventilation of my own egotisms"? And in fact, according to the dean of a journalism school, "the controversy over Sinclair himself" minimized the impact of the book when it appeared. Even the editors of a recent reprint who praise it as the first "systematic structural critique of U.S. journalism" find the personal emphasis self-indulgent. They conclude that the book remains worth reading in spite of its unfortunate lapse into personal experience.[73]

I argue, to the contrary, that *The Brass Check* is important precisely because of its personal approach. Sinclair's method anticipates a key premise of the 1960s New Journalists such as Tom Wolfe and Truman Capote who, contemptuous of how mainstream news was disseminated, believed they achieved a "higher . . . objectivity" precisely by revealing their own personal bias.[74] *The Brass Check* illuminates Sinclair's opposition to personality-mongering and desire to keep his personal life private, but it also makes a very different point: that enduring social criticism can grow out of personal experience. That, of course, had been Meta's overriding point in "Corydon and Thrysis."

The organizing metaphor of *The Brass Check* reveals how sexual phobias continued to plague Sinclair. The title refers to prostitution: a man pays his fee, receives a brass check, and then gives it to the prostitute. Encapsulating so much that Sinclair loathed—economic exploitation, the dangers of sexuality, the fear of personal and social contamination—prostitution provides Sinclair the ideal metaphor for focusing his hatred of the press. After explaining "the Brass Check is the price of your shame," Sinclair describes a gruesome contamination by venereal disease: "running sores and bursting glands, rotting lips and festering noses, swollen heads and crooked joints, idiot gabblings and maniac shrieks, pistols to blow out your brains and poisons to still your agonies." Despite the second person pronoun, Sinclair himself suffers also: "I, who wish to attack these high-priced advertisers, am forced to publish what I have to say in a paper which can only exist by publishing the advertisements of cancer-cures and headache-powders. This is very humiliating, but what can I do? Stop writing?" By casting the press as a prostitute and himself as one valiantly trying to maintain purity in a corrupt world, Sinclair not only repeats the opening scene of *Love's Pilgrimage*—in which young Thrysis defends his virginity from a beckoning prostitute—but also exemplifies Loren Glass's contention that twentieth-century authors, both courting and condemning fame, find celebrity "threatening the 'stable ego boundaries' of the male author." Glass concludes that celebrity thus "figures as a psychosexual trauma in many careers of the modern era."[75]

The Brass Check sheds considerable light on Sinclair's emotional makeup as well. Meta Sinclair, as discussed above, makes the case that he suffered from what might be called emotional frigidity. He was evidently, however, quite capable of an emotion that could blow as hot as love can—anger. Sinclair excelled in portraying himself as a suffering victim—whether of a nymphomaniacal wife or the degenerate press. In doing so, he exemplifies the "cultural narratives of masculine suffering" traced by literary scholar Jennifer Travis. The wounded, anguished man, according to Travis, illustrates how emotion gets recoded in surprising ways as masculine around the turn into the twentieth century.[76]

THE REFORMER REFORMED

Sinclair says that his views about marriage never altered, but his memory is selective. Significant changes are evident as early as 1913, in articles he wrote for Bernarr Macfadden's *Physical Culture* that reframe Sinclair's own youthful sexual ignorance as typical of white middle class American naiveté. The newly remarried Sinclair starts presenting himself as a sex-and-marriage guru, writing to counter "mistaken prudery" and "actual *ignorance*." Concentrating on the "hygienic and sexual aspects," Sinclair now puts "the body first." Astoundingly, he now sympathizes with sexually unfulfilled wives and considers sex the engine driving evolutionary progress, making "apes into savages, and savages into civilized man." "Real Marriage" results from what Samuel Johnson had defined as the triumph of hope over experience, and Sinclair now endorsed: a second try. Needless to say, his second marriage in 1913 lies beyond the scope of this book, but Sinclair attributes his changed perspective to Mary "Craig" Kimbrough, who provided tales about her Southern past that Sinclair used in novels while gratifyingly taking a back seat to his genius. They remained married until her death in 1961—at which point Sinclair, at age eighty-three, promptly remarried.[77]

Sinclair's magnum opus of personal reform, *The Book of Life* (1921), is surely one of the most ambitious how-to manuals ever published. The intent is to delineate a "code" for living that can be practiced, not just theorized.[78] *The Book of Life* contains forward-looking discussions about the merits of a diet limiting starch, fat, and sugar, alongside crackpot ideas such as that tight hats cause baldness and alcoholism causes capitalism.

And *The Book of Life* significantly rewrites once again Sinclair's marital reform agenda. Now Sinclair maintains "the mind and body are inextricably interwoven." He criticizes ideas he had held a decade earlier, such as that celibacy increases one's power and that the only acceptable form of contraception is abstinence. "Nonsense," he snorts! Embracing the views of Ellis, Key, Carpenter, and his own first wife—without crediting any of them—Sinclair trumpets that the highest purpose of marriage is to perpetuate romantic love. Women are harder to arouse than men, he lectures, and husbands must learn to gratify wives. Sinclair even repackages Ellis's distinction between chastity and abstinence as if it were his own discovery: chastity is "a preparing for" love; celibacy "a perversion of life." Once again, conjugal sexuality emerges as central to reform, only the tune has changed: "it is here, in the marriage bed, that the divorce problem is to be settled, and likewise the problem of prostitution." Sinclair now advocates what he calls, curiously enough, "progressive polygamy." He concludes, "Passion is a part of us, and a fundamental part. If we do not find a place for it in marriage, it will seek satisfaction outside of marriage."[79] As he, of all husbands, should know.

Although Sinclair intended *The Book of Life* as a revolutionary sex manual, Floyd Dell perceptively observes that "one sometimes feels that it is to his [Sinclair's] youthful self that this whole book is addressed." That would be quite a narrow audience indeed—yet the reformer does seem to have succeeded in the most difficult project of reforming himself. Moreover, through

The Book of Life, Meta's viewpoint finally makes it into print, although under her ex-husband's name, of course. It is unclear, finally, which of the Sinclairs got the last word.[80]

The "Sinclair Affair" illustrates how the Progressive era campaign to reform marriage was a battle of the books. Scenes of reading are integral to Upton Sinclair's *Love's Pilgrimage*, as to Meta's "Corydon and Thrysis"—with each offering distinct conclusions about what the Sinclairs did with the books they read. Given the central role that both assign to books in promoting marital reform, it isn't surprising to find them so interested in becoming, themselves, writers—even writing self-reflexively about the process of authorship. But when their marriage became subject matter for countless journalists, the Sinclairs found themselves, rather than their compositions, being read.

Upton Sinclair's attempt to produce a companionate novel that would fairly embody his wife's viewpoint clearly did not succeed. What we have instead are dueling accounts. But Meta claims that Corydon and Thrysis considered a more thoroughgoing co-authorship. "They frequently talked of a book that they would some day write together concerning their own lives," Meta explains, "They would call it 'A Guide Book for Lovers.' Strange travesty."[81] Is the "travesty" that Corydon and Thrysis never achieved an egalitarian sense of marriage as jointly authored? Or perhaps that they wanted to think of themselves as experts who knew enough to write a "guide book" for others?

Travesty or not, their guide book would have found a ready audience. One likely reader is Theodore Dreiser, who wrote his own fiancée Sara White, "I wish there were houses already furnished for lovers, and a book to buy which would tell husband and wife just what to do. I should read it diligently just now."[82] In the next chapter I turn to Dreiser's own dueling accounts of his marriage. Only in that case, the husband wrote both versions himself.

CHAPTER FOUR

Theodore Dreiser on Monogamy, Varietism, and "This Matter of Marriage, Now"

One man had unusually intimate knowledge about the early years of Theodore Dreiser's first marriage. Shortly after Dreiser and Sara Osborne White married in December 1898, they lived on two separate occasions with Arthur Henry, an editor, novelist, nature writer, and close friend of Dreiser's. The first time, they occupied Henry's decrepit mansion in Maumee, Ohio, where Dreiser, under his friend's urging, began *Sister Carrie* (1900). The second time was in the much tighter quarters of the New York flat where Dreiser completed that first novel. "Up to a certain point," Henry recalled, the two men "had share and share alike" in Sara, and he joked with Dreiser about "my half of our wife." In the first instance of cohabitation, the Dreisers shared domestic quarters not only with Henry but also his wife and daughter. In the second, the platonic "*ménage à trois*," as biographer Richard Lingeman calls it, was disrupted when the still-married Henry fell for an older woman who ran a typing service in New York. Dreiser, who had dedicated *Sister Carrie* to Henry and said of him, "if he had been a girl, I would have married him," was jealous of his friend's defection, one of several incidents that drove a wedge between them.[1]

When Henry published *An Island Cabin* in 1902, offering a remarkable portrait of Dreiser as a new husband, it drove a deeper wedge. In this thinly fictionalized account of Dreiser's visit in the summer of 1901 to a small island near Noank, Connecticut, "Tom"—as Henry calls his friend—is finicky and whiney about the rustic accommodations. Squeamish about gutting fish, complaining about damp bedclothes, Tom brings his "bugaboos and anxieties" to Henry's island paradise.[2]

After "the delicate charm of the place" finally works its magic on Tom, in a moment of uncharacteristic serenity he ruminates aloud on how marriage has changed him. "A few years ago," Tom remarks, "I would have slept on a bare floor and not noticed it, and I thought nothing of my food. Ruth has certainly spoiled me for that. She makes me so comfortable in a thousand ways that I'm lost now when I must take care of myself." At least ten times a day, Henry writes, Tom would "sigh" for his wife. Were she to join them on Dumpling Island, Tom says, "I could stay forever." When the Sara Dreiser figure does arrive, she quickly whips the cabin into order. The food improves dramatically, acquiring "the delicacy and sweetness of her own nature." Henry praises Ruth as "the best wife I know, devoted to the comfort of her husband." Tom agrees: "When Ruth is in a place two minutes, it begins to look like home."[3]

In Henry's account this domestic goddess is no frail angel in the house. While the men expect her to recoil at the dirty cabin and declare the mattresses on the floor unfit for sleeping, she surprises them by proclaiming the cabin "lovely" and concluding it would "be foolish to buy cots." Tom, "bewildered" by his wife's willingness to rough it, goes off alone, at which point Ruth explains to their host, "he is not used to camping out . . . and I am. He'll be all right now. He needed me, I guess."[4]

This portrait contradicts Dreiser's claim that within six months he realized his marriage was "a disaster" which escalated to "torture" within another year. It is not simply the timeline that is at stake, but more importantly Dreiser's sharply conflicting feelings about marriage as seen when Henry's account is placed alongside his own. Considerable evidence confirms that before, during, and after marriage, the novelist craved marital domesticity as much as he chafed at it. For instance, the courtship letter in which Dreiser wishes he could find a book to teach him how to be a good husband, which I quoted at the end of the previous chapter, demonstrates at least as much eagerness as anxiety over the prospect of marriage.[5] And the diaries he kept during marriage, while substantiating the promiscuity widely associated with Dreiser (e.g., "it would almost kill me . . . to be faithful to one woman"), also point in a different direction. "All the desire of my heart is centered on getting well" from a nervous breakdown, he writes in 1902, "on getting my wife back, on having a home." Dreiser's diaries, indeed, contain as many details about such domestic matters as buying curtains, the cost of groceries, and meals eaten as they do rakish accounts of his sex life with an array of women.[6]

Dreiser never forgave Henry for *An Island Cabin*. Years later, Dreiser would retaliate in *A Gallery of Women* with "Rona Murtha" (1929), which portrays the Henry figure "Winnie" as a sponge on women. The cause of Dreiser's anger interests me. Precisely because Henry's portrait of "Tom" as a dependent, happily domesticated hubby contradicts the persona Dreiser was developing—just as he launched his novelistic career—as an iconoclast contemptuous of bourgeois mores, publication of *An Island Cabin* strained Dreiser's friendship with the man he had once considered a soul mate. Literary renditions of an actual marriage became deadly serious business for Dreiser—although in a different manner than I traced in the previous chapter.

I have argued that for Upton Sinclair, maintaining his reputation as a progressive reformer depended on portraying his first marriage to Meta Fuller in ways that discredited her. Dreiser has a similar inclination, but while Sinclair believed he could protect his reformist credentials by maintaining a public image of purity, Dreiser based his own reputation on defying purity, at least conventional notions of it concerning marriage and sexuality. That defiance informs Dreiser's sympathetic portrayals of characters who decline conventional matrimonial relationships. The title character in *Sister Carrie*, for instance, rejects the constraining domesticity of her sister and brother-in-law, preferring to live with two men out of wedlock, while her second partner, George Hurstwood, is a casual bigamist. In *Jennie Gerhardt* (1911) and *The Financier* (1912), Dreiser portrays the common law marriages of Jennie Gerhardt and Lester Kane and of Frank Cowperwood and Aileen Butler, respectively, as providing sexual, emotional, and even spiritual fulfillment that transcends what occurs in official marriages. Dreiser's well-known novelistic critiques of matrimony have helped to underwrite, and also been reinforced by, his own reputation as a Don Juan constitutionally unable to remain faithful to any woman.

How did Dreiser evolve from the moony domesticity captured by Arthur Henry to what biographer Thomas P. Riggio terms "radical domestic politics"? How did a man once so dependent on marriage achieve renown as a fierce critic of the institution? And why has Henry's portrayal of his friend, while referenced in all the biographies, had no impact on how the novelist is seen? This chapter teases out the answers by excavating the cultural and literary history surrounding Dreiser's favorite of his novels, *The "Genius"* (1915). Specifically, I read that autobiographical novel—which consolidated Dreiser's image as a literary and social rebel precisely because it soundly rejected marriage—through the lens of an earlier version he composed in 1911 but which was not published until I edited it for the Dreiser Edition in 2008.[7]

When Dreiser revised the 1911 *The Genius* for 1915 publication as *The "Genius,"* his main project was to make the autobiographically-inspired character represent not simply progress but actual insurgency. (In its first incarnation, the title lacked the qualifying quotation marks.) The revised character necessitated a major thematic change, from reforming marriage to rejecting it—which is also to say, as this chapter will show, a shift from progressivism to bohemianism. Those literary and ideological revisions enabled Dreiser, in turn, to reinvent himself as author and public figure. The project succeeded magnificently when *The "Genius"* of 1915 became a *cause célèbre* once the New York Society for the Suppression of Vice condemned it for promoting profanity and vice. That well-publicized attack secured Dreiser's reputation as a crusader for sexual liberation and personal freedom. It also helped obscure earlier, more moderate, self-presentations as a domesticated progressive. Before proceeding, I repeat my disclaimer: throughout this chapter, I use the term *progressive* as a historical descriptor, not a term of judgment or endorsement.

VERSIONS

Again I track competing fictionalizations of a marriage, only in this case, Dreiser himself composed the different versions. Unfortunately, very little remains of Sara White Dreiser's own words; many of her letters have been destroyed or, if extant, have sections obscured by dark ink. However, Dreiser's fictionalization of her as Angela Blue in *The Genius* of 1911 suggests a very different personality than what emerges from *The "Genius"* of 1915, and a more nuanced portrait of Sara emerges from examining those differences.

A few words about the better-known 1915 version of the novel can help to set the stage. Shortly before publication of *The "Genius,"* H.L. Mencken wrote his friend, singling out a handful of exemplary realist novels that he felt Dreiser could not afford to miss, among them *Love's Pilgrimage*. The parallels between Sinclair's 1911 novel and *The "Genius"* are astounding. To begin with the narrative arcs, in both novels, a troubled marriage, and particularly a husband's plunge into sexual overindulgence with his wife, threatens to derail his rising artistic career. But whereas Sinclair, in shifting from fact to fiction, obscures his own adultery and makes the wife into a nymphomaniac so as to disgrace her, Dreiser trumpets infidelity for the husband so as to discredit both the wife and the institution of marriage. Perhaps tearing a page from the dreaded Arthur Henry's *An Island Cabin* (which cast "Tom" as a painter), Dreiser presents his own protagonist Eugene Witla as a visual artist: initially an Ashcan painter, later a crafter of advertising images, and finally a muralist. That occupation meshes nicely with Dreiser's placing the newlyweds in Greenwich Village, a site of sexual experiments far more critical of marriage than were those of the progressives. As a Village observer (like Dreiser transplanted from the Midwest) recalled the scene in the early 1900s, "In the world which opened before me, poets seemed to have special privileges with respect to their love affairs. . . . But not poets alone had these special privileges in the matter of love affairs—'Genius' in every field had them."[8]

The wife of Dreiser's "genius," however, refuses him these privileges. Portraying compulsory monogamy within proprietary marriage as destructive, the 1915 "Genius" positions Eugene as a rebel against a conventional wife cast as the embodiment of conformity. At novel's end the author resolves the marital problem by killing off Angela. Eugene's nubile but spineless girlfriend Suzanne Dale abandons him, and then when a chance encounter reunites the two, he snubs her. The novel concludes with Eugene returned to his art after years of lucrative commercial work, cynical about marriage, and raising a daughter as a single parent while sleeping with an unnamed string of women. Dreiser had no children (and was in fact sterile), but otherwise this portrayal of Eugene corresponds with the popular image of the novelist.

Given its trajectory, The "Genius" has long been seen as a transparently self-serving paean to male promiscuity. More precisely, the text seems to celebrate what Dreiser calls "varietism" (the word was popularized by his friend Emma Goldman, about whom I will have more to say shortly). A Chicago reviewer captures the distaste of generations of readers: "Mr. Dreiser Chooses a Tom Cat for a Hero." Or as the Printer and Publisher reviewer had it, Dreiser "has plumbed . . . every beastliness of human conduct. His pig nature delights to wallow in lustful imaginings."[9]

However, the novel as Dreiser originally composed it in 1911 has a different, less polemical, and arguably less porcine trajectory. Far from rejecting matrimony, The Genius of 1911 embraces it, both as personal ideal and as appropriate resolution for the plot. Comparing the two versions clarifies how the marital and sexual ethics of progressivism and bohemianism overlap—as well as how they diverge. The differences emerge particularly clearly in the endings. In the 1911 text Eugene reunites with Suzanne after Angela's death and the two marry, presumably to live happily ever after. This conclusion may perplex readers familiar with Dreiser's protests against marriage, but the 1911 text consistently endorses marriage as an institution suitable for progressive reform. The novel as revised for 1915 publication, by pitting husband against wife, externalizes the debate between liberal and conservative views while also polarizing those views by gender. But in the 1911 version the debate had been internal. That is, in 1911 Dreiser focuses on the conflicts of a confused male protagonist who ultimately resolves his problems not by rejecting marriage but by finding, and also marrying, his ideal mate.

Donald Pizer, a leading scholar of American literary realism, has observed that "the principal value of *The 'Genius'* is its dramatization of a disastrously bad marriage." But I argue here that Dreiser does not simply fictionalize negative feelings about Sara. More importantly, he enters the debate about marital reform, as suggested even by his working title, "This Matter of Marriage, Now."[10] The problem that the novel (in both versions) sets out explore is less personal than institutional. Angela correctly identifies the difficulty when she tells her restless spouse, "I know what it is with you . . . it's the yoke that galls. It isn't me only—it's anyone. It's marriage" (581). [11]

While I will have things to say about the characters' reading habits, I am not arguing that Dreiser translates the ideas of particular marital theorists into fiction as do Upton and Meta Sinclair. But both versions of *The "Genius"* engage fundamental tenets of marital reform and, taken together, do so in an unusual way. Simply put, from the 1911 version of the novel to the 1915, Dreiser takes opposing positions. In 1911 the message aligns with progressive marital reform goals: marriage can thrive when monogamy is voluntary and spouses enjoy spiritual unity, but not when monogamy is compulsory and the unit merely formal and proprietary. In 1915, however, Dreiser radicalizes the message, rejecting marriage altogether, and thus aligns himself with Greenwich Village bohemianism. This revision is interesting for what it reveals about an author who, as critic Ellen Moers says, is best understood as "two Dreisers," with one face looking backward to the Victorian era and the other forward into the twentieth century.[12] But Dreiser's revision is more important for what it illustrates about the transitional nature of Progressive era marital reform itself. The two versions of *The Genius* serve as my test case for examining how the new ideas about marriage grow out of Victorian values and into bohemian ones.

A VICTORIAN LAMB IN WOLF'S CLOTHING

Toward the end of *The Genius*, the narrator explains that Eugene appeals to his young girlfriend Suzanne Dale because he is "subversive of conventionality." On the surface the artist appears "a lamb of conventional feelings

UNIVERSITY OF WINCHESTER
LIBRARY

and appearances, whereas inwardly he was a ravening wolf of indifference to convention" (684). That description makes sense for the Eugene of 1915, at least by novel's end, but does not fit the indecisive character of 1911. In a passage appearing only in the earlier version, the narrator offers the important qualification that his hero's "thoughts were far more revolutionary than his deeds" (206). Bridging the gap between thoughts and deeds, theory and practice, was precisely the challenge for progressive marriages, including, as the previous chapter explored, Upton and Meta Sinclair's. In addition, Dreiser's exaggerated claim that the 1911 Eugene is "revolutionary" illustrates a now-familiar tendency of the marital reformers to overstate the reach of their agenda.

In his aptly titled memoir, *A Victorian in the Modern World*, Dreiser's sometime-friend Hutchins Hapgood describes a spiritualized view of sexuality as characteristic of their generation. "In the person in whom Victorianism persists," Hapgood says, "sex still remains a mystic symbol."[13] While there is plenty of sex in the 1915 *"Genius,"* it rarely seems mystical or symbolic. Dreiser portrays conjugal sex, unforgettably, as draining Eugene of his artistic potency and leading to a neurasthenic breakdown—while extramarital sex remains far more animating.

But the 1911 version maps much more closely onto Hapgood's mystical view of sex, for Dreiser frames Eugene's illness as also a spiritual crisis. A passage in *The Genius* just before the marriage shows Eugene's immersion in the ideal of spiritualized sexuality—and his understanding that union with Angela betrays it:

> The truth was that Eugene, excited by his carnal experiences with her and having found her of a temperament which answered his present mood, was eager for more of what had proved to be so delightful. She ran through his mind now not for any spiritual qualities, though these were dimly in the background, but unfortunately for her gross physical ones. Two natures being at war in him, one spiritual, the other carnal and fleshy, it was possible to appeal to either. He responded quickest at most times to the appeal of the flesh. (180)

This account resembles the marriage-as-prostitution argument à la Gilman and Schreiner, with the significant difference that Dreiser emphasizes the corruption of the husband. Rather than bringing two individuals together in spiritual union, marriage sets off a Manichean conflict within Eugene. The marriage is legal and formal without being authentic or natural. Precisely as the marital theorists warn, obligatory intercourse actually cripples Eugene's spirit.

As in *Love's Pilgrimage*, *The Genius* locates sexual anxiety, even sexual loathing, within an inauthentic marriage. Because Eugene "was not doing anything to overcome the one fault which was most destructive to him," collapse is inevitable. A particularly melodramatic (and nineteenth-century-sounding) passage warns,

> If he had had the physique of a gladiator, the nerve-tensity and toughness of steel, the sex-energy of a satyr, his nerves could not have withstood the persistent assaults he made upon them. This incessant contact was out of all proportion to necessity or any normal desire. Because passions grow with what they feed upon, this grew, and each failure to restrain himself made it harder so to do. It was a customary remark of his that "he must quit this," but it was like the self-apologetic assurance of the drunkard that he must reform. (263)

This censorious tone hardly suggests the wail of a "tom cat." Eugene's inability to control himself and the comparison to a drunkard (again reminiscent of *Love's Pilgrimage*) highlight what Riggio calls the novel's "residual Puritanism."[14]

Such passages also help bring into focus the latent Victorianism in progressive ideas about the place of sex in marriage. Dreiser's logic in the 1911 novel precisely follows the progressive reformers' challenge to a Victorian conspiracy of silence even while extending the very understanding of sexuality they claimed to dispute. Dreiser's descriptions of the marriage bed read like pages torn out of Edith Ellis, who expresses disgust with the belief that "the mere word of the clergyman or registrar sanctions . . . what is in the majority of unions adultery on the man's side and a plunge into animalism on the woman's side." Edith Ellis also blames social mores for framing marriage in formalistic terms which, she claims, undermine the very morality they claim to uphold: "Society demands the ring, the parchment, and the vow as a preliminary to the knowledge and experience—hence adulteries, the divorce court, home prisons, and the increase of cant and pruriency." She maintains that in a "finer marriage" independent of church or state, sex would become "as much an affair of the soul as of the body." Upon realization of that ideal, spouses become, in her own husband Havelock Ellis's words, "spiritual comrades."[15] In Dreiser's 1911 version of the novel, the protagonist knows his first marriage defiles him and continues to seek spiritual comradeship—and ultimately finds it in a second marriage.

In Chapter 2, I discussed how the reformers rejected church jurisdiction over marriage even while routinely using spiritual, even religious language to bolster their own agenda. A few examples make the relevance of that strategy to Dreiser's novel quite clear. Edward Carpenter, for instance, hoped to see sexuality "rehabilitated again with a sense almost of religious consecration." Olive Schreiner, likewise, called intercourse "the great sacrament of life." According to Ellen Key, experientially grounded and self-validated marriage exemplifies "the new morality," a code superior to "Christian morality." Key maintains that "it will one day be admitted that the auto-da-fés of marriage have been just as valueless to true morality as those of religion were to the true faith." The progressives' persistently spiritual, even Christian rhetoric confirms Julian B. Carter's point that self-described sexual moderns continued to draw from the Victorian concepts they deplore. According to historian Peter N. Stearns, in fact, for the Victorians, "religiouslike intensity was love's hallmark."[16] Although there is a difference between Victorian and progressive ideals, it is less absolute than the progressives maintained. That fact does not discredit progressivism but does indicate what might be called its "in-betweenness": much like Dreiser's novel, marital reform looks back and forward at the same time.

Eugene maintains the ideal of a spiritual yet secular union while knowing his marriage to Angela will never match up. He wonders why the relationship couldn't be "something higher—a union of fine thoughts and feeling" but knows Angela will never be his "true mate," "the be all and the end all of his existence" (193; *"Genius"* 198, 197). Eugene longs for "someone who was more in accord, mentally and spiritually, with his deepest and most inmost spiritual convictions" (488). Since he and Angela are not spiritual comrades, their marriage lacks the "divine fire" of the higher, voluntary monogamy (193; *"Genius"* 197). As in progressive marital reform, so in *The Genius*, marriage does not make sex morally correct or spiritually viable.

Understanding the tenets of progressive marital reform clarifies the relationship of ideas that otherwise seem discordant—including the logic of Dreiser's 1911 novel. On one hand, Dreiser casts Eugene's descent into carnality as a grievous spiritual lapse. On the other, that descent happens within marriage, extending the novel's challenge to the traditional view that law and religion validate marriage. The views the 1911 novel dramatize would appear perfectly consistent to progressive marital reformers, who saw external authority as irrelevant and internal authority (such as emotion and spiritual kinship) as necessary to true marriage.

The Genius of 1911 follows the tenets of progressive marital reform in other ways as well. Immediately after Angela and Eugene's wedding, while the bride revels in her new status as Mrs. Witla, Eugene silently rejects the notion that a piece of paper or vow authenticates their union (194). Doubting the "generally accepted interpretation of marriage" as permanent, he still believes that "union ought . . . to be based on a keen desire to live together and nothing else" (194). Eugene follows here the critique of traditional marriage as, in the words of Havelock Ellis, a "fiction" which is "narrowed down to a kind of legal sex-contract" and "promise of exclusive and permanent mutual love."[17] Such discredited formalism appears, in fact, as the novel's ironic epigraph, in which Eugene declares the vows that will make Angela his wife in the eyes of the state and God, but never in his own.

OLD-FASHIONED MEN, NEW WOMEN

Stereotypes about Dreiser as a womanizing tom cat obscure how instructive his novels can be about a critical era in women's history. While presented through the vantage point of a confused young man, *The Genius* documents a time when many white middle-class women found exciting new possibilities for economic, intellectual, and personal independence. A passage that appears only in the 1911 novel captures Eugene's fascination with such unconventional, free-spirited women. Looking back on two early girlfriends, he admires how "they dared to do the things they wanted to do and were not mere chattels." "Most women," Eugene reflects sympathetically, remain "tied by a thousand ties; afraid to turn their heads, afraid to call their names their own" (141). But as an artist living in Greenwich Village, he encounters "the newer order of femininity, eager to get out in the world and follow some individual line of self-development and interest" (158). In a passage Dreiser wrote but then crossed out of the 1911 holograph manuscript, he correctly identifies this emergent cohort as "new women," and described them as "eager to . . . smash the traditions in regard to women's place in the universe" (860). Various New Women in the novel seek self-definition independent of marriage: artists like Christina Channing and Miriam Finch, professional women like Norma Whitmore, even divorcées like Carlotta Wilson. They inspire Eugene with "their radical ideas, their indifference to appearances" (249). More important, these New Women challenge Eugene's repressive views about sexuality while tutoring him in erotic pleasure.

The singer Christina Channing proves an especially important educator. She meets Eugene on their common ground as artists, then initiates him into "life among the radicals and bohemians" (190). Christina has decided not to marry because, she informs Eugene, it would interfere with her musical career (147–48). She whisks him off to a mountain retreat where they commence a short but passionate affair while Angela pines for her fiancé. Although Dreiser draws upon old-fashioned language of a woman "yield[ing]" her virginity (153), a passage that appears only in the 1911 novel explains that Christina enters the sexual relationship "solely because of her intense desire" (153). Her passion is, I might say, a matter of principle, and she regales Eugene with talk about free love outside of marriage (153–54). He finds this attitude shocking because "he still had a profound reverence for a home" (154). But Christina's most consequential action turns out to be dumping Eugene. She had warned that singing was her priority, so he has no reason to be disappointed and confused when she leaves him for a European tour—but he is anyway. While he understood they might not "eventually husband and wife," still "it irritated him to think she could be so calm about a thing which to him seemed so important" (165). Given this offense to his ego, Eugene not surprisingly starts seeing "Angela's fidelity . . . in a much finer light" (165). In comparison with his New Woman girlfriend, Eugene seems rather an old-fashioned man.

This dynamic of progressive woman and conservative man, reminiscent of the Sinclairs, also structures Eugene's relationship with Suzanne Dale. The least effectively realized of Dreiser's female characters, Suzanne nonetheless plays a critical role in the sexual ideology of the 1911 text, for she is the New Woman targeted for a permanent union. Advocating voluntary monogamy, Suzanne tells Eugene, "I want you to love me only so long as you want to love me. When you are tired of me, I want you to leave me. I wouldn't want you to live with me if you didn't love me" (592). As such, Suzanne resembles Ellen Key's "erotically noble person" who would never remain with a partner who no longer loved her, as explained in *Love and Marriage*, translated into English the same year that Dreiser wrote the first version of *The Genius*.[18] Suzanne also, of course, rejects proprietary sexual relationships such as Olive Schreiner defines as female parasitism and Charlotte Perkins Gilman terms sexuo-economic, for Suzanne has "no desire to profit by, hold, or exact from him anything which he did not . . . wish to give" (683). Her credo, "'My life is my own'" (602), captures the individualism that progressive marital theorists defined as the hallmark of the modern person—especially the modern woman.

Suzanne's views could come straight from any number of progressive marital reform sources, perhaps especially Elsie Clews Parsons's advocacy of trial marriage in *The Family* (1906). If Suzanne's mother is correct, then the girl's shocking intent to live with a married man in fact reflects the influence of "some outré book" the girl has read (602). Unlike with Eugene (or for that matter, Upton and Meta Sinclair), Dreiser says nothing about Suzanne's library. But whatever her inspiration, the trope of the New Woman reading her way to advanced views was common at the time. As Christine Stansell explains, "Just as bohemian identity was intimately intertwined with its representation in print, so was being a New Woman: what one read shaped how one lived."[19]

Dreiser emphasizes Suzanne's principled forwardness also by contrasting the girl with her mother. Mrs. Dale, a self-proclaimed liberal, enjoys "question[ing] the marriage system but only in a philosophic way" (565), showing once again the discrepancy between theory and practice. While she talks about wives having affairs and of unmarried couples living together, Mrs. Dale's tolerance is of the not-in-my-backyard variety. In comparison with her daughter, Mrs. Dale seems, to paraphrase William Dean Howells, a theoretical liberal but a practical conservative.

Suzanne's sexual progressivism trumps her mother's, but it more significantly trumps her boyfriend's also. In the 1911 *Genius*, the young woman—not the man—represents future trends. While Suzanne consistently urges that they live together, Eugene keeps fantasizing that their still-platonic love affair will culminate in the most traditional sort of ending: "It was all a delightful courtship which was to end in a still more delightful marriage" (593). And notwithstanding his foray into bohemia, Eugene remains unable to think outside of the matrimonial box. Nor, apparently, could Dreiser do so for his autobiographically inspired male character in 1911, a fact particularly surprising given the marital unorthodoxy of so many of his characters in other novels.

ANGELA BLUE, SARA WHITE DREISER, AND THE LURE OF DOMESTICITY

That Angela embodies traditional wifely virtues surely needs no proof. She longs to become Eugene's "true wife" (230) and, like Dreiser's wife Sara, proves an "ideal housekeeper" (200). It is also clear how Dreiser takes care from the start to align Angela's feelings about marriage with her pervasive conservatism.

What may be less obvious—given the resonance of the Dreiser stereotype consolidated by the 1915 *"Genius"*—is how attractive Eugene finds domestic comforts and traditional virtues, and how sexually conservative he is as well. These tendencies are more obvious in the 1911 version. The first time Eugene visits New York he finds the city vital and stimulating (as many

Dreiser characters do). But he also longs to retreat to the bucolic life that his country girlfriend represents: "He felt lonely. He wished now he were back with Angela where her soft arms could shut him safe" (94). Even after he learns to enjoy the city as a bachelor artist, Eugene relishes when his new bride brings domestic comforts. The morning after arriving in Washington Square and settling into a rented studio, the newlyweds purchase groceries from Italian street vendors and Angela prepares a breakfast causing Eugene to feel he has arrived at heaven on earth: "after the . . . commonplace restaurant dining . . . this seemed ideal. To sit in your own private apartment furnished in comparative luxury, with a charming wife opposite you ready to render you any service, and with an array of food before you"—it all "seemed perfect" (201). Admiring looks and comments from friends confirm the appeal of domestic comforts even to the urban male artist (203).

Eugene's attraction to domesticity reflects a powerful lure felt by his creator. An 1897 courtship letter entreats Sara, "Do you want to keep a little flat for me[?] Personally I am awfully weary of this Bohemian existence of mine. I have tired of restaurant and hotel dinners. . . . I should like to take a cozy flat and have a whirl at keeping house." Dreiser's letters to Sara are filled with promises of sexual ecstasy (although unfortunately Sara or someone else blacked out many of the details) linked with dreams of cozy domesticity. One letter closes in anticipation of

> Delicious nights in which our arms shall enfold each other and our lips be sealed in one long, passionate kiss when

> "your little shoes and my big boots
> are under the bed together."

In a very material way, Sara stands at the source of Dreiser's career as an author; he would later describe his courtship letters as "my first and easiest attempt at literary expression."[20]

Dreiser's craving for Sara's pampering domesticity continued even after he began chafing at the matrimonial bit. Although he dated their separation to October 1910 (after his unconsummated affair with Thelma Cudlipp, the daughter of a coworker and model for Suzanne Dale), the break was far from clean. For nearly four years Dreiser and Sara continued to live together intermittently, an arrangement that biographer W. A. Swanberg describes as on a "'hotel' basis." As Swanberg sums up this period during which the author rebelled against matrimonial confines even while unable to let go of his wife, Dreiser was "essentially opposed to all aspects of marriage save its comforts."[21]

FIGURE 8. Sara Dreiser bends over her husband in an intimate gesture, while the domesticated Dreiser's thoughts are difficult to fathom. Courtesy of Theodore Dreiser Papers, University of Pennsylvania Rare Book and Manuscript Library.

Marriage appealed to Dreiser not only because of its comforting domesticity but also because he believed it could help him socially. Encouraging young men to marry so as to advance their careers formed a staple of Horatio Alger stories and was echoed in the popular press of the period. More to the point, Dreiser's masterpiece *An American Tragedy* (1925) would fuse dreams of marriage and social ascent as they crystallized in the mind of an impressionable young man. By the time of that novel (published the same year as the similarly themed *The Great Gatsby*), Dreiser had developed a sharply critical view of the dream of ascent through of marriage.

In the early years with Sara, however, it was a different story. She attracted Dreiser in part because she stoked his ambitions, in part because she could provide a haven from the harsh, competitive world. As he wrote her, "none ever stirred the desire in me to be something and to do everything possible for my welfare. That was left for you." In another courtship letter he brushes away morbid thoughts with a fantasy that fuses domesticity, affluence, and sex: "I want a little quarter of our own, with you and pretty furniture in it to make it lovely. I want money to buy you rich dresses and soft luxurious lingerie and best of all I want you with me, in warm, voluptuous embrace for nights and nights, unending." Given the extreme poverty of his youth, Dreiser can perhaps be forgiven for hoping to turn his fiancée into the sort of conspicuous wife satirized by Thorstein Veblen:

> I feel equally distressed when I think that up to the present year I have never felt as though I could marry you and still afford to maintain you as our taste and my own would suggest. I know that if you had elegant clothing, a few splendid jewels, and suitable surroundings you would be queenly in appearance, and it is the ambition of my life to so surround you. I have a desire to make your garments elegant, not only that you may be pleased but that I may gloat over my prize.[22]

Such human "prizes" have a way of becoming less desirable once won.

By the time he wrote *The Genius*, however, Dreiser had concluded that marriage à la Veblen could confine the husband as well. The most memorably unpleasant trait of Angela is intense jealousy, which Dreiser takes care to shape as reflecting her proprietary interest in her husband. Following a scene about Angela's attempts to stop Eugene's roving eye, a segment that appears only in the 1911 novel discusses "the feminine mind, which at this time could thus reason in regard to the husband or children or both . . . as property." In this curious account of men's entrapment by marriage, the husband, "historic lord and master," becomes a mere "chattel[]" to the possessive wife. The narrator generalizes that such a wife's "theory of duty in marriage was stringent," overturning "the serfdom imposed by man upon his domestic partner in earlier centuries" (298–99). In a related scene, a socialite's comment about the Witlas as an exemplary couple prompts Eugene to criticize Angela's materialism: "A nice house, a nice income, plenty of pleasing friends, good clothes, stability, the dignity and comfort that comes from being the loved and honored wife of a prosperous man—these were the things that she wanted and that she felt to be her right." The word "right" captures the problem. Eugene resists his wife's view that "men, ever weak and fickle, should be compelled by law to conform to the principles which they accepted in marriage. Everything said at the altar must be literally fulfilled" (489). From the standpoint of the progressive ideal, Angela's legalism, rigidity, and possessiveness demonstrate the invalidity of her notion of marriage. As Dreiser put it in a 1912 symposium on divorce published in *Hearst's Magazine*, "Marriage runs deeper than man-made laws."[23]

Two more appealing qualities of Angela's character, as Dreiser first shaped her in 1911, become weakened or eliminated in the 1915 edition. While prevailing opinion of the 1915 *"Genius"* laments the celebration of male sexual exploits, the women characters in the 1911 version in general, and Angela in particular, are more passionate and forthright about their sexual desires than Eugene. While the singer Christina Wilson, discussed above, provides some indication of that general point, Angela does far more. From the first she has "as much if not more . . . sex desire" as her future husband (58). Her "astonishing sex virility" and ability "to meet his utmost passionate desires" never cease to amaze Eugene (242; cf. the very different passage in *"Genius"* 245). (While the word *virile* now conjures up potent masculinity, in Dreiser's day it carried the now obsolete sense of *nubile*.) Little wonder that "on her passional side Angela appealed to him more than any woman" (162). Insofar as the Witlas' erotic indulgence makes the husband literally sick, it is interesting to find no such adverse effects for the wife.

As I have argued elsewhere, Dreiser deserves recognition for often liberal views about female sexual desire even if he still subscribed to objectionable double standards.[24] His forthrightness about women's sexuality aligns him with the views of Havelock Ellis, who marshals considerable evidence to dismantle "the modern tendency to underestimate the sexual impulse in women." Ellis's description of the disproportionate effects of sexual activity on men and women provides a useful gloss on *The Genius*. "Sexual intercourse is undoubtedly less injurious to women than to men," Ellis says. "Other things being equal, . . . the threshold of excess is passed very much sooner by the man than by the woman."[25] Eugene unquestionably passes that threshold more quickly than Angela.

An additional characteristic of Angela's that appears only in the 1911 edition involves what Eugene calls "emotional genius" (271). The term is particularly significant given the novel's interest, from the title forward, in male genius. Angela's sexual passion, jealousy, and intense if possessive love all feed into and draw force from her "emotional genius." When the artist recognizes this quality in his wife, he realizes that there are "two kinds of greatness possible in an individual—intellectual and emotional." The emotionally great individuals he ranks with Angela are all women, and mostly literary and operatic constructs—Carmen, Camille, Manon Lescaut, Trilby, Héloïse, and Dante's Beatrice—to which Eugene later adds actresses Sarah Bernhardt and Clara Morris (138, 255). Even in comparison with the attractive, independent New Women of the city, Angela, her husband admits, can "more than hold[] her own emotionally" (138).[26]

Does Dreiser's schema of the two types of genius, emotional and intellectual, provide grounds for applauding Angela or of censuring her? Studies of emotion provide intriguing ways to approach that question. Cognitive theorists, neuroscientists, psychologists, and other researchers have challenged the long-held belief that emotion is opposed (and inferior) to reason. That value judgment has underwritten another, according to which women are subordinate because they are more emotional, less rational than men. Recent research blows up both of those appraisals by reconceptualizing emotion as instrumental and even crucial to cognition and decision making. Armed with that insight, let me reformulate more bluntly the question with which I began this paragraph: Is Dreiser's idea of emotional versus intellectual genius more a sexist or a feminist construct? On the one hand, Dreiser does posit emotion as separate from intellect—and each instance he gives of emotional genius is of course gendered female. On the other hand, Eugene (and, I think, also Dreiser) clearly admires Angela's "emotional genius," perhaps in spite of himself. That feature is, after all, given the honorific tag of "genius."

Research into what might be called the epistemological validity of emotions provides further ways of answering these questions. One of the emotions that Martha Nussbaum analyzes is empathy, which can, she says, be "accurate" or "inaccurate." Her point is that while any emotion has an inherent truth content (insofar as it is real to the person experiencing it), what causes the emotion—its prompt—can be legitimate or not. Empathy, for instance, could be "inaccurate" if the person feeling it does not adequately imagine the experience of the other. Psychologist Jon Elster makes a similar point, finding emotions fundamentally different from "beliefs" (the latter an affair of the head, not heart) and yet "analogous." He explains: just as "beliefs are rational if they are adequate or appropriate, given the available evidence," so Elster finds the same holding for emotions, which can be "appropriate or adequate" and in that sense "rational," or they can be irrational.[27]

Let me apply this way of thinking about emotion to the intense jealousy of Dreiser's character Angela. If emotional reactions are "rational" and "appropriate" when they correspond with "evidence," then Angela's jealousy appears quite justified. Eugene does in fact lust after other women, frequently pursues them, and when possible (except for with Suzanne), sleeps with them. Angela's jealousy is fierce but soundly based in reality, and she has considerable emotional intelligence. Angela is, indeed, an emotional genius. While I do not think Dreiser intended for the character to be viewed in this light, emotion research provides a way of understanding how the answer to my earlier questions are: sort of yes and sort of no. Dreiser's insistence, in 1911, on Angela's "emotional genius" is both somewhat sexist and also somewhat feminist, a way of containing her and a way of celebrating her.

The elimination of Angela's "emotional genius" from the 1915 edition is typical of how Dreiser simplifies her character to heighten his anti-marriage polemic. In stripping Angela of genius and some of her sexual intensity, the 1915 revision makes her into more of a virago; her plot function shifts from being a relatively autonomous and sympathetic character to simply her husband's foil. Likewise, passages asserting the spouses' compatibility are expunged from the 1915 novel. Only the 1911 version contains a passage such as this: "Temperamentally they were suited in many ways—a mutual love of order, a mutual admiration for the odd in character, a sense of humor, a sense of pathos in themselves and life in general,"—qualities which, the passage significantly concludes, "made for a comfortable home life which is so important in any union" (384). In exactly the same way that Dreiser broke with Arthur Henry in outrage at the portrayal of "Tom's" affection for domesticity, so he revised The "Genius" to hide that side of himself.

VARIETISM AND ITS DISCONTENTS

The timing of Dreiser's writing and rewriting of The Genius is critical. First there is the professional backdrop. In June 1907 he had taken a well-paying job ($5,000 per year, or $120,000 in today's dollars[28]) as chief editor of Butterick's trio of women's magazines. His work there was, in the words of general editor of the Dreiser Edition, Jude Davies, "feminist and Progressive." The Delineator in particular was involved in numerous reform causes.

A 1910 article published under Dreiser's editorship explains that when the magazine sought to assume a socially conscious role, it entered the "general discussion of marriage and divorce which was looming large at this time." One of Dreiser's own editorials sounds two familiar notes: optimism and alignment of progress with women. "*The Delineator* message is human betterment," Dreiser wrote; "Its appeal is to the one great humanizing force of humanity—womanhood."[29] Dreiser held the Butterick position until he was fired in October of 1910 over the Thelma Cudlipp scandal. (Overlapping with his day job, in 1909 Dreiser briefly and secretly edited the aptly named *Bohemian*.)

Then there is the romantic backdrop. Dreiser wanted to marry Thelma—not just sleep with her—and implored Sara for a divorce in 1910. In the last chapter I discussed New York divorce law in some detail. Recall that the only statutory ground for divorce in that state was adultery, and that the law was structured so as to require one guilty defendant and one innocent plaintiff. Hence Dreiser needed the unimpeachably moral Sara to file against him. She refused. Yet in a January 1911 letter to an assistant at *The Delineator*, three months after the Cudlipp scandal, Dreiser discounts the "silly report abroad . . . that I have deserted Mrs. Dreiser & am going to marry some one else. There's nothing in it. If [you] hear anyone say so contradict it from me."[30]

Finally, there is the domestic backdrop. When he composed *The Genius* in the first half of 1911, the Dreisers were living uptown, at 3609 Broadway, on the corner of 149th Street. After over a decade together, their marriage was on the rocks. Because of the autobiographical basis of the novel, Dreiser felt he could not publish it for several years. By the time he returned to the novel in the fall of 1914, however, Dreiser had left his wife and moved to an apartment on West 10th Street, in Greenwich Village, that would remain his home for five years (although, as I've said, he continued to visit Sara on a "hotel basis" during this time). An unpublished piece, probably composed in the 1920s, captures Dreiser's memories of the Village atmosphere of "youth and enthusiasm and a love of freedom" as well as "garret barrooms or basement studios, or restaurants, or art shops, or art galleries, or book shops or art parlors used betimes for the dispensation of everything from batik or drama to psycho-analytic readings and ukuleles."[31]

Dreiser had not been a stranger to bohemia before moving to the Village. Since the early 1890s he had been drawn to the studio life of artists and writers, which he felt offered the freedom and creativity that he craved, even as he also wanted domestic comforts. Immediately upon glimpsing the

St. Louis studio scene through his friendships with artists Peter McCord and Dick Wood, Dreiser found the camaraderie, interest in art, and personal freedom intoxicating. He imagined the art world might even provide a solution to the financial concerns that vexed him: "This was Bohemia! This was that middle world which was better than wealth and more heavenly than simple poverty. It was the serene realm in which moved freely talent, artistic ability, noble thought, ingenious action, and . . . absolute freedom of thought and conduct! The creed of Bohemia," Dreiser enthuses, makes religion irrelevant, marriage and family optional, while enshrining art and "a fine liberty as to personal conduct," including the freedom to "solace your poverty and lonely hours with any such charming figures—male or female—as were artistically suitable. In my case," he adds, "it would have preferably been female."[32]

Despite these early experiences, his move to West 10th Street in July 1914 marks a turning point that would influence his revisions to *The "Genius."* Mencken describes (with exasperation born of his contempt for what he saw as Village pretenses) Dreiser's personality changes upon moving downtown. As long as Dreiser "lived uptown with Sarah [sic] he led a thoroughly bourgeois life, though he was already practicing a Latin Quarter promiscuity," Mencken recalled, "but once he got down to 10th Street he took to the life of art, and was soon a painful figure to his old friends."[33]

Bohemia, however, provided Dreiser with a new set of friends. Floyd Dell, who would later edit *The "Genius"* for publication, was a Village personality, having moved from Chicago to New York in 1913 where he worked as assistant editor of *The Masses* under Max Eastman. Notwithstanding Dell's bohemian creds (which he would later repudiate), in 1909 he married Vassar-educated schoolteacher Margery Currey. Dell's description of their relationship will sound familiar: "Of course, we agreed in disbelieving in marriage," that "stupid relic of the barbaric past." Rather than the traditional marital vows, Dell proclaims, "These were our vows—to be courageously candid in our expected and inevitable unfaithfulness." Such openness would establish the couple as "reasonable, intellectual, modern young people" who were "superior to the common run of mankind." Simply put, "We were going to behave *better* than any husband and wife!" Dell did not live up to his promise. When he had the anticipated affair, he did not come clean right away, and his secrecy rather than his adultery caused a permanent estrangement. Margery told Dell, as he recalls, "bitterly—that I had treated her as though she were a wife."[34]

Other bohemians went further and advocated varietism. Hapgood, who was friendly with Dreiser during his Greenwich Village years (although Dreiser would later write him off as a "parlor or library radical"), explains this emerging sexual ethic: "Marriage on principle was not tolerated since it was an enslaving institution." It therefore became "obligatory on the part of the male not only to tolerate but to encourage the occasional impulse of the wife or sweetheart toward some other man; or, on the part of the woman, a more than tolerant willingness to have her man follow out a brief impulse with some other woman. This was called varietism," Hapgood concluded, "and was supposed to be hygienic and stimulating to the imagination."[35]

Varietism is easy to dismiss as a jazzy — or even pretentious — euphemism for promiscuity. Taking varietism seriously is especially difficult since a watered-down idea of casual "hook-ups" has become yawningly familiar in American culture today, without improving relations between the sexes. To many politically inclined varietists early in the twentieth century, however, the new sexual ethic was, in the words of sociologist Ellen Kay Trimberger, "far more complex than its hedonistic image."

What might be called principled or philosophical varietists believed nonexclusivity broke down the patriarchal view of women as property, challenged the conspiracy of silence about sex, affirmed the healthiness of women's erotic needs, and freed sexuality from reproduction. They considered these principles essential to personal freedom, especially the freedom of women. As a historian of the Village feminist group Heterodoxy sums up, "a woman's sexual right to make love with whomever she wishes without troubling to get a marriage license beforehand was basic to all her other rights as a human being." Varietism was so integral to the culture of Heterodoxy that it appeared as the subject of a 1919 spoof called "Marriage Customs and Taboos among the Early Heterodities." This faux ethnography of the feminist club, citing as its source Heterodoxy member Elsie Clews Parsons's "iconoclastic" *The Family*, anatomizes the "three types of sex relationships," calling them "*monotonists, varietists,* and *resistants.*" The author describes "monotonists" as those who "mated young and by pressure and circumstance have remained mated"; varietists as those who have "never been ceremonially mated but have preferred a succession of matings"; and "resistants" as women who avoid "mating" altogether.[36]

The principled nature of varietism becomes especially clear in the writings of anarchist-feminist (and friend of Dreiser) Emma Goldman. Extending the progressive condemnation of patriarchal marriage as prostitution, Goldman declared that "nowhere is woman treated according to the merit of her work, but rather as a sex. It is therefore almost inevitable that she should pay for her right to exist . . . with sex favors. Thus it is merely a question of degree whether she sells herself to one man, in or out of marriage, or to many men." Gilman had made a similar point, but whereas progressives invoked the analogy with prostitution in order to reform marriage, Goldman did so to argue for its abolishment. She urged that people—particularly women—must reclaim the love that had been deformed by marriage. Precisely unlike the progressives' affirmation of a higher monogamy and better marriage, Goldman declares love and marriage "antagonistic." She recommends that any woman so foolish as to marry adopt the legend that Dante found over the gates of the inferno, counseling entrants to abandon all hope.[37]

Goldman defines the philosophical core of anarchism as "voluntary co-operation," and she believed varietism exemplifies that ideal. She celebrates love as "the defiler of all laws, of all conventions; love, the freest, the most powerful moulder of human destiny," and asks, "how can such an all-compelling force be synonymous with that poor little State- and Church-begotten weed marriage"? In an essay with the provocative title "The Tragedy of Woman's Emancipation," Goldman urges that no amount of attention to suffrage or jobs (causes dear to middle-class feminists), important as those goals were, could free women. Equal rights were important, but "the most vital right is the right to love and be loved." Casting love as anarchism writ large, she declares, "yes, love is free; it can dwell in no other atmosphere." Goldman believes that "every love relation should by its very nature remain an absolutely private affair. Neither the State, the Church, morality, or people should meddle with it." Support for varietism, in fact, differentiates "the thoroughgoing radical" from the "half-baked." Adopting similar terms as the progressives in differentiating between voluntary and compulsory monogamy—but taking the idea further, to abandon marriage altogether—Goldman distinguishes varietism (open, honest, and promoting spiritual union) from promiscuity (hidden, illicit, and purely carnal).[38]

Goldman delivered a popular lecture titled "Is Man a Varietist or Monogamist?" at the Liberal Club, which Dreiser had joined in 1913. Whether or not he heard it, Goldman's conclusion would have been familiar to him. The text of her lecture has not survived, but it is clear how she would have answered the question she posed. In an essay that has survived, she argues that "monogamy is a much later sex form which came into being as a result of the domestication and ownership of women, and which created sex monopoly and the inevitable feeling of jealousy." Goldman's claim that monogamy was a relatively late product of human evolution linked with jealousy and possessiveness further differentiates her view from the progressives', who considered monogamy, as I have shown, both the origin and the goal of heterosexual relationships.[39]

Late in *The Genius*, Dreiser alludes to another important contemporary voice in the debate over monogamy. "Someone," the narrator says, "had written a two volume treatise on it — *The History of Human Marriage* or something like that — and in it animals were shown to have mated only for so long as it took to rear the young" (701). The unnamed author is Finnish sociologist Edward Westermarck. Dreiser gets the title right, but his characterization of the book suggests highly selective reading. Westermarck uses ethnography to establish that throughout human history, heterosexual coupling had taken many forms. However, far from providing a biologically informed argument defending varietism or suggesting humanity was evolving away from marriage, as Dreiser implies, Westermarck attacks the idea that "primitive promiscuity" prevailed in "savage and barbarian races" before the much later evolution of monogamy. He counters that "monogamy, always the predominant form of marriage, has been more prevalent at the lowest stages of civilization than at somewhat higher states; whilst, at a still higher stage, polygyny has again, to a great extent, yielded to monogamy." In other words, in logic that the progressive reformers would embrace (and Westermarck was in fact a major source for George Elliott Howard and Havelock Ellis), monogamy was both the original and the highest form of human sexual relationship. The intricacies of *The History of Human Marriage* need not detain us, but Westermarck concurred with Herbert Spencer (another source that Dreiser apparently read selectively) that monogamy constitutes the "ultimate form" of heterosexual union.[40]

I wouldn't want the task of arguing for any deeply philosophical basis for Dreiser's varietism. But he did believe the practice furthered personal growth as well as multiple orgasms, and he did think women needed passionate sex lives as much as men. In *Newspaper Days*, Dreiser's autobiography of his young manhood, he alludes to "future years" in which he would "discover that there was little true intellectual growth for either man or woman outside a certain amount of sexual experimentation. Under strict monogamy the mind seems to wither and take on working formulaes."[41] In other words, he wants women to embrace varietism — in theory. But in practice, and like many another male liberal and radical, Dreiser expected fidelity from his lovers even while sleeping around himself.[42]

Little survives to provide access to Sara Dreiser's perspective on her marriage, apart from such tidbits as a 1919 letter to a friend asking, "Are you married! Or are you like me—Never Again!" But an extraordinary set of letters survives from Kirah Markham, Dreiser's lover with whom he lived in the Village from the summer of 1914 until the middle of 1916, the period which saw the revisions to and publication of *The "Genius."* (In fact Kirah's handwriting appears on several holograph pages of the 1911 novel.) Born Elaine Hyman, this talented actress, involved with Chicago's Little Theater and the Provincetown Players, took the stage name of Kirah Markham. A series of letters she wrote Dreiser document a rich and full love, but one that could not survive Dreiser's inconsistencies concerning varietism (which he felt to be his right) and monogamy (which he expected from women involved with him). The relationship is especially significant because it was part Village salon shared by cohabitating artists while also being, in the words of Riggio, "as close to a domestic household as Dreiser would have after his first marriage" and before he met actress Helen Richardson, who would become his second wife in 1944. Mencken, recalling visits to the 10th Street flat, writes with pleasure about the excellent food Kirah cooked and with exasperation about the "arty candlelight" and pretentious "nonentities" such as "third-rate painters, . . . bad poets, worse novelists" who joined him at table.[43]

Much of the lovers' quarrel revealed in the letters centers on what Dreiser implausibly maintained was his innocent correspondence with other women. Kirah told him in March 1916 that she did not object to his letter-writing, but "I most decidedly declare my aversion to sharing my and your emotional life with a third emotional life." The very fact of his concealing the letters, Kirah informs Dreiser, belies his claim of their insignificance. By May she had concluded that his complaining both when she clung to him and when she went off on her own indicated Dreiser did not know what he wanted. Later that month, explaining she could no longer participate in an "intellectual harem," Kirah sadly concluded they must part. Her career, while no doubt initially attractive to Dreiser, seems also to have caused friction. Kirah could not fit herself into the mold of dependent wife that she felt Dreiser continued to seek, and she told him, "there are women who are unimportant enough to simply minister to a big man by a doting, self-sacrificing, dog-like devotion . . . I am not one of these women. My work seems sufficiently important to me to make me feel that I have no energy above what it requires to give to any arrangement where my love is treated as a soothing drug and no more."[44]

The final straw seems to have been when Kirah claimed the same sort of personal (and probably also sexual) liberties that Dreiser considered his due. In May 1916 she responds to a letter from him that she calls "the most astonishing document of monopoly I ever saw. You say that if I claim the privileges for myself which you have claimed for yourself there is no point in our living together. I wonder do you realize how completely that statement gives you away." Hoisting Dreiser on his own petard, Kirah then tells him, "That which is food for the male is food for the female, and if you propose to eat exquisite things at other women's tables and keep me on bread and milk I would be pretty dull if I didn't remonstrate, wouldn't I?" (One of the spurs of Dreiser's jealousy was Kirah's earlier relationship with Floyd Dell, who continued to pursue her despite the actress's preference for Dreiser.) Kirah also identifies how easily bohemian relationships could drift into traditional patterns: "if we were married and I were expected to run the house and look after the children and never see a man except when you invited one home to dinner, and you stayed down at the club when you felt like it—*supposedly* at the club—we could not be more conventionally mated than we are."[45] If Dreiser felt varietism was the spice of life, he apparently still wanted a woman to do the cooking.

BOHEMIAN'S PROGRESS

The years between Dreiser's marriage to Sara in 1898 and publication of *The "Genius"* in 1915 mark the period during which he recreated himself from a Midwestern naïf into a cosmopolitan public figure. The period between his 1911 drafting and 1915 rewriting of *The "Genius,"* which coincide with his initial separation from his wife and move to the Village, are critical to this self-transformation. Dreiser's shift toward bohemianism, which included shedding the progressive ideal of voluntary monogamy and embracing varietism, accounts for the changes between *The Genius* of 1911 and *The "Genius"* of 1915. My point is not that Greenwich Village *made* Dreiser change, as if the author were some inert mass acted upon. To adapt an old adage, if the Village had not existed, Dreiser would have had to have invented it.

A chapter appearing only in the earlier version of *The Genius* suggests Dreiser's continuing ambivalence about bohemia as late as 1911. A scene tracing Eugene's bachelor party attended by the typical Village mix of artists and radicals allows Dreiser to stage the contrast between varietism and monogamy. Women smoke cigarettes in a crowded room where everyone drinks cheap wine. Eugene is torn between fascination and judgment, particularly when it comes to the women. He finds one "socialist agitator" lovely but doubts any "true mental reciprocity could exist between them"

(190). Eugene concentrates especially on pretty socialist Elizabeth Stein, who "would take up with any man according to her predilections but it was a phase of philosophic belief with her—a problem in individual liberty" (189). Although initially, Eugene tepidly endorses her varietism as "worthwhile," once he recalls an earlier party at which her date had encouraged Elizabeth to act upon her beliefs, the narrator remarks that Eugene "did not care for this open and aboveboard declaration of principles. It seemed too loose—at least for his personal practice" (190). Yes, surprising as it may sound, Eugene declines to sleep with a beautiful and willing woman because it seems "too loose." The whole atmosphere of his bachelor party, in fact, while intoxicating, strikes Eugene as "unduly gay," "broad and noisy—in some of its phases a little coarse" (189). In sum, he is ambivalent about these "representatives of Bohemia" and their hallmark varietism (191). And so was Dreiser in 1911, still enjoying the stability and comforts of marriage, even while his relationship to Sara was proving unsustainable.[46]

In this context let us revisit the different endings of the two versions of the novel. In the 1911 *Genius*, recall that Suzanne figures as New Woman leading her more traditional lover beyond compulsory marriage to enter into a blissful, nonproprietary, and voluntary union. In contrast the trajectory of the 1915 *"Genius"* culminates in "Revolt" (the last of three section titles added to the published version). The 1911 version, far from ending in revolt, traces Eugene's "slow return to a normal point" (736). The 1915 text, in keeping with the rejection of middle class mores, qualifies that normality as "his [Eugene's] kind of normality—the artistic normality of which he was capable" (*"Genius"* 724). Corresponding with its celebration of the bohemian artist, the conclusion of the 1915 edition adds passages stressing Eugene's artistic talent and reputation. His one-time dealer, the Frenchman M. Charles, reappears to praise Eugene's artistic vision, predict that he will transform American art, and encourage him to exhibit new paintings (*"G"* 728–29). Other artists concur, sealing Eugene with the imprimatur of bohemian genius: "strange, eccentric, but great" (*"G"* 732).

The two endings also endorse different philosophical beliefs which illustrate Dreiser's progressivism in 1911 and bohemianism in 1915. In the 1911 *Genius*, when Eugene picks up a volume of Spencer (a philosopher who greatly influenced the young Dreiser) and reads his reflections on the Unknowable, he concludes, "that thought could never trouble me anymore. I think it is full of kindly wisdom," while in the later version, Eugene applauds Spencer for providing "the sanest interpretation of the limitations of human thought" (*Genius* 746, *"Genius"* 736). The earlier version stresses balance and redemption, for Eugene "reached a metaphysical basis of peace"; in the later text, however, he adopts "almost a belief that a devil ruled the world, a Gargantuan, Brobdignagian Mountebank" (*Genius* 736, *"Genius"* 726). In 1911 Eugene concludes "there is a ruling power . . . and it is not malicious," but in 1915 decides one of God's faces must be "fantastic and swinish evil" (*Genius* 746, *"Genius"* 726). The description of Eugene as "pagan to the core," needless to say, appears only in the 1915 novel (*"Genius"* 734). The narrator throws his weight on the side of agnosticism in the 1915 edition with a famous passage discrediting religion which begins, "If I were personally to define religion I would say that it is a bandage that man has invented to protect a soul made bloody by circumstance" (*"Genius"* 734).

In 1911 Dreiser resolves—or perhaps dissolves—conflicts by replacing a traditional, formalistic marriage sanctioned by law and church with a reformed progressive marriage. Eugene's philosophical quest throughout the 1911 novel for "something better and higher" (737) culminates in his reunion with Suzanne. Unlike the narcissistic, opportunistic, flighty creature she would become in 1915, in 1911 Dreiser describes Suzanne as "meditative, philosophic, introspective" (745). The language describing their reunion confirms their mating as the spiritual comradeship (to recall Ellis's phrase) that eluded Mr. and Mrs. Witla. Eugene and Suzanne, in contrast, enjoy a "basic unity of soul . . . which held them together" (745). Suzanne even "brought back a lost paradise to him," a description recalling what I discussed in Chapter 2 as the progressive theorists' Back-to-Nature prelapsarianism (744). In addition, she proves an acute critic of his art, thereby gesturing toward the reformers' ideal of spouses supporting each other's work.

The 1911 conclusion is hard to swallow today, resembling the obligatory happy ending to many a Hollywood movie. However, the fuzzy utopianism which may seem like some failure of artistic vision on Dreiser's part actually illustrates his immersion in progressive views of marriage at the time. A particularly apt analogy can be found in Ellen Key's prediction that "the everlasting conflict" between the sexes "will one day end in the conclusion of peace." As I have shown, Edith Ellis contended that spiritual comrades would attain this blissful state only by experimentation with various partners, a premise that certainly fits Eugene. The trajectory of Dreiser's 1911 novel follows the movement anticipated by marital reformers in that the "evolved relationship of the future will [likely] be monogamy—but a monogamy as much wider and more beautiful than the present caricature." Eugene evolves from what Edith Ellis calls the "disguised polygamy" of traditional marriage which breeds adultery to find the "new romance *in* marriage and not only outside it."[47]

Reviews of the very different version published in 1915 as *The "Genius"* focused on Dreiser's challenge to traditional morality, particularly regarding sex and marriage. Depending on the observer's politics, the author's insurgency demonstrated revolutionary genius or craven depravity. A *Little Review* critic praised how "calmly, aloofly, with a consummate dispassion Dreiser has thrust his magic pen home into the heart of American Puritanism." For this reviewer *The "Genius"* signaled a watershed in literary history since Eugene Witla marks the first American hero who was neither a puritan nor a punished sinner. A reviewer for the *Brooklyn Eagle*, however, aghast at the novel's "orgy of lust," declared it unfit for youthful readers and likely to "do more harm among boys than among girls, to whom at least it conveys a warning to beware of fascinating married men." Two additional reviews reveal especially polarized judgments: whereas the *St. Louis Post-Dispatch* felt *The "Genius"* was "all a huge orgy of the flesh without the slightest touch of the divine," Villager Randolph Bourne wrote in *The New Republic* that "Mr. Dreiser writes of the erotic with an almost religious solemnity."[48]

The terms of these reviews recapitulate basic issues informing the Progressive era debate over marriage. Should the nineteenth-century ideal of keeping sex within marriage be modified or discarded? Which endangered society more, frank discussion about sexuality or the conspiracy of silence surrounding it? Was disengaging sex from marriage the problem or the solution? The way reviewers measured *The "Genius"* against their own marital, sexual, and moral norms illustrates how the novel became a lightning rod for the changing views. Progressive ideals which had challenged Victorian views were themselves challenged by bohemian ones.

The novel's cultural importance and Dreiser's reputation as a pioneer of sexual frankness were consolidated when *The "Genius"* was banned. Ironically, the same year the novel was published, anti-vice crusader Anthony Comstock "died and went to hell," in the words of Floyd Dell. Comstock, excoriated by Emma Goldman as a "moral eunuch" and "old fossil[]" who practiced "bigoted censorship," was succeeded by John S. Sumner, Executive Secretary of the New York Society of the Suppression for Vice. In July 1916, this "Comstock the Less," after diligently locating seventeen profane and seventy-five lewd passages, demanded that *The "Genius"* be pulled from the stores.[49] Fearing prosecution, the New York office of publisher John Lane recalled all copies.

The ban immediately became a rallying-point for advocates of free speech. No fan of bohemia, as we have seen, Mencken hated the Comstocks more, and mocked their "going through the volume with the terrible industry of a Sunday-school boy dredging up pearls of smut from the Old Testament." Turning a complaint he had made earlier about the novel's verbosity against the vice crusaders, Mencken mock-innocently noted that even if one accepted the Comstockian tally, "the profanity thus works out to somewhat less than one word in 10,000." Mencken helped organize 458 writers (including Upton Sinclair, Susan Glaspell, Ezra Pound, Max Eastman, Willa Cather, Walter Lippman, Abraham Cahan, Amy Lowell, and Harriet Monroe) who signed "A Protest against the Suppression of Theodore Dreiser's *The 'Genius.'"* The document articulated the national significance of the ban which "must inevitably do great damage to the freedom of letters in the United States, and bring down upon the American people the ridicule and contempt of other nations." As biographer Richard Lingeman observes, this campaign marked an unprecedented show of support for an American author. Across the Atlantic, Arnold Bennett and H. G. Wells telegrammed: "We regard *The 'Genius'* as a work of high literary merit and sympathise with the Authors League of America in their protest against its suppression."[50]

Even more than the content of the book, its banning consolidated Dreiser's reputation as a literary and sexual pioneer. As Mencken explained, "It gives an author a romantic glamour to have a suppressed book on his list." Dreiser scholar Louis J. Oldani notes that during the "suppression," at least five newspapers, including the *Los Angeles Times* and the *Chicago Examiner*, declared Dreiser the leading American novelist. Yet Mencken grew concerned that his friend might be seduced by all this glamour. Just two years into what turned out to be a seven-year ban on the 1915 *"Genius,"* Mencken warned that "the danger of the combined Comstockian professorial attack, to Dreiser as artist, . . . [is] that it will convert him into a professional revolutionary." Mencken worried about the novelist's "contaminat[ion] by various so-called 'radical' purposes"—in other words, by Villagers eager to align themselves with the *"Genius"* controversy so as to further their own careers. Although not as political as he would become in the 1930s, Dreiser was in fact leaning in just the direction that Mencken feared.[51]

Shortly after the ban on *The "Genius"* began, Dreiser started work on a manuscript that would be published in 1922 as *A Book About Myself* and reissued in 1931 as *Newspaper Days*. This autobiography covers his early years as a journalist and also his courtship of Sara. It continues the rebuttal of Arthur Henry's portrayal of "Tom"—and also continues rewriting the marriage as Dreiser himself had portrayed it in *The "Genius."* In *Newspaper Days*, Dreiser writes, "I can imagine no greater error of mind or temperament than that which drew me to her, considering my own definite varietistic tendencies and my naturally freedom-loving point of view." Sara was convention incarnate, worshiping at the altar of traditional marriage: "'To have and to hold, in sickness and in health, in poverty and in riches, till death do us part.' I think the full force of those laws must have been imbibed by her with her mother's milk." Dreiser naturally also downplays his own desire for domesticity as well as his dependence on Sara. According to *Newspaper Days*, even the Sara-bashing *"Genius"* of 1915 underestimates the severity of the marital problems as well as the extent of Dreiser's intransigence. "Some of these [marital] difficulties and their result I have long since outlined in *The "Genius,"* Dreiser writes, but "in the main, I fancy I have been a far different creature to Witla—less pliable—more direct and even aggressive at times."[52]

The "Genius" was reissued in 1923, but the mystique generated by its seven-year suppression lived on. As literary scholar Joseph Katz observes, "Dreiser's position as a twisted man, or as a creative hero, depending upon who was speaking, became solidified" with the Comstock attack. Hence Sinclair Lewis, upon winning the Nobel Prize in 1930, paid tribute to Dreiser, who, "marching alone, . . . has cleared the trail from Victorian and Howellsian timidity and gentility in American fiction to honesty and boldness and passion of life. Without his pioneering, I doubt if any of us could, unless we liked to be sent to jail, seek to express life and beauty and terror." Dorothy Dudley's *Forgotten Frontiers: Dreiser and the Land of the Free* (1932) articulates the pivotal role the controversy over *The "Genius"* played in establishing Dreiser's reputation. Because of it, Dudley maintains, "All of those who could not dare but wished they might, found solace in Dreiser. And those born to dare found precedent in him. He became a source of thought and of action."[53] According to this account, then, *The "Genius"* inspired theory as well as practice.

Sensing the cultural importance of his own failing marriage, Dreiser dramatized "This Matter of Marriage, Now" in 1911 with a hero torn between Victorianism and progressivism. He re-dramatized it in 1915, its hero now a proponent of varietism. Yet the resonance of the novel owes much to forces outside of Dreiser's control—the conflicted reviews, the Comstock attack, the literary rally in his defense, the development of Greenwich Village as a center of rebellion. All of these factors contributed to Dreiser's self-dramatization—and the culture's dramatization of him—as a pioneer bravely crusading for a new sexual frankness. The transformation of *The Genius* of 1911 into the anti-marriage polemic with its "Tom Cat" hero that it would become in *The "Genius"* of 1915 reflects Dreiser's embrace of ideas about marriage and sexuality that would go far beyond the progressive ideal of voluntary monogamy.

The couple I turn to now had their own intricate history of voluntary monogamy. Unlike the Dreisers, Neith Boyce and Hutchins Hapgood left a gratifyingly egalitarian archive that allows equal access to the wife's perspective. As I will show, they crafted a different interpretation of the place of varietism in "this matter of marriage, now."

CHAPTER FIVE

Organic Marriage in the Life Writings of Neith Boyce and Hutchins Hapgood

Neith Boyce (1872–1951) never intended to marry. A series of autobiographically inspired "Bachelor Girl" columns that she wrote for *Vogue* in 1898 suggests the course Boyce imagined her life would take. Then as now, *Vogue* was a high fashion magazine (three years before running Boyce's sketches, it scored a coup in publishing drawings of Consuelo Vanderbilt's $3,000 trousseau), and so the appearance of the bachelor girl in its pages indicates the figure had achieved real cachet. Marking a new understanding of the single woman quite unlike the pitiable "spinster" whom no man wanted, the bachelor girl deliberately chose her single life; she was independent, attractive, and self-directed. But symbolic figures aside, actual women still felt pressure to marry, and so Boyce's "Bachelor Girl" must, in her words, "convince the world that she is possible." Boyce presents this New Woman as wedded to her work rather than a man. She feels "fated" to pursue a career in journalism and irritated by the "matrimonial epidemic" striking her women friends.[1]

In addition to publishing journalism, Boyce went on to establish a national reputation as a novelist and playwright. In 1904 a reviewer called her one of "the two most interesting young writers," Edith Wharton being the other. Boyce's career had been fostered by parents involved in publishing: her mother edited the woman's monthly magazine *LOTOS* for several years (it later became the *Bookman*), her father co-founded the *Los Angeles Times*, and Boyce placed early work in both of those venues. After Boyce's four siblings died in a diphtheria epidemic, the family left Milwaukee for Indiana and then Los Angeles. They moved to Boston in 1891, and then

FIGURE 9. Neith Boyce, cigarette in hand, as Bachelor Girl. Courtesy of Frances Benjamin Johnston Collection, Library of Congress.

to New York in 1896. Around the time of the move east, when Boyce was twenty, she published her first book, *Songs*. In 1897 she landed a position as the only woman working for Lincoln Steffens, then city editor for the *Commercial Advertiser*. Part of the new cohort of women entering metropolitan news work in significant numbers, Boyce soon moved out on her own to the Judson Hotel on Washington Square, a boarding house favored by other writers. In addition to writing for the *Advertiser*'s supplement, Boyce was charged with editing some of her co-workers, among them Hutchins Hapgood (1869–1944). The handsome and charismatic Hapgood, who had graduated at the top of his Harvard class in 1892, said that when he met this smart, poised, green-eyed redhead, "one glance was enough for me to know that my day had come."[2]

Lincoln Steffens's *Autobiography* assigns Boyce the leading role in the courtship, describing her as "an unsentimental, pretty girl, who ran a romance through the city room by editing Hutch and his copy till he fell in love with and married her." While Steffens inaccurately suggests his only female journalist was on the lookout for a husband, he correctly frames the relationship as inseparable from their writing. Attracted by Hapgood's "immense energy," Boyce finally accepted his proposal because he promised, in the words of one commentator, "an unusually negotiated marriage" that would accommodate both of their careers.[3] While continuing to write journalism most of his life, Hapgood would also achieve renown as the author of urban ethnographies and memoirs.

In 1899 when they wed, according to Hapgood, "We still lived in the Victorian era, when marriage . . . was supposed to be indissoluble." The couple, however, planned a more flexible arrangement along the lines recommended by the Progressive era marital reformers. "It was to be tentative," Boyce explained in her autobiography, "it was not to be till death did them part. If either of them didn't like it, retreat must be easy." (Boyce wrote her autobiography in the third person, calling the figure modeled on herself "Iras," the name of Cleopatra's attendant.) Despite the affluence of the family into which she married (Hapgood's father was an exceptional businessman who had made a fortune), Boyce continued to work. She further maintained her independence by retaining her surname. Hapgood, who supported all this, wanted their marriage to stand "independent of any of the conventional expressions of fidelity."[4]

Hapgood's phrasing is revealing, for the couple maintained what would now be described as an open marriage. But today's phrasing does not quite capture it. More precisely, Boyce and Hapgood's marriage was punctuated by continuous, but lopsided, breaches of "conventional . . . fidelity." Having numerous affairs which he insisted had no impact on his marriage, Hapgood was consistent enough to encourage his wife to seek other lovers, yet not consistent in his reaction, which was jealousy and possessiveness. His response provides an interesting instance of Carol Z. Stearns and Peter N. Stearns's claim that "emotional standards. . . . change more rapidly and completely than emotional experience does."[5]

Previous commentators have zeroed in on the adultery, concluding that

FIGURE 10. Hutchins Hapgood as a young man. Courtesy of Hapgood Family Papers, Yale Collection of American Literature, Beinecke Rare Book and Manuscript Library. Reproduced with permission of Fred Hapgood.

the husband's double standard inhibited the wife's writing, and have been justly critical of his hypocrisy. Such readings lay important groundwork for all subsequent work on the couple (including my own).[6] But this concern with Hapgood's sexual practices has unfortunately distracted attention away from his sometimes remarkable writings. There has also been a greater casualty: the focus on Hapgood's actions has restricted interpretations of Boyce's own agency. Simply put, she has been cast as more the put-upon victim than I think the facts warrant. Through the 1920s Boyce continued to publish short stories and other work in prominent magazines such as *Lippincott's*, *Scribner's*, and *Harper's Weekly* (the latter edited by Hapgood's brother Norman). All told, she published nine books—an impressive achievement by any standard.

The argument that Hapgood squelched Boyce's career dovetails with the tendency to see their relationship as a product of Greenwich Village. Hapgood's inconsistency has been described as typical of supposedly "radical" men's ambivalence toward feminism. Greenwich Village was indeed a major source of Hapgood's ideas about varietism and anarchism (both of which he also investigated in Chicago as well). Among the couple's intimates were such Village icons as feminist anarchist Emma Goldman (as discussed in the previous chapter, *the* leading proponent of varietism); millionaire Mabel Dodge, whose legendary Fifth Avenue salon, partly Hapgood's own brainchild, attracted iconoclasts of all stripes; innovative playwrights Susan Glaspell and George Cram Cook; novelist and critic Carl Van Vechten; and socialist poet and journalist John (Jack) Reed. Boyce and Hapgood cemented their importance to this avant-garde group as founding members of the Provincetown Players. Writing and producing pioneering drama in defiance of New York's growing commercialism, the Players gave Eugene O'Neill his debut in 1916. The year before O'Neill joined the Players, two productions launched the group. One was Boyce's *Constancy*, a sendup of Dodge's affair with Reed that I will discuss later. Notably, the Players' debut took place at Boyce and Hapgood's rented summer house on 621 Commercial Street in Provincetown.[7]

I find it significant that their household should host such an important event. By opening the door into their shared domestic space, I present an alternative framework for understanding the cultural significance of this couple. That space was not always harmonious but, contrary to prevailing opinion, sustained the creativity of each. Hapgood explains in a memoir that the patterns of their life differed from those of their bohemian friends due to his "almost constant presence in the family." "All day and all night," he wrote, Boyce and he would be "writing, she and I at the same time, I taking my share in care of the children, in teaching them, in the thousand details of the domestic situation." He sums up, "It was a close partnership." "Constant presence" is something of an exaggeration as the two often lived apart, sometimes dividing up responsibility for their four children. Yet during extensive sojourns together as well as times apart, they sought, in Hapgood's words, "to keep house wherever we went. . . . we could bear nothing except keeping house."[8] And when work, finance, or other matters would separate them, Boyce and Hapgood wrote letters longing for the day they would reunite.

The very fact that they stayed married substantiates their only partial allegiance to Greenwich Village mores. While Boyce and Hapgood shared what a recent historian terms "the ultimate bohemian ideal: the fusion of love and art," they parted company with the Village's rejection of marriage as, in the words of one of its spokesman, "spoil[ing]" that ideal. Intriguingly, a Village couple in one of Boyce's novels pretends to scorn marriage while actually cherishing it. They don as a "mask" the chic bohemian view of "domestic happiness . . . as an amusing or pathetic myth." But a friend who knows them intimately says, "you are the most domestic people I know."[9] Boyce and Hapgood's own Village connections provide an important but only a partial context for understanding their lives and writings. They lived with one eye on that innovative world while practicing the sort of marriage theorized by the Progressive era reformers. Boyce and Hapgood's relays between these two ideals exemplify progressivism's interest in changing limits as well as in limiting change. (Once again, the disclaimer: I use the word *progressive* as shorthand for the Progressive era; the term does not signify my endorsement.)

Boyce and Hapgood achieved another sort of blending: between family and work. And key to their achievement—both as writers and as partners—was conceiving of marriage as an archive upon which both drew liberally for their writing. While there was plenty of conflict in their marriage (and differences in their literary reshapings of it), their sense of joint authorship was more egalitarian than I have traced in the case of the Sinclairs, who likewise attempted to sustain dual literary careers. As writers, Boyce and Hapgood might best be described as competitive collaborators.

I center here on Boyce's *The Bond* (1908) and Hapgood's *The Story of a Lover* (composed 1914, published 1919). Both are hybrid forms of life writing—*The Bond* a work of fiction infused with biography, *Story* a memoir self-conscious about its fictionalization. As Shari Benstock puts it, "marriage provided the plot of their lives and the narratives of their fictions."[10] Using Ellen Key's discussion of the conflict inherent in marriages of two "geniuses," Havelock Ellis's idea of marital love as an art form, and Edward Carpenter's construct of the "amalgamated personality," this chapter explores the complications that arise from Boyce's and Hapgood's treating marriage simultaneously as creative process, organic form, and written text. In doing so I want to show how marriage was a generative force, in fact, *the* generative force, in their lives and works, and also how through their writings, Boyce and Hapgood maintain a dialogue with each other.

CAUTION: SPOUSES AT WORK

Of all Progressive era marital reform goals, one remains a particularly familiar challenge for couples today. As I have shown, the theorists sought to reform proprietary marriage in order to meet the economic and psychological need of wives to work. They asserted that such reform would not only improve the lives of women but also the institution of marriage, thus benefiting husbands while regenerating society. Historian Leon Fink defines this aspiration as typical of progressivism generally: "how to weave love into the fabric of one's work and political activity."[11]

From the start, Boyce and Hapgood sought a doubled connection as romantic partners and co-workers. A letter he wrote before their marriage characteristically fused the two roles. They were working at the *Commercial Advertiser* together, and Hapgood mailed Boyce copy to edit—along with a note anticipating the weekend when the two of them "shall no longer be newspaper men." (This playing with gender roles is something to which I will return.) Throughout his courtship letters, Hapgood complains about the "grind" of newspaper work and predicts that marriage would facilitate better writing. Hapgood "hope[d] to be able to concentrate my energy on you at easy range and my work at easy range." Boyce shared his expectations. When she finally agreed to a June 1899 wedding, Boyce suggested that shifting from newspapers to magazines might allow him "more regular hours and no demand on your evenings!—The latter you can spend at home scribbling at one side of the table while I scribble at the other—and our united efforts will probably fend off the wolf!"[12]

Whatever may be said against Hapgood, he understood the depth of Boyce's need to write. She "needed to build," he said, and he understood that "her personal work, her writing, had been the way in which she felt she was herself" (*Story* 175). Through decades of marriage he admired her writing and supported it in practical ways, such as scouting out appropriate venues for her stories like a literary agent. Hapgood never doubted that Boyce "was an artist" and work "her deepest passion" (*Story* 12, 175). He broadcast this personal conviction as a general principle in an early newspaper article reporting on Bryn Mawr's first president M. Carey Thomas, who had recently asserted that "women who work independently are, as a rule, more capable mothers and more interesting and attractive wives." Hapgood endorsed Thomas's controversial position, declaring, "the choice between a woman's work and marriage is a horrible choice and ought not to exist." He understood work, for women as for men, to be fundamentally innovative and creative, an "instinct to loosen up the old forms and traditions, to dynamite the backed and hardened earth so that fresh flowers can grow."[13]

In writings across many genres, Boyce described work as a fundamental need. A memoir explains that she "adored the creator" and "liked to feel herself a worker among workers." Her "Bachelor Girl" sketches depict a young woman delighted with the "newspaper view of life," proud that she can "concentrate[] her brain-energy." In Boyce's play *Winter's Night* (1928), a farmer's wife decides immediately upon the death of her husband to start a dressmaking business, not because she needs the income but because she craves the satisfaction of work. (The widow also refuses a surprise offer of marriage from her brother-in-law.)[14]

Boyce also wrote numerous stories about couples in which one or both partners were artists.[15] *The Bond* centers on one such pair, Basil and Teresa Ransome, who launch what Edith Ellis would term a "semi-detached marriage" structured so that each spouse has time as well as space for independent labor—an arrangement that Ellis believed promoted greater intimacy as well as autonomy.[16] Initially both Basil and Teresa maintain private studio space while sharing a New York apartment: "He had his work separately, she had hers, and they met at the flat on equal terms" (*Bond* 50). Anticipating Virginia Woolf's *A Room of One's Own* (1929), Teresa understands that the separate studio helps her maintain the autonomy she needs to be creative.

Although most interested in the psychological effects of labor, Boyce describes the actual artwork of both characters. Detailed descriptions of Basil's aesthetic are clearly inspired by the work for which Hapgood is best known, ethnographic urban nonfiction about marginalized populations such as *The Spirit of the Ghetto* (1902) and *Autobiography of a Thief* (1903).[17] Much as Dreiser fictionalized his own realism into Ashcan painting in *The*

"*Genius,*" *The Bond* translates Hapgood's nonfiction into visual form: Basil's paintings are sparse, graphic, and composed "with hard simple lines." Basil favors the "rougher aspects" of the city, such as "two tramps on a bench in the park" and "street scenes in the Jewish and Syrian quarters" (15).

Teresa also, the narrator explains, "had her work to do" (45). Modeling bronze and clay miniatures and crafting jewelry, she has what the narrator terms with faint deprecation a "slender but real artistic gift" (47). While her artwork generates a "microscopic income," the real benefit is, as Charlotte Perkins Gilman or Olive Schreiner might predict, the satisfaction of labor (47). Teresa integrates family and work in various ways, such as by making a statuette in memory of a stillborn baby and modeling a series of figures from her toddler. Most intriguingly, Basil and Teresa pose for each other, suggesting that each provides inspiration for the other and, more fundamentally, that marriage and creative work can coexist.

A marriage of two artists provides an ideal test case for the Progressive era ideal of egalitarian co-workers. There is an inherent challenge in balancing the privacy and autonomy (perhaps even selfishness) to produce art with the companionship and collaboration (sometimes requiring compromise) to sustain marriage. Ellen Key provides a useful discussion of marriages of creative workers, and the limited options she identifies continue to challenge couples today. Key divides "genius" marriages into three types defined by the wives' choices. In the first, women adopt the "lesser conflict" of marriage without having children, making it easier to keep working. The second group of wives subordinates their creativity to their husbands' and enjoys what Key defines as the compensatory creativity of motherhood. (Although admitting that choice could be difficult, Key finds it the superior option, leading to many of the "happiest marriages of the present time.") Third, a woman may embrace motherhood while continuing to practice her creative work. [18]

Boyce and Hapgood's marriage followed that third path. Carol DeBoer-Longworthy sums it up in noting that, between 1900 and 1910, Boyce had four children and published four books. Such a balancing act inevitably creates conflicts. Ellen Key characterizes the problem thus: since "all creation requires selfishness . . . while all love's solicitude requires active attention to the needs of the loved ones, the conflict must remain permanent and insoluble."[19] Boyce and Hapgood did not resolve that tension, but they found ways to use conflict creatively, as a stimulus for their writings and means of sustaining intimacy.

In *The Bond*, Boyce draws from what she describes as her own "panicky feeling" before marrying—her fear of "melting in [Hapgood's] warmth."[20] In the novel, marriage confounds the ego boundaries that Teresa had so happily maintained as a Bachelor Girl and artist. *The Bond* begins on the couple's first anniversary, with Basil radiantly declaring he feels as if he had been "born married." But the marital unity so delightful to the husband disrupts the wife's equilibrium. As she tells Basil, "you are the same as you were before, but I am different. . . . The centre of gravity has been changed, and I am tottering!" (34). He insists she remains "the same cool little person that you were when I made you marry me," but she disagrees: "No, I'm not. I'm in love with you now" (36). Teresa dislikes the "creature" love has made her become; she feels "blind, primeval, essentially a slave" (50). Disliking the effect on her subjectivity as well as on her marriage, she expresses to Basil a sense of internal division: "I am rational, but she is blind instinct. I know you belong to me, but she doubts it" (97). When Teresa becomes pregnant, the balance tips toward instinct and dependence as she "conscious[ly] yield[s]" to Basil (134). Hapgood's *Story of a Lover* suggestively describes the dynamic: "Before she knew me she needed nothing. I had taught her to need" (26).

FROM CONVENTIONAL BONDAGE TO ORGANIC BOND

Boyce's late historical novel *Proud Lady* (1923) depicts a conventional marriage that provides an instructive counterpoint. The conflict here originates with the protagonist's marrying a man solely because she feels bound by her earlier engagement to him. When the beau, Laurence Carlin, returns from the Civil War, he anticipates marriage will create a "mystic bond." But because Mary Lowell does not love him, their marriage never rises above a formalistic contract. Laurence's disappointment leads him—in narrative logic that modern readers will likely find distasteful—into the arms of a lower class woman who adores him. But Laurence continues to love his wife, and when his terminal illness brings her face to face with his mistress, Mary blames herself for the "unbending pride" that not only kept her husband at arm's length but also caused her to "hold fast to the form [of marriage] long after the substance of feeling had gone."[21]

This distinction between specious form and authentic substance, as I have shown, grounds the Progressive era marital reform agenda. What Boyce and Hapgood add to that antiformalist position is a perspective on how marriage can endure, in substance rather than form, over a lifetime. People, by definition, change over time—and in fact the reformers believed marriage could foster the individual growth of each spouse. Boyce and Hapgood extend those ideas by portraying marriage as organic—a living entity that grows and evolves over time in reaction to changing experiences. But sustaining this organic bond becomes particularly difficult when children enter the picture. As discussed in Chapter 2, the progressive reformers abandon their concern for the privacy of the couple with the birth of children, at which point, they conclude, marriage becomes a matter of public interest.

Boyce's *The Bond* dramatizes how the birth of children exposes this equivocation at the center of the progressive marital ideal. When Teresa discovers she is pregnant, her first thought is that their egalitarian marriage as independent co-workers must end, for the child will terminate the voluntary basis of their union. They will *have* to stay together, as Teresa tells Basil: "Now, you're bound. . . . Now you can never get away from me, nor I from you." Children will make them both, she says, "slaves" to each other (135).

Boyce focuses in particular on how pregnancy creates conflicts for the wife. That occurs internally (between a woman's need for love and for creative work), and also interpersonally (between the desire for autonomy and for intimacy). Teresa, whose "joy had always lain . . . in the free expression of her will," as a mother must "resign[] her own clear individual preferences" (144, 143). It is not that Teresa experiences pregnancy as a diminishment, though; to the contrary, she feels a new "touch of mysticism" and that the world has become a "greater, . . . more terrible, but more inspiring" place (143, 144). So the point is hardly that as a mother, a woman becomes confined to a limited sphere.

In fact, pregnancy augments Teresa's autonomy as a spouse. That is because pregnancy emphasizes by contrast her essential distinctness from her husband. The absolute connection she feels with the unborn child demonstrates that she and Basil are, to the contrary, "one and . . . another" and that she will be "forever outside" of him (145). She also realizes she does not "need" her husband so much as she had thought. Thus the pregnancy which initially had seemed to shackle them together ends up providing a new psychological space in which Teresa gains another sort of independence. The "bond" of the title becomes even more a work in progress, to be renegotiated on a new basis between two free agents—or discarded.

An additional complication occurs as Teresa starts suspecting Basil of having an affair. While she feels their bond has been destroyed, Basil (again inspired by Hapgood), maintains that "only emotional infidelity counted" and that he has not done anything wrong (162).[22] Acknowledging only "spiritual infidelity" as producing a crisis for a marriage (264), Basil posits that extramarital sexual relations *per se* do not harm a marriage as long as the straying partner does not become emotionally attached to the lover.

This variant of varietism can be self-serving, but it can also represent a principled ideal. That principle originates in the progressive reformers' opposition to proprietary relationships. Elsie Clews Parsons, as I discussed in Chapter 2, categorically rejected that marriage granted a person sexual "monopoly" over another. Edward Carpenter provides an extended explanation of how sexual exclusivity born of a proprietary attitude can lapse into "stagnant double selfishness." Because "love is fed not by what it takes, but by what it gives," Carpenter maintains, "the love of man and wife too must be fed by the love they give to others." In one of Carpenter's more-difficult-to-imagine scenarios of marital bliss, a spouse could be intimate with an outsider while remaining "perfectly true" to his partner. (He calls this possibility a "triune" relationship.)[23] Like Carpenter and Hapgood, Boyce's character Basil justifies his sexual "theories" on the grounds of "absolute freedom." All well and good, except that "Teresa distrusted all theories" (162).

Interestingly, the novel neither confirms nor denies Basil's affair. While he insists he has not consummated his relationship with his wealthy patron, Teresa remains convinced that he has. The uncertainty arises because Boyce uses the wife as the novel's primary center of consciousness, letting the reader perceive for the most part only what Teresa herself perceives. I believe Boyce uses this ambiguity strategically. The uncertainty about Basil's affair shifts the emphasis away from what may (or may not) occur outside a marriage toward if, and how, a couple deals with conflicts that inevitably arise within it.

Teresa responds by testing out her identity separately from her husband. Taking their toddler, she leaves for Europe, staying with her conventionally wedded sister, who is content to remain in a loveless marriage because she believes the institution serves exclusively social needs. Teresa, reaffirming her individuality and what she will not compromise, tells her sister, "You've given up too much. . . . I must have my life" (261). As Teresa later looks back on this period, she realizes that believing Basil was having an affair allowed her to differentiate from him in a new way. Regaining further independence, she realizes "that she was separate from him; he was one person and she was another" (379).

Teresa, who has had her own admirers in the states, develops a more significant relationship abroad with a faintly Orientalized Englishman who lives in Cairo. The curiously named Crayven is married but only, as he puts it, "in the least degree possible" (306), and he develops a friendship with Teresa that their friends assume to be sexual. The relationship, erotically charged but not in fact consummated, helps her further differentiate from her husband. "She no longer felt that they belonged absolutely to one another," Teresa thinks, "the bond that was too strong to break, that had been too strait to bear, was in some way loosened. She no longer felt accountable to Basil for herself" (297).

But again Boyce is interested not so much in adultery as in the impact of a secondary relationship on the primary one. Teresa's flirtation spurs her realization that while certain bonds to Basil have loosened, a more powerful, emotional bond still unites them. Crayven thinks she is "satisfied," with "no need of anyone," and so regretfully concludes that she doesn't want him (338). Chafing at his correct deduction that she remains consumed with her husband, Teresa provokes Crayven to kiss her passionately—and then she recoils. As intriguing as she had found Crayven as an intellect and companion, she is repulsed with him as a potential sexual partner. Teresa's instinctive reaction prompts further reappraisal of her marriage. Again she apprehends her "bondage," that she is "not free for a moment" (349). But she no longer understands this bondage as resulting from having a child with Basil; she is, after all, living thousands of miles away. Nor does the bond reflect, as we have seen, Teresa's feeling "accountable" to him, for she does not. Theoretically (and we have seen Basil's keenness for theories), she knows she could have an affair—only she also discovers that she doesn't wish to. That is because "something far deeper than convention" binds Teresa to Basil (349). Not because of conventional notions of female chastity, but because "a passion of the soul" joins them, Teresa decides to return to Basil (350).

If aspects of the Ransome marriage seem troubling, then thinking again about the sort of work emotion does helps to clarify what Boyce is portraying. I have referred earlier to psychologist Keith Oatley's contention that emotions arise when a person must readjust a "plan" because something gets in the way of its fulfillment. For that reason, Oatley says, "emotions are communications to ourselves arising as evaluations change. As such, they produce feelings. . . . they allow us to continue, relinquish, or modify our plans and goals."[24] The work that emotion does is, therefore, deliberative, even rational, allowing one to weigh competing goals so as to further the most important ones. With that point in mind, let us reconsider Teresa's decision to go back to Basil. It is disturbing when she realizes, along with the depth of her soul-passion, that while *he* may have affairs, *she* cannot. But readers owe Boyce and her protagonist the courtesy of considering these conclusions as the rational, emotionally grounded choices that they are. Teresa chooses not to sleep with Crayven, and she chooses to return to Basil, even while accepting who he is. Those decisions, made by a very logical character, do not mark Teresa's submission to a husband's will but rather deliberate assertion of her own. Emotion helps Teresa make a deliberate, conscious decision about what is best for her own happiness.

The final chapter of *The Bond* does not resolve all problems nor provide pat answers. Categorical answers would, in fact, conflict with the premise of marriage as an organic, continually negotiated entity, different for each couple and even for a single couple every day. But the novel's conclusion does reaffirm a mutually sustaining, deliberately chosen connection— demonstrating, in other words, how to keep renegotiating a progressive marriage. The only thing "certain" is "that [Teresa] and Basil were not to separate." The precise shape their relationship will take remains unclear but she believes it will be on "her terms" (419). This qualified optimism seems justified, given Basil's own recent epiphany: once believing he could get along without Teresa, he now realizes "I can't get away from you. You're in my blood" (421). The metaphor presents their marriage as an organic process, each spouse as necessary to the other as blood.

A marriage is a living entity. It can be wounded or killed outright by neglect, indifference, disrespect, or betrayal. An organic marriage must, as *The Bond* dramatizes, remain in flux. When Basil doubts that they will regain their former intimacy, Teresa replies, "Then we shall get something better." Her next words echo the traditional wedding vows, only instead of asking "do you take this man . . . ," Teresa says, "You take me with my weaknesses, as I take you with yours." Instead of "in sickness and in health," she adds, "I don't say it will be all peace and sweetness—we're too near one another for that." Their nearness, in fact—their intimacy—means that each will "hurt or irritate" the other. Accepting their own and each other's fallibility and the contingency of their relationship, Teresa concludes not with "until death do us part" but rather a "promise . . . to leave you as free as possible" (424). With these updated vows, Teresa affirms durability within mutability, love within conflict. Their reunion after each has hurt the other (and with full knowledge that, as flawed and selfish beings, each will continue to hurt the other) marks the deliberate, free choice that Progressives era reformers believed sanctioned true marriage.

The novel's end also reaffirms the initial premise of an egalitarian marriage of two co-workers and (to quote Gilman once again) "class equals." Basil explains that during Teresa's absence, he has been unable to paint. His creativity, it turns out, is sustained by their marriage and now that they are reunited he can "work with more interest, more intensity" (422). Teresa, in turn, plans to create a new series of silver objects. Their mutual inspiration includes financial parity, for Teresa, along with Basil, will earn money to support the family. Economic interdependence will help sustain creative, psychological, and emotional interdependence.

Through its narrative arc, *The Bond* tracks a couple's evolving understanding of marriage. The novel begins on the Ransomes' first anniversary, marking the ticking of one couple's marital clock. When they wed, Teresa had a naïve and static view that marriage would require no change in her, but be "very simple. You married a person you liked, and did just as you liked, exactly as before; and the person adored you, and even if he lost his temper sometimes over a beefsteak, or a missing shirt, he was still the most charming person in the world" (81). But people modify each other; indeed, "two people can't live together intimately without influencing one another, and deeply" (195). Several years in to the relationship, Teresa has learned the "law of struggle and change" applies to marriage as to everything else (391). The Darwinian language points to competition within and between spouses—"a combat, a struggle to keep what they had conquered, a fight against those things in one another, in themselves, that tended to destroy" (391). Intimacy necessitates change, which produces greater intimacy. It also generates conflict, which *The Bond* folds in as an essential part of the process of sustaining marriage. While capturing a transitional period in the lives of a couple, the novel also marks a new way of thinking about marriage not as a vow good for all time but as a continual work in progress.

Hapgood's *The Story of a Lover* extends Boyce's portrait of organic marriage. The narrator describes his marriage as sustaining and indeed bringing him life: "the sap of my life, which has urged the slender stalk into the full-grown tree with its many branches" (198). According to Hapgood, a "human relationship is never finished, as long as it remains alive. There is a never-ceasing, strenuous remaking, re-creating" (45). This language casts partners as active, creative workers. Echoing Teresa's putting aside her youthful view of marriage as uncomplicated, Hapgood explains, "if our relation had remained simple it might not have endured. It could not have endured had it not developed, changed, and taken into it the richness of the outside world" (121).

Like Boyce, Hapgood describes marriage as a continual struggle for both to "realize [their] own individuality," their independent, "egotistic need" (97). A central challenge of the Progressive era marital ideal—and one that persists for many couples today—is how to individuate while maintaining connection. If a couple succeeds, marriage can theoretically continue to grow and remain creative. In a striking passage, Havelock Ellis explains the connections among marriage, individuation, unity, and creativity:

> Each of the partners is called upon to carry forward the task of self-develop-
> ment, not merely for his or her own individual sake but for the sake of the
> higher creative unity which together they constitute. . . . For the same rea-
> son a certain distance and reserve are called for in the two partners, . . . 'the
> more intimate they are the more strictly should they cherish their own indi-
> viduality.' . . . In that way marriage . . . may reach its highest point of creative
> spiritual unity.[25]

This account suggests a solution to the problem of a marriage of two "ge-niuses" of concern to Ellen Key that I discussed at the start of this chapter. Rather than autonomy and connectedness representing antagonistic goals, to Ellis, "distance and reserve" facilitate the personal growth necessary to make marriage a "higher creative unity." Such an organic relationship survives by embracing conflict and continuing to evolve.

EMPATHY AND THE RADICAL ARTIST

As its title suggests, *The Story of a Lover* defines the protagonist in terms of his primary romantic relationship. Hapgood described the novelized autobiography as "one long gesture of passion" about "my relation to her [Boyce]—the central relation of my life." The book records an epic struggle to achieve intersubjectivity, as Hapgood seeks to understand his ego as well as the creative process through the lens of his marriage, while seeking also to understand an often-inscrutable wife. This obsession with intersubjectiv-ity makes *Story of a Lover* a strange sort of autobiography—one that, for instance, identifies no author on its title page or elsewhere in the text. In fact, there are few proper names anywhere in this fascinating and mad-dening book, which identifies the couple simply as he and she (the latter sometimes She or the Woman). The figures should be understood as both mythologized versions of Hapgood and Boyce and as historically emblem-atic of their era.[26]

In other respects, *Story* is highly particularized. For one thing, it focuses on the marriage during a period of particular turmoil, around 1908, the year *The Bond* appeared. Around that time Boyce fell in love (with one of

Hapgood's best friends, Arthur F. Bentley) and hoped to retain parallel, and open, relations with the two men. The strain of that effort led her to a breakdown. Hapgood did not compose *Story* until 1914, but because he felt his father would disapprove, delayed publication until the older man's death. Upon publication in 1919, *Story* was promptly attacked as pornography by the New York Society for the Suppression of Vice, the same organization that went after Dreiser's *The "Genius"* in 1915. In this case, however, the judge threw out the charge as absurd. Throughout his life, Hapgood retained a special fondness for *Story*, in 1939 identifying it as "the very best thing I have written," immodestly adding, "from the point of literary style it is, . . . as perfect in form as anything we Americans have ever written."[27]

Providing a reverse image of *The Bond*, in *Story* the wife retains her autonomy, equilibrium, and creativity while the husband struggles over his. Indeed, the husband's repeated complaint is precisely the wife's self-possession, which he interprets as indicating her insufficiently loving him. And so while *The Bond* explores a woman artist's attempt to maintain subjectivity within a relationship, *The Story of a Lover* depicts a male artist's exploration of how marriage muddles ego boundaries in a way that, he ultimately concludes, is profoundly generative for his art. Hapgood never acknowledges much conflict between love and work: for him, marriage "helped us to express ourselves impersonally, has helped our writing, our understanding, our culture and our human connections," ultimately giving them both what he calls "social sympathy" (*Story* 71).

In clarifying that rather vague assertion, Hapgood makes a remarkable point. Through his profound connection with her, Hapgood claims, he attains a higher level of consciousness that transforms his writing. Long drawn to urban underdogs such as thieves and revolutionary immigrants, he had always seen them as objects for literary study. Yet marriage establishes what might be called an empathy bridge, allowing Hapgood to grasp the subjectivity of those who had earlier seemed only fodder for his writing (72–73). As he explains the transformation, "writing became for me a human occupation. . . . A thief was a human being, not a thief" (73). *Story* presents Hapgood's commitment to political, philosophical, and personal reform, then, as growing organically out of his marriage. In a remarkable articulation of the notion that marriage could transform society, he asserts, "my love for my wife . . . led me step by step into what is called radicalism, into an infidelity to the conventions of my class" (73).

Without becoming embroiled in a terminological debate over "radicalism," I would like to consider Boyce's commentary on her husband's politics. As she explains, Hapgood had

> an exploring temperament, but tradition was very strong in him. To him "radicalism" . . . meant return to the deepest-rooted instincts and values; not rooting out of traditional inherited values, but clearing away from them of superficial growths to leave free what was vital. He held no brief for any fixed status in society, nor any profession; he saw profound failings in the present system of education and in the social system. But he ardently wanted his sons to have what was good in these; he didn't want them to throw over the whole thing.

Boyce's organic language emphasizes roots, growth, and vitality. In addition, her description of Hapgood's longing to return to a natural, Edenic state, as well as his desire to conserve even while transforming existing social structures, reflect precisely those objectives that I have been tracing as central to progressive marital reform.[28]

Hapgood's idea that marriage incites "radicalism" is intriguing also in how he frames it as "infidelity" to his "class." I will return later to infidelity *per se*; for now, I want to examine Hapgood's belief that marriage could transform political consciousness. He generalizes, "He who has never desired a re-valuation of all values, who in his deeper emotions is not a revolutionist, has never fully loved a woman, for in the closest personal relation there lies a challenge and a threat to all that is meaningless or lifeless in organized society" (*Story* 102). This claim embodies the hope of Charlotte Perkins Gilman and others that reformed marriage could reconnect the isolated private family with the social world.

In *The Bond*, however, Boyce suggests an alternative interpretation of Basil's radical consciousness. As noted above, Boyce renders Basil's paintings in *The Bond* as visual equivalents of Hapgood's own urban ethnographies. In a curious chapter, *The Bond* traces the Ransomes and some friends as they take a "slumming expedition" into New York's Tenderloin and Bowery districts, with Basil serving as guide (178). Teresa finds the bars, music halls, Turkish coffee houses, and Chinese restaurants unnerving. While her reaction reflects her elitism and genteel racism, it also suggests that she grasps the misery of the lives she witnesses. She finds "pleasure . . . the least discoverable element" in a group of partiers and recognizes the smile of a young abandoned woman as "a piteous attempt at bravado" (179, 180). Descriptions of Tenderloin denizens are menacing, such as a man with a "half-extinct black eye" and a female addict with puncture wounds (181). A prizefighter acquaintance of Basil's, accustomed to "innumerable slumming parties," exchanges whispers with Chinese waiters, after which Teresa detects "a shade which might have been a smile" passing over immovable, ominous faces (181). The Orientalizing is distasteful, yet the chapter deftly marks the artists as tourists witnessing a performance of the underworld staged for their benefit.

This curiously naturalistic chapter, unlike anything else in *The Bond*, registers significant doubts about Basil's aesthetic. First, he seems unaware of the make-believe. Basil's oblivion is particularly incriminating since he prides himself on grasping urban realities. But the most serious doubt takes shape when the scene is read alongside Hapgood's ecstatic description in *Story* of the empathy bridge connecting him with the underworld. In *The Bond*, Basil simply sees copy: "the mass of misery did not move him. He dissociated himself from it completely" (188). Teresa sees his "impersonal interest in the scene" and thinks it "cruel to enjoy the sight of such a world, to use it as material for art" (187, 188). She sees her husband's aestheticizing of the underworld as ethically and artistically objectionable.

FEMINISM, ESSENTIALISM, AND MALE SUBJECTIVITY

The Bond provides further critical analysis of Hapgood through the allusive name of its male protagonist. The similarity in name of Boyce's Basil Ransome to that of the protagonist/antagonist of Henry James's *The Bostonians* (1886)—Basil Ransom, without the terminal "e"—cannot be coincidental. *The Bond* is in many respects a Jamesean novel, privileging interiority over external events, focalizing a single center of consciousness, and using interpersonal relationships to examine gender roles at a time of acute transition. Even more to the point, Henry James's brother William was a household god for Hapgood, who had studied with the philosopher at Harvard. The organicism of James's pragmatism struck Hapgood as exemplary philosophy: "fixtures were not a part of his philosophy," Hapgood enthused, "he flowed." Boyce's character's name, therefore, provides a way of embedding private communication with her husband within a public medium. But this palimpsest also provides an opportunity to examine how tenets of Progressive era marriage reform bear a distinctly conflicted relationship to ideas just then coming to be known as *feminist*.[29]

Basil Ransom of *The Bostonians* is a conservative Southerner occupying one corner in an unconventional triangle. In the other two corners stand Olive Chancellor, a strident woman's rights advocate and spinster (the word is offensive but captures how James portrays her); and Verena Tarrant, a beautiful young woman whom Olive and Ransom both find irresistible. For much of *The Bostonians*, Olive persuades Verena to use her rhetorical powers to advance women's rights, but Ransom eventually steals her from the public stage, luring her away as his wife. Through it all, Verena seems passive, even pawn-like, in a high-stakes competition between Northern feminism (and implicit lesbianism) represented by Olive, and Southern anti-feminism (and patriarchal marriage) represented by Ransom.

The Bond includes a loveable if doctrinaire feminist as a minor character, but Teresa's Aunt Sophy does not provide a substantial connection to *The Bostonians*. Boyce's recycling the name of James's character makes an explicit link, and it reflects, I believe, a private joke with Hapgood. Like many private jokes that couples return to time and again, this one involves serious business.

In early 1907, when Boyce had just begun writing *The Bond*, she was caring for three small children, one of them chronically ill, and living just outside of Florence. Hapgood had recently gone to Paris to research a book. From there he wrote her excitedly about a woman's rights speaker, "a *feministe* [sic] and anarchist—a beautiful, charming being, very eloquent: she made me think—for the time, at any rate—that women are slaves and that the great injustice of society begins there. . . . I feel that I belong to the oppressive sex! And I have thought of you a hundred times to-day as a dear victim of me and Man." In response, Boyce denied she was a slave—or if so, she cryptically added, "it is to something much more radical than society." She was "amused" by Hapgood's "conversion by the beautiful + eloquent feminist." Boyce teased "that a beauty, whether eloquent or not, can convert a man to anything." She predicted, however, that Hapgood would soon "revert" and would not long "carry[] the banner for Women's Rights!"[30]

Certainly Hapgood never became a Verena Tarrant, but this epistolary exchange suggests why Boyce thought of *The Bostonians* while writing her own novel. Another letter provides an additional clue as to why she named her male protagonist after James's. Around the same time, Hapgood wrote that he had been thinking about marriage in general and theirs in particular. Was her "scheme," he wondered (referring to her novel-in-progress, *The Bond*), "broad enough to take in several different aspects of the institution?" If so, he offered some literary fodder: "the difference in sexual temperament between the man + the woman who live together. . . . You + I have often touched upon this, but I have some side-lights on it that will interest you—and perhaps fit into your book."[31] The "difference" in men's and women's temperaments, of course, is precisely one of Boyce's primary concerns in

The Bond. Earlier chapters in *Until Choice Do Us Part* have considered other literary transformations of actual marriages. But unlike Theodore Dreiser's revisions to the character based on his wife so as to promote a particular image of himself, or Upton Sinclair's appropriation of shared marital experience as his exclusive literary property, Hapgood encourages Boyce to use their shared life as her copy.

Hapgood's message, however, remains mixed. As Boyce continued to work on the novel, he was urging her against overextending herself. She was nursing their youngest child, and Hapgood suggested that the chronic health problems of their middle child might have been caused by Boyce's overworking during the boy's infancy. Not surprisingly, Boyce was annoyed. She retorted that the hour or two a day she wrote provided "great pleasure," never a "strain."[32]

The moments in which Basil Ransome of *The Bond* behaves like a bossy patriarch—that is, when he most resembles his namesake in *The Bostonians*—suggest Boyce's resistance to that tendency in her own husband. It is precisely when her male protagonist feels threatened or vulnerable that he issues doctrinaire patriarchal statements. At one point he even wails that women now "own" men and that "it's all the fault of feminism." The solution he proposes is to reestablish traditional gender hierarchy: "The line ought to stand where it was drawn for all time, sharp and clear. Trying to rub it away is folly." He also accuses his wife of trying to become a man, a charge that she calmly denies, calling men "poor, foolish creatures" (196). Teresa even uses the same French form of the word that Hapgood had used to describe the charming speaker: "You a *feministe*!" she exclaims incredulously (171).

Hapgood is not Boyce's Basil, nor is he James's, but he harbored conflicted feelings about feminism. With notable exceptions such as the complaint about Boyce's writing while nursing, he generally supported married women's working, both as a theoretical proposition and as a practical matter. In addition to (mostly) supporting his wife's career and sharing in child care—causing Lincoln Steffens to call Hapgood the "mother of the family"—Hapgood wrote in favor of women's suffrage, describing anti-suffragists as "consciously or unconsciously interested in the maintenance of special privileges." His own daughter, in a memoir, calls Hapgood one of the few men she had ever known who is not "a male chauvinist." Miriam Hapgood DeWitt goes on to add, "I just grew up taking it for granted that women were the equals of men." But where Hapgood drew the line was with feminists who promoted what he considered "Sex-Antagonism."[33]

A fascinating unpublished manuscript provides an index of Hapgood's ambivalence about feminism. "The New Bohemia" differentiates the Village from its "Old World" counterparts such as the Latin Quarter in Paris. What Hapgood terms its "spiritual geography" is "bounded on the North by the Feminist Movement, on the East by Old World Bohemia . . . , on the South by the Artistic Temperament and on the West by the I.W.W." While feminism gave the New Bohemia "ferocity," its men remained "sentimental." New Bohemian men understood their own hypocrisy in having advocated women's freedom only until their wives and girlfriends began claiming it. A series of interesting analogies follows: feminists have,

> like the lowest laborers, "nothing to lose but their chains." And emancipated slaves have never shown sentiment or delicacy when dealing with their former masters. The guillotine of the French Revolution has its spiritual counterpart within the territory of the new Bohemia, and the aristocracy that is led to the scaffold is what used to be called male. The victims are men.

While the argument of male victimhood smacks of the most tedious sort of antifeminism, the analogies with a Marxist revolution, freed slaves, and the French Revolution all dignify the cause of feminism.[34]

Critics have linked Hapgood's conflicted views about women to the essentialist conception of gender promoted by such writers as Key, Carpenter, and Ellis.[35] *Story of a Lover* indulges in plenty of gender essentialism—and yet spends as much time inverting as upholding gender polarities.[36] The narrator describes himself as "more of a mother, more of a housekeeper," indifferent to men's "usual ambitions" (98). He describes his wife, in turn, as uninterested in "domestic and wifely qualities" and masculine in "go[ing] out to the larger world in her thought, her imagination, and her work" (99). And while Hapgood claims that pregnancy "completes" women, he also wishes, "if I could only have been with child myself!" (52). Jealous that he could not carry any of their children, Hapgood explains his attempt "to impregnate myself in a figurative sense" by "giving birth to ideas" (52, 53). The equation of male writing with female childbirth recalls Sinclair's *Love's Pilgrimage*, but Hapgood has the humility to admit his literary children are but "pale consolations" (53). Hapgood's insistence that in their marriage "neither of us has felt any limitation of sex" may exaggerate the facts but the affirmation of equality seems sincere (99). Nor is there reason to doubt his claim that he and Boyce approached their writing "as if there were no conventional career for either man or woman" (99). It also should be emphasized that much of *Story's* dichotomizing proceeds independently of gender. The narrator describes himself as noisy to her silence, hot to her cold, young to her old, needy to her self-sufficiency, theoretical to her practical, and so on.

Moreover, *Story of a Lover* portrays the husband's subjectivity in a manner that has traditionally been understood as "feminine." The narrator casts his identity as a void—a fundamental lack he hopes she will fill. He complains that She does not reciprocate his gaze: "She did not see me—and I sometimes think she has never seen me since," after fifteen years of marriage (7). The narrator's subjectivity, thus, can be constituted only by her recognition. And it is "terrible," he confesses, "to be dependent on another being" (54). The narrator explains he could have tolerated anything, "had she *seen* me, once and forever!" (18). Asserting that while he has "no crude lack" physically or mentally, and "could meet her desires in every obvious way," what he ambiguously terms (perhaps thinking of his beloved Whitman) "the Real Self is not [so] obvious." And it is precisely "*that* she never saw!" (19). What Edward Carpenter describes as "the great need" generated by profound love sustains Hapgood as it impels *The Story of a Lover*.[37]

Jessica Benjamin's theory of intersubjectivity helps to clarify what Hapgood seeks in his marriage. According to Benjamin, we can use our "marvelous capacity for identification with others to either further or impede our recognition of others." As discussed above, Hapgood and Boyce provide precisely those two different interpretations of what I called his empathy bridge: according to *Story of a Lover*, he perfectly recognizes urban outsiders, but according to *The Bond*, Basil turns them into aesthetic objects. The stakes are higher for Hapgood in his marriage, which implicates, after all, his "Real Self." Benjamin explains that "the different other is a threat to the identity of the self or ego that wants to be all there is." There are two ways of dealing with otherness, she says, only one of them marking the intersubjective union that Hapgood mostly craves (but also partly fears). In the lesser way, the ego can be "constituted by the identifications with the other . . . in an ongoing way"—but as a means of avoiding "the loss and uncontrollability that otherness necessarily brings." A person may experience mutuality, in other words, while still forestalling the threat to the ego that comes with an embrace of radical otherness. In the second way, which Benjamin defines as intersubjectivity, the ego recognizes its own contingency upon realizing it "depend[s] on the other's recognition, which it cannot have without being negated, acted on by the other, in a way that changes the self."[38]

Story of a Lover suggests both of these paradigms. On one hand, the book could scarcely be more ego-driven, a fact that, along with Hapgood's complaints that She does not see him, suggest that intersubjective union must remain a fantasy. Yet Hapgood also craves precisely the loss of ego-bound self, the dissolving of self into other, and even manifests the radical recognition that his self ultimately depends on Hers that, according to Benjamin, constitutes intersubjectivity. In such a relationship, the self would apprehend, as she puts it, "the other as more than the self's object," or a subjectivity in its own right. Hapgood's insistence on Boyce's otherness and autonomy, as well as his desire for an absolute merging, it seems to me, indicates that he realizes she is far more than his object, however much he might wish to contain her as his subject.[39]

Oatley's analysis of marital conflict provides an additional way of seeing how Benjamin's psychoanalytic frame pertains to the Hapgood-Boyce marriage. Finding emotion arising most frequently when two people's goals or plans conflict, Oatley calls marriage an exemplary "joint plan" that will inevitably—because of what I would call its dual authorship—involve conflicts and repeated renegotiations. Oatley particularly attends to what happens when one spouse's personal plan collides with the joint plan of the marriage, noting that both plans are deeply implicated in the spouse's sense of subjectivity. At such moments of conflict, "the incongruence is experienced not as a cognitive problem to be solved but as an insult that threatens the foundations of the self." Consequently the "model" of the self, of the other, and of the marriage all become precarious. The ensuing struggle is as much about renegotiating "a sense of who one is" as it is about resolving conflicts with one's mate.[40] *Story of a Lover* illustrates all of these struggles as its narrator/protagonist strives for ecstatic, intersubjective fusion with Her.

And as the narrator of *Story* experiences his own subjectivity as tenuous, he depicts his wife as serenely maintaining hers. She responds to his "dependency" with "her indestructible aloofness" (139). *Story* depicts her as having an "unconscious completeness" and "integrity" at which Hapgood marvels (92). Her "inalienable independence," he says, "filled me with passionate respect" (180). This perception of her wholeness is especially important because the highest ideal of *Story* is unity: of love and work, of the different facets of the self, of husband and wife, of self and other. (Again, the echoes of Whitman are palpable.) "I imagine that at the root of every real love," Hapgood speculates, "is this almost metaphysical passion—this deep emotional insistency on unity" (*Story* 114). And, just as he attributes his radicalism to marriage, so he locates his access to transcendent unity:

"In her arms only have I been able to feel united with something . . . bigger than myself" (*Story* 63). Thus I propose a modification to Christine Stansell's reading of *Story* as subordinating Boyce's voice to Hapgood's. I do not find an "obliteration of the heroine's subjectivity in the name of the narrator's superior powers to elucidate her character."[41] Hapgood does at times, as I will show presently, attempt to fix Boyce as a literary subject. But rather than ever elucidating his wife, Hapgood finds her endlessly mysterious; and as to his obliterating her subjectivity, that would be, by his own admission, like an atom obliterating a planet.

Letters flesh out the biographical context for Hapgood's sense of his "feminine" dependence and Boyce's "masculine" qualities. In 1919 he explained the role she had played in his life over two decades as a reversal of gender expectations: "The woman's life is more determined as a rule by the man with whom she lives + has children by than the man's. But, in my case, the effect of you on me has been quite as compelling and determining a thing as ever happened to a woman." Ten years later he wrote Boyce that he never could have endured thirty years with "any woman who was a female before all else." But she "differed enough from the so-called normal to make it possible for me (also differing to some degree from the normal) to live with you."[42]

LOVE-ARTISTRY AND THE INTERSUBJECTIVE BOOK OF MARRIAGE

Story of a Lover riffs on Havelock Ellis's idea of marriage as the "art of love," but with different consequences than I traced in Chapter 3 regarding Upton and Meta Sinclair. Edith Ellis wrote of her husband that "love and Art are his keys to the Universe," but notes that "every artist must learn technique, even the Love-Artist." Hapgood likewise considered love "one of the highest expressions of imagination," and there is strong internal evidence that he drew the idea directly from Ellis's best-selling *Sex in Relation to Society* (1911). In an often-quoted passage, Ellis calls the woman "on the physical side, inevitably the instrument in love; it must be [the man's] hand and bow which evoke the music."[43] Commentators have cited this passage as evidence of Ellis's gender essentialism, a point that cannot be denied. Yet the phrasing is also remarkable for stressing the importance of a woman's sexual pleasure—and for placing the responsibility for it on her husband. In *Story*, Hapgood adopts Ellis's metaphor to suggest a duet rather than a solo:

Each human being is a peculiar, irreproducible instrument, different from all other instruments, capable of giving out music of an original quality but needing the right touch, the right player, who understands the particular instrument upon which he is playing. If he plays artistically, beautiful spiritual harmony results. (*Story* 66)

Besides suggesting that men as well as women need their perfect musician, Hapgood extends the image in another way. Conflict, according to him, creates greater intimacy: "the deeper disturbance of our mutual life" begins with "undertones," but quickly develops into "clear motifs in the symphony of our relation" (100). As their "essential discord" intensifies, it "make[s] the harmony more difficult" but also "render[s] it deeper; as it does in the operas of Strauss and Debussy" (100–101). Hapgood's adaptation of Ellis's musical metaphor casts discord as producing the higher harmony of creative intersubjectivity.

The Story of a Lover depicts the process by which marriage, in Hapgood's account, made him into what I will call a love-artist. Becoming this love-artist entails the husband's sexual education—not in the techniques of intercourse, which he already knew, but in appreciating lovemaking as an enactment of intersubjective creativity. Hapgood describes himself before meeting her as sexually experienced but lacking in "spiritual emotion" (66). Their lovemaking, he writes, at first was "light . . . , playful and athletic" but also "to her[,] a little foolish and unmeaning" (66). Eventually, Hapgood realizes that Boyce's "pleasure and emotion" and his own were not separate but "inextricably dependent, one upon the other" (67). At this point the "sexual embrace" assumes, as Hapgood intriguingly describes it, "aesthetic meaning" (65).

While Hapgood believes the love-artist is made, not born, he imagines an artistic hierarchy among romantic relationships. Thus while love constitutes the highest creative achievement, he traces a continuum running from the casual sketch to the masterpiece. In "the art of love as in the minor arts—those minor arts being poetry, painting, sculpture and music—the rule in love is the sketch." A sketch may show talent but remains secondary to the "finished thing." Only love-artists with "enduring power" and "artistic patience" can create that "essential form" recognized as a masterpiece (45–46). *Story* records how Hapgood believed he "live[d] artistically" (45) with Boyce and how their love created an almost Platonic "essential form" (45). Their "bond," he therefore claims, "is aesthetic first and last" (157).

Hapgood's views of love-artistry lead him to flirt with the idea of autobiography as an intersubjective genre. Going further than Upton Sinclair's attempt to write a companionate novel, Hapgood suggests that *Story* was not authored by him, exactly, but rather by a third personality constituted by the marriage. The book was, Hapgood says, the "artistic product of a state of being rather than of an individual man" (410). Elsewhere he explains, "just as my love for Neith was stronger than I, so this book [*Story*] was much better than anything I was able to write as Hutchins Hapgood."[44] And he admits that intersubjectivity is more difficult to capture in writing than in lovemaking. That is, the book he authored as half of a marriage (rather than rendered as an individual writer) cannot represent Boyce's subjectivity as accurately as his own. Such an authorial failure is hardly surprising, but Hapgood believes that Boyce withdraws from him emotionally precisely because of it: "if she could have felt that our relation was her construction, not mine, she would have loved me more!" (*Story* 175). That admission perfectly captures the constructed nature of the marriage. Hapgood admits that as he re-reads *Story*, "it seems like fiction, even to me" (91).

Intersubjectivity and creative authorship compete in other ways in their marriage. Boyce and Hapgood bristled at even while encouraging each other's textualizations of the marriage. She referred to *Story* as providing "a very different truth from *my* truth" and said she did not recognize herself in it. "Nevertheless," Boyce added, apparently speaking as an artist rather than a wife, "it is both true and beautiful."[45] Hapgood, in turn, charges Boyce with aestheticizing him as a means of keeping emotional distance: "she felt aesthetically my qualities," he complains, but "she did not love Me" (*Story* 17).

Boyce dramatizes the consequences of turning one person's life into another's creative product in an interesting scene toward the end of *The Bond*. Teresa has returned from Europe to Basil, but he flies into a rage when letters arrive from Crayven, the man who had courted her. Teresa confesses what there is to confess (not much), and Basil asks "infinite questions" in what seems to her like an effort "to wring more out of the facts than they contained." Basil's over-reaction leads Teresa to feel that he is "trying to construct, quite impersonally, a drama, in which she figured merely as an actor" (388). If intersubjectivity is, as Jessica Benjamin says, a "double action" that entails "recognizing the other's subjectivity and one's own," then Basil here betrays it.[46]

Yet other evidence suggests that Boyce believed her own husband did succeed as a love-artist. Three years after publication of *The Bond*, she offered Hapgood her own cache of love letters from someone else. Given Basil's posturing over Crayven's letters to Teresa, Boyce's cover letter to her husband is worth considering in some detail:

> I am enclosing Ben's love-letters which will be of more use to you than to me — They are interesting but I don't see any story in them — only the old story! How much alike love-letters are — I would give a lot to see some original ones — but know it is hopeless — Love is the same today + forever — and its expression too — don't you think so? I could take these letters and some of Cora's and make a romantic series that nine women out of ten would think I stole from them!

While Ben and Cora have not been identified, it is clear that Boyce offers their letters to Hapgood in the spirit of their compact to share intimacies. In doing so, she presents the letters and the emotion inspiring them as predictable, inferior texts, all relaying the same "old story." From her vantage point as a critical reader of love-writing, Boyce praises Hapgood: "There is novelty though in some of your letters to me — to think you can write them after 13 years!"[47] The love-artist pleases her as an unusual lover *and* as an original writer. As Hapgood imagined a hierarchy among love-artists, so Boyce believed they were literary aristocrats of love.

Boyce and Hapgood produced a collaborative work which may take the idea of intersubjective writing as far as it is possible to go. In the summer of 1916, they co-wrote and subsequently acted in *Enemies*, a one-act play that literally stages their marriage. First produced by the Provincetown Players, *Enemies* features a married couple identified (as in *Story of a Lover*) simply as He and She. The opening establishes them as a literary couple: She sits reading while He writes — or, rather, tries to write, with a pen in hand and pages scattered around him. Reiterating Hapgood's real-life complaints, He attempts to pick a fight by grumbling about her "spiritual infidelity" and not truly seeing him.[48] As He baits and insinuates, She teases him (notably, by quoting William James against him) but remains calm, which of course further annoys him.

As in *The Bond* and *Story of a Lover*, *Enemies* dramatizes conflict as symptomatic of a living marriage and, as such, productive of sexual intimacy. In the words of She, "the shock and flame of two hostile temperaments meeting is what produces fine children." Through most of the play, He personalizes their conflict while She generalizes, accepting disagreement as part of the heterosexual compact: "men and women are natural enemies, like cat and dog, only more so." But the climax occurs when She personalizes, charging that his love-artistry can be despotic: "you have wanted to treat our relation, and me, as clay, and model it into the form you saw in your imagination. You have been a passionate artist. But life is not a plastic mate-

FIGURE 11. Boyce and Hapgood acting in *Enemies,* a play they co-authored based on their marriage. Courtesy of Hapgood Family Papers, Yale Collection of American Literature, Beinecke Rare Book and Manuscript Library. Reproduced with permission of Fred Hapgood.

rial. *It* models us." He admits that He has the "egotism of the artist." But critical as She is, She also makes clear that She will never divorce him. After fifteen years of marriage, She exults, they have never bored each other: "to be still for one another the most interesting persons in the world! How many people can say that?" Aroused by her question, He "seiz[es] her" and the play concludes with an embrace and wordplay.[49] *Enemies* portrays tension as enhancing passion as well as literary acuity, thus fostering intimacy. In this way, love-artistry keeps marriage organic.

Although readers may generate endless interpretations, texts themselves are finite objects, which places them at odds with the fluidity of organic forms. That contradiction is embedded in Hapgood's differentiating the "sketch" of love from the "finished" work he calls a "masterpiece" (*Story* 45-46). In a newspaper article he tries to finesse the incongruity: "Love is like a tree that grows from a seed in the ground. . . . The leaves and the branches develop into complex and beautiful expressions." He links organic growth with the love-artist—"we paint and write beautifully because we love"—but the logical connection remains elusive, and so he reverts to the empathy bridge: "Our desire becomes the love for art, for justice, for perfection of workmanship, for men, women, and children, for all of society, for all of Nature."[50] The connections linking marriage as text, organic form, and creative work are fragile, but Hapgood and Boyce cast marriage in all these terms.

The generation that pursued new ideas about marriage in the Progressive era, as I have shown, loved their books. Dreiser's *The Genius* endlessly references texts that influenced the protagonist, even attributing Suzanne Dale's nonproprietary views about sex and marriage to her reading habits. Upton and Meta Sinclairs' dueling accounts, *Love's Pilgrimage* and "Corydon and Thrysis," provide running commentaries on books that shaped the couple's views. Dreiser also, as I discussed in the previous chapter, was encouraged by Mencken to examine *Love's Pilgrimage,* and it also appears that Hapgood himself read Sinclair's novel soon after it appeared. In a letter written to Boyce the same month *Love's Pilgrimage* was published, Hapgood discusses an unnamed book of Sinclair's, adding, "though now that I have read it, I have more sympathy for it, yet seems silly to me, just because it has ideals. Freedom is an illusion and one who seeks for it all his life has more energy than brains."[51] While Hapgood's assessment of Sinclair is cryptic, it is clear that he and Boyce envisioned marriage literally as text, at times co-written, but more often produced by independent yet intertwined artistic visions.

Is writing—ultimately a solitary endeavor—incommensurable with marriage, necessarily a relationship? Can marriage ever be co-written like a book? I don't believe that either Hapgood or Boyce provides answers, but rather that their writings, when read side by side, keep those questions alive in productive tension.

MONOGAMY'S ESCAPE VALVE AND THE "AMALGAMATED PERSONALITY"

Hapgood's discussion of adultery in *The Story of a Lover* illuminates a sticking point in Progressive era marital theory. As I have shown, the reformers enthusiastically supported monogamy—even while arguing (to varying degrees) for acceptance of sexual experimentation before marriage and (uniformly) for divorce by mutual consent. In addition, many defended sexual experimentation within marriage. Variety-within-monogamy is contradictory (if not inconsistent), but if the history of sexuality has taught us anything, it is that norms as well as practices change, and that what sounds commonsensical to one generation may strike another as absurd. The prevalence of this ideal in Progressive era texts suggests that it appeared neither so contradictory nor ideologically suspicious then as it does now. Hapgood affirms both components of the paradox of variety-within-monogamy in *Story of a Lover*. We might call this paradoxical ideal monogamy's escape valve.

Ellis provides the most logical explanation. In a discussion of "erotic comradeship," he explains that spouses might have "an exclusive mutual erotic devotion"—monogamy as commonly understood. But Ellis also maintains that "the natural prevalence of monogamy as the normal type of sexual relationship by no means excludes variations." (As I explained in Chapter 2, Ellis emphasizes *variations* to keep *natural* and *normal* from becoming tyrannical.) He believes a healthy "elasticity" of mind recognizes sexual pluralism, including "variations from the general monogamic order." According to Ellis, erotic comrades understand that exclusivity is by definition limited. He recommends spouses understand it is "natural and instinctive to tell each other of their feelings towards other persons." By "shar[ing]" each other's "new affections," he believes erotic comrades can "increase . . . their affection for each other." Moreover, Ellis asserts that "marriage . . . is without any high mission unless it brings those who contract it into a many-sided contact with the greater world, and that contact cannot be real and intimate if it excludes at the outset the possibility of other relationships that are affectionate."[52] Once again, a marital theorist asserts that reforming marriage could lead couples to interact more meaningfully with the "greater world."

Hapgood and Boyce, as this chapter has shown, shared intimacies they had with third parties. For Hapgood especially, marriage should connect a couple to the greater world, not isolate it. The same idea informs his rationale for extramarital affairs. He explains that because of the "mysterious bond which held my spirit" to Boyce, he found it "impossible to give my real self to another" (*Story* 146-47). He calls this condition "inevitable monogamy," a matter not of physical but "spiritual" faithfulness. Hapgood believed that affairs heighten the dynamically experimental quality of marriage, with the subsequent return to the spouse heightening the union–a logically comprehensible if emotionally challenging proposition. For instance, in a memoir he dictated to Boyce, Hapgood candidly discusses his affair in 1917-1918 with Greenwich Village's beloved actress Mary Pyne and the jealousy of her husband, poet Harry Kemp (formerly the lover of Meta Sinclair). In contrast to Kemp, Hapgood maintains, "the deep and beautiful Neith understood it perfectly."[53] They remain committed, he says, to a "monogamy deeper than . . . convention or law" (*Story* 116).

UNIVERSITY OF WINCHESTER
LIBRARY

Carpenter, that advocate of so-called inner laws, makes a similar point in *Love's Coming of Age*. Rejecting that a past vow could bind a couple indefinitely, he still favors long-term relationships. In fact, Carpenter believes outside relationships strengthen a bond, which becomes "concentrated and intensified by years of linked experience, of twined [sic] associations, of shared labors, and of mutual forgiveness." The last item is particularly significant as it emphasizes that travails as well as delights deepen a relationship, an idea that Boyce and Hapgood clearly shared. Carpenter maintains that a "free" and "spontaneous" marriage that does not exclude either partner from having other relationships becomes "by its very freedom . . . all the more poignantly attractive." Such an open relationship would be no less than "indestructible," Carpenter says, letting loose his most ecstatic language, "like the relation of two suns which, revolving in fluent and rebounding curves, only recede from each other in order to return again with renewed swiftness into close proximity—and which together blend their rays into the glory of one double star."[54] According to this logic, intersubjectivity is sustained precisely by a couple's departure from and reunion at their common center.

Carpenter calls this ideal union the "amalgamated personality." In *Story of a Lover*, Hapgood endorses and strives to exemplify that sort of unity. He traces the couple's evolution from "lighter amorousness" into everlasting love "built on a fortress which nothing but a double death can destroy, and perhaps not even that!" (200). *Story* thus captures Carpenter's wistful hope for "a permanent and life-long union—perhaps a many-life-long union." As the amalgamated personality constitutes what Carpenter calls "a natural fact, independent of any artificial laws" (97), so for Hapgood, union with Boyce establishes "the impertinence of law and conventional morality which insists on a condition already inevitable if of the spirit—and if it is not of the spirit it is nothing" (147).

Boyce's musings on adultery bring together many of the conflicts between theory and practice that I have explored in this book. In response to a 1905 letter from Hapgood relaying interest in Chicago's varietist-anarchist scene, she called it "crude + unlovely" to "erect[] into a principle what ought to be regarded as a breach." Crucially, Boyce frames her opposition to varietistic "principles" as a violation of art: her objection, she stresses, is "more aesthetic than moral."[55]

A remarkable series of letters illuminates Boyce's complex attitudes about adultery. Late in 1915, Hapgood wrote that he had "fallen in love with Lucy Collier but not in the way I am with you!" This new love was a Smith College graduate, reporter, and first wife of the reformer and immigrant activist John Collier. Hapgood's affair generated deep conflict in his own marriage, and a letter Boyce wrote him several months later captures her anguish over his repeated affairs. That letter has gotten considerable circulation since it was reprinted in a collection of the couple's writings edited by Ellen Kay Trimberger in 1991.[56] But filed with the Hapgood Family Papers at Yale's Beinecke Library is a cache of typewritten copies of letters that Boyce had written to their close friend Mabel Dodge (later Luhan) dating from 1915-1916, during the time of Hapgood's affair with Collier. In one, Boyce writes that Lucy Collier had been growing too possessive of Hapgood and thus overstepped boundaries that the trio had agreed upon, or more likely that Boyce and Hapgood had agreed upon. Lucy was wrong, Boyce writes Dodge, to think Hapgood could ever be her "primary" relationship, for "both Hutch and I feel that we are free to love other people — but that nothing can break or even touch the deep vital passionate bond between *us*." Disdaining sexual possessiveness, Boyce ridicules Dodge's interpretation of Lucy "and me fighting over Hutch's body! How enchanting! But I really think you're wrong there. I don't care so much about the sexual act as you think — it's not of primary importance! If she wants that with him she can have it, naturally." Boyce accuses Dodge of taking a "primitive view of the situation — of what started out to be a very civilized arrangement!" Dodge may be right as to Lucy, "but Hutch isn't primitive and neither am I." In this extended discussion with an intimate friend, Boyce does not admit to any grievous problem in her marriage, but only in Lucy's possessiveness and Dodge's "primitive" assumptions and interference. Boyce even affirms that a triangle might work "if the third person were all right for it." Moreover, she refuses "any business of 'struggling' with another woman for him (as if he were a piece of goods at a bargain counter!)"[57] These letters show Boyce's principled opposition to sexual possessiveness — and certainty that an unbreakable bond links her to Hapgood.

Private letters are such useful sources of information because they capture a moment in time. They also capture a particular instance of self-presentation, whether conscious or not, fashioned for a designated recipient. My point is not that the letters Boyce wrote Dodge deserve priority over other correspondence. But they do provide one of numerous instances when Boyce's reaction to her husband's affairs shows none of the pain emphasized by Trimberger and other commentators. While some of Boyce's letters express anguish, others treat Hapgood's straying as a joke between them, an unfortunate but inconsequential personality quirk, or a daily order of domestic business like reading the paper or brushing one's teeth.

What makes the cache of letters to Dodge even more intriguing is a handwritten note that prefaces them from Boyce and Hapgood's second son Charles. The date (15 December 1944) places the note the month after Hapgood died and nearly three decades after Boyce and Dodge's correspondence. The intervening years had further tested the marriage, particularly when their eldest son (named Boyce Hapgood) died in 1918 from influenza and when they lost thousands after the stock market collapse in 1929. But the couple continued to collaborate, working together on a book that related their family history to US history in broad terms. (Covering the years 1648 to 1917, *The Story of an American Family* was published in 1953, after both of their deaths.) Through these and other conflicts, they also remained married. Charles Hapgood wrote of the correspondence with Mabel Dodge, "Dear Mother—This is marvelous stuff—a complete novel—and *what* a novel."[58] Whether Boyce ever had any thoughts of constructing a book out of the letters, her son's description of them as a literary opportunity indicates he understood his parents' methods of composition—and the terms of their relationship.

Constancy, Boyce's one-act play that opened the Provincetown Players, responds directly to Dodge's own love life and indirectly to Boyce's own. Known as a satire of Dodge's affair with Jack Reed, the play's emotional dynamics also reflect Boyce's own marriage.[59] In the play Rex returns to Moira, whom he had left for another woman. Moira (played by Boyce when the play opened) cheerfully welcomes him, displaying none of the histrionic jealousy that Rex expects—and which it soon becomes clear that he craves. Suggesting that men and women have different definitions of "constancy," the play positions Rex as silly in his alternately bitter and gloomy, but always self-pitying, complaint that Moira no longer loves him. Absurdly taking the position of jilted lover, Rex flings at Moira the idea that her poise demonstrates she never truly loved him. But Moira keeps reminding Rex of inconvenient facts: *he* left *her* for another woman; *he* wrote *her* that he was no longer in love.

Boyce projects onto the screen of Dodge and Reed's well-known affair her own experiences with a promiscuous and inconsistent mate. *Constancy* juxtaposes the man's egotistical sentimentality with the woman's clearheaded realism. The following exchange is typical:

> REX: Moira, I was always faithful to you, really. I always shall be. I would always come back.
> MOIRA: That is your idea of fidelity. You would always come back.

Boyce and Hapgood went over the same ground many times. In addition, Moira's explanation that she had felt "absorbed" in Rex echoes Boyce's description of her own fear of losing herself in Hapgood. Moira leaves, telling Rex she "can't endure love without fidelity" and that she refuses to be "head of a harem."[60] One might expect Boyce likewise eventually to leave Hapgood, but she never did. Among other things, he provided incomparable copy.

Years before meeting his future wife, Hapgood wrote a friend that the institution of marriage was "very imperfect"—in many respects even "outworn." He would prefer, he breezily suggested, living with a woman and thus removing "the idea of compulsion which is annoying to highly organized beings." But Hapgood hastened to distance himself from the enemies of marriage. Although "unideal, marriage may be now necessary and even permanently necessary." Rather than "cry out for its abolition," Hapgood urged, "we don't want to abolish marriage . . . , but to modify it."[61] That ardent desire to reform marriage, combined with an equally ardent commitment to preserving it, exemplifies what this book identifies as central to progressivism. Ironically the recipient of these musings, Arthur F. Bentley, was the dear friend with whom Boyce would fall in love in 1907 or 1908. Yet Boyce and Hapgood's marriage survived that and other romances. Both of them even remained close friends with Bentley.

Unlike many couples drawn to Progressive era marital reform (including the others examined in this book), choice never parted Boyce and Hapgood. Thirty years after their 1899 marriage, Boyce had her engagement ring re-set and wrote her husband, "now we are engaged!" He responded with delight: "Yes, we must be together hereafter. . . . So, at last, you feel engaged to me? Almost married? Perhaps you will put on the wedding ring soon?"[62] Boyce and Hapgood sustained the sense of courtship that progressives considered essential for a happy marriage. Their decision to remain together signals not a compromise, a failure of nerve or principle, but rather a principle of its own. While their dedication to remain together would make sense to Victorians and their apprehension of the mutability of relationships would appeal to bohemians, the blending of these sentiments exemplifies Progressive era marital reform. Boyce and Hapgood's union illustrates why Havelock Ellis considered "the art of marriage . . . one of the most difficult of the arts."[63]

Perhaps love-artists alone need apply.

Epilogue

At the end of *Antony and Cleopatra*, as the queen of the Nile prepares for suicide, she speaks to Antony, across the vale, calling him "husband." The word is startling in a play that consistently pits love and passion *against* marriage. Antony's first wife was a scheming, jealous shrew; the second a pawn he married solely because she was the sister of Caesar, whose mounting antagonism threatened Antony's position in the triumvirate. The singular Cleopatra has nothing in common with such standard-issue wives. The lover of countless men, she is wife to none. That is, until she decides, without benefit of any ceremony, that she and Antony are married. Defying the laws of Rome and Egypt, their love transcends all law. In this incomparable love story, not even death can part Antony and Cleopatra. They will remain defiantly together, in the best of all possible ways—on their own terms—in their "new heaven, and new earth."

While finishing revisions to this book, I saw an exceptional production of *Antony and Cleopatra* in the small fishing village of Stonington, Maine, which made it perfectly clear: *of course* Antony and Cleopatra are married. Not in the domestic sense of armchair comfort, nor because their families approve or it is politically expedient, but because they are equals and their commitment to each other unbounded.

Nothing, in literature or life, can approach the perfection of that love. But the Progressive era marital reformers I have examined sought to translate some of those soaring ideas into the far less exalted world that the rest of us inhabit. Unlike characters in plays who live forever, the marital theorists and the creative writers who reworked their ideas were, like us, creatures of a particular moment, embroiled in conflict, and imperfect. Accordingly they needed to allow for the fact that love can change over time, and that even the most passionate of lovers may one day choose to part. But still they believed, like Antony and Cleopatra, that no bourn could be set on marriage.

According to psychologist Robert J. Sternberg, the best way to understand love is by considering it as story. All of us learn about love through stories— from Shakespeare to fairy tales, from soap operas to art house films. We learn also by observing the trajectory of our parents' and other people's relationships, which play out like real-life narratives. Based on what we see, we develop a story of our own. Over the years, we may revise it, as we discover new stories and have romantic experiences, including with partners whose stories of love may diverge from, even demand changes to, our own. Alternatively, we may remain stuck in some story, which can undermine efforts to realize it in actuality. Sternberg breaks down stories of love into twenty-six patterns. For instance, the "fantasy" involves one who "expects to be saved by a knight in shining armor or to marry a princess and live happily ever after," while the "horror" story occurs when a lover believes "relationships become interesting when you terrorize or are terrorized by your partner." Sternberg does not offer his twenty-six stories as exhaustive, nor does he present some top-down theory according to which individual lovers have no choice but to follow some preauthorized script. Rather, he emphasizes a complex "interaction of our personal attributes with the environment—which we in part create—[that] leads to the development of stories about love that we then seek to fulfill."[1] What is important here is that people negotiate their way in love through stories learned, repeated, and changed.

What kind of story about love does progressive marital reform tell?

It shares elements with several of Sternberg's stories, particularly the "democratic" (in which "partners share power equally"); "gardening" (according to which relationships must be cultivated and tended); and also "travel" (according to which "love is a journey").

But a more complete version of the story that progressive marital reform tells would go like this: marriage, when freely chosen, enhances personal development while also providing inestimable companionship and sexual satisfaction. In order to be so valuable, marriage must be freely chosen— not once for all time, but day after day. Partners must be equal, and divorce available. (As Sternberg puts it, our story of love is most likely to last if we find a partner whose story resembles ours.[2]) Monogamy is conducive to the greatest intimacy, but again only if freely chosen. In five words: Until choice do us part.

Progressive era writers—both those I have called the marital theorists and the literary figures—rendered their stories of marriage literally into texts. In doing so they provided public accounts that readers could add to their own collection of possible stories of love. Indeed, the driving force of Progressive era marital reform, as I have argued, was the belief that the right kind of story about marriage could not only make couples happier but ultimately transform society. While the progressives could not achieve that ambitious goal any more than other generation has, they did help capture and render into language a new, and still prized, story about marriage.

Given the reach of this particular story, it is not surprising to find some of its core elements structuring ongoing debates over marriage, debates that are far from concluded. Accordingly, I would like to close by sketching what might be called a tale of two Progressive eras, then and now.[3]

Despite the open secret of "Boston marriages" between women, and also what Foucault calls the invention of homosexuality, legalized same-sex marriage was not on the table in the Progressive era. Nevertheless, that era's debate about marital reform provides invaluable historical context for the history of homosexual rights in general and, in particular, the controversy over gay marriage a hundred years later. To illustrate the first part of that claim, about the relevance of progressive marital reform to the history of gay rights, I draw upon brief histories of a few authors central to *Until Choice Do Us Part* and the books they wrote.

The publication history of *Love's Coming of Age* (1896) exemplifies the complex and overlapping histories of marriage reform and homosexuality. Edward Carpenter's bestseller originated in three pamphlets that appeared in 1894. The following year, Carpenter (himself a homosexual) published a fourth, *Homogenic Love, and Its Place in a Free Society*, a defense of homosexuality that would later become a chapter in his *Intermediate Sex* (1908). But in addition to marking the initial publication of *Homogenic Love*, 1895 was the year Oscar Wilde was arrested for sodomy. As a result, although *Love's Coming of Age* had been accepted for publication, the Wilde scandal scared Carpenter's publisher away from printing a book dealing with sex—even marital sex—and Carpenter had to find a new home for *Love's Coming of Age*. Further complicating matters, when he brought out the fifth edition (1906), Carpenter expanded it to include his later writing on homogenic love—thus queering a book once focused on heterosexual marriage. According to cultural critic Beverly Thiele, Carpenter felt that combining these treatises made perfect sense because he believed "as a homosexual[,] he was closer in spirit and practice to progressive female sexuality."[4] Such assumptions have not worn well, and recent commentators have emphasized what they see as Carpenter's regressive view of homosexuality rather than his often forward-looking view of marriage.

While the lives and writings of Havelock and Edith Ellis deserve a book of their own, here I can at least glance at how their marriage provides another chapter in the interlocking histories of marital reform and homosexuality. Mrs. Ellis was, in her husband's words, "more or less homosexual." What she promoted as "semi-detached marriage," in which spouses spend considerable time living apart, thus reflects a practical response to needs that could not be met in marriage. Her husband also had relationships with women outside the marriage. The Ellises' agreement on that score should be understood as in addition to—not instead of—their principled commitment to a marital ideal of autonomy balanced with intimacy. Despite her sexual orientation, Edith Ellis identified as a married woman, frequently publishing and giving lectures under the name "Mrs. Havelock Ellis." During her US lecture tour in 1914, she made headlines when, in addition to urging marital reform, she defended lesbianism. Moreover, the first volume of Havelock's *Studies in the Psychology of Sex*, the one which prompted the obscenity trial that George Bernard Shaw called "a masterpiece of police stupidity and magisterial ignorance," focused on homosexuality.[5] The case studies Ellis references in that book (*Sexual Inversion* [1896]) include his wife and his close friend Edward Carpenter. In these ways, book history and biography link marital reform with the history of homosexuality.

Given my focus on autobiographical constructions in *Until Choice Do Us Part*, it is significant also that the bulk of Havelock Ellis's memoir *My Life* (1939) centers on his marriage to Edith, who had died in 1916. Much as I traced with Hutchins Hapgood's and Neith Boyce's characterizations of infidelity in the previous chapter, *My Life* asserts that neither of the Ellises' liaisons ever "undermined" their unshakable intimacy. The memoir indicates, in fact, that the couple's unusual marital practice instantiated what they considered a more moral and humane marital theory. As Havelock Ellis puts it, in pursuing extramarital relationships, both of them "were struggling towards ideals which would be truer to the nature of each of us, and our deeper union, far from being destroyed, was being consolidated." Defining their marriage, in its very capaciousness, as superior to " the narrow self-absorption of domestic love," the sexologist claims it existed "beyond even the imagination of those conventional couples who proclaim the duty

FIGURE 12. Havelock and Edith Ellis believed their unusual marriage represented a new ideal.

and the beauty of mutual devotion." But such unimaginative couples, Ellis claims, actually "loathe the ideals of freedom and independence" so important to himself and Edith. (Such couples often, he says, also secretly loathe each other). His marriage with Edith, he writes, embodied their shared "ideals of freedom and independence, both in theory and in practice."[6]

A different sort of connection between homosexuality and marital reform, and one with enormous consequences, is that the rhetorical terms dominating debates on gay marriage at the start of the twentieth century were established in the Progressive era debate. Before pursuing that point, I will pause over two flashpoints in the current controversies: the Defense of Marriage Act and covenant marriage.

The 1996 Defense of Marriage Act (DOMA) was signed into law by President Clinton, who would infamously have to defend his own marriage once his affair with intern Monica Lewinsky broke in 1998. Prohibiting federal recognition of same-sex unions, DOMA defined marriage as possible only between one man and one woman. Thus while it is gratifying that my home state of Connecticut (among several others) recognized same-sex marriage, it is appalling that gay widowers still could not receive Social Security benefits available to surviving heterosexual spouses, take advantage of the larger estate tax exemption for married couples, nor receive other benefits routinely granted heterosexuals. Since President Obama took office, DOMA has faced serious challenges. First, in February 2011, Obama ordered the Justice Department to stop defending DOMA against lawsuits claiming it discriminates against gays (which, of course, it does). The message the president thereby delivered, that DOMA is unconstitutional, marks an unusual, but not unprecedented, instance of the federal government deciding not to enforce a federal statute. Second, along with Obama's reelection in 2012, Maine and Maryland joined seven other states that (in addition to the District of Columbia) recognized gay marriage. Third, in June 2013 the Supreme Court restored same-sex marriage in California (where it had been blocked by Proposition 8) and more importantly struck down central provisions of DOMA as unconstitutional. As of August 2013, thirteen states recognize gay marriage. Still, it is far too early to assume that "the straight state," as historian Margot Canaday calls it, will have to bend.[7]

While not overtly targeting gays, so-called "covenant marriage" derives from many of the same ideological assumptions as DOMA. As its name suggests, however, covenant marriage looks to Christianity rather than the federal government for its authority. Originating in Louisiana in 1997, covenant marriage has since spread to Arkansas and Arizona, and many other states have legislation pending to recognize it. Couples electing a covenant marriage renounce their right ever to divorce unless one partner commits adultery or another act from a short list of specific offenses seen as violating the scriptural ground of union.

In addition to springing from similar values and fears, DOMA and covenant marriage represent legal landmarks. DOMA marks one of very few instances in US history in which the federal government has trumped state jurisdiction over marriage and divorce. (Another was what Nancy Cott terms the "federal campaign" against Mormon polygamy.[8] Various acts passed in the 1860s through the 1880s criminalized polygamy, prohibiting citizenship on the basis of a type of marital practice. Only after the Church of Latter Day Saints renounced polygamy in 1890 [officially, at least] was Utah granted statehood.) Covenant marriage marks another important chapter in legal history. By repudiating no-fault divorce, which began in California in the 1970s and has since become accepted in every state, advocates of covenant marriage seek, in effect, to reverse legal history. And also, I am tempted to say, reverse progress.[9]

I turn now to how the Progressive era debate over marital reform set the terms for these and other recent debates. Two pairs of quotations will illustrate the continuation of the same distinctive rhetoric over one hundred years. The first set is framed in apocalyptic language; the second uses imagery of violent weather. Here is the first pair:

> Barring a miracle, the family as it has been known for more than five millennia will crumble, presaging the fall of western civilization itself. (2004)

> It is not unusual to hear those persons who dispense salutary advice and admonition . . . to express themselves forcibly upon the far-reaching pernicious effects which the community would suffer from such relatively slight changes as . . . an increased facility of divorce, adoption of female suffrage, . . . etc. Any one of these innovations would, we are told, "shake the social structure to its base," "reduce society to chaos," "subvert the foundations of morality," "make life intolerable," "confound the order of nature," etc. (1899)

The language in these passages is jarringly similar. In the first, a fundamentalist preacher in 2004 laments proposals for legalizing gay marriage. The catastrophic rhetoric is so distinctive a feature of recent diatribes against gay marriage that it may come as a surprise that the second passage dates from 1899. In it, Thorstein Veblen parodies conservative fears that more liberal divorce provisions would destroy society. Veblen underscores the madness of that idea by describing the free divorce campaign as marking only a "relatively slight" social change. While the fundamentalist is deadly serious and Veblen satirically droll, both use apocalyptic language to represent what Veblen aptly calls "the revulsion felt by good people at any proposed departure from the accepted methods of life."[10] For ill or for good, reforming marriage would supposedly usher in the end of the world as we know it.

A second set of parallel passages uses imagery of violent weather worthy of *King Lear* to characterize a social trend as perilous. The landmark 1908–1909 study published by the Department of Commerce and Labor, *Marriage and Divorce 1867–1906*, supplements its piles of statistics with some strategic illustrations. In one of them, maps of the United States render the increasing number of divorces by region in 1870, 1880, 1890, and 1900 as ominous, dark patches. Captions editorialize that "a dark cloud [is] gradually gathering over the country" (see illustration 3, page 28). In addition to suggesting there is no safe port in the storm, the report locates a quantifiable basis for American exceptionalism—although of an unsavory sort—because the statistics document the divorce rate in the United States exceeding that of any country in Europe.[11]

Both the rhetoric of the "dark cloud" and assumption of American exceptionalism inform recent assaults on gay marriage. "Gathering Storm," a 2009 television ad sponsored by a conservative action group, the National Organization for Marriage (NOM), features a group of conspicuously multiethnic citizens in front of a portentously dark sky. "There's a storm coming," one warns; "The clouds are dark, and the winds are strong," frets another. That menacing storm, of course, is gay marriage. The NOM supporters then denounce gay marriage as a radical effort to impose wickedness on innocent heterosexuals. The citizen-speakers insist that same-sex marriage threatens freedom, religion, parenting—even, somehow, jobs for heterosexuals. NOM's fiendishly inspired proposal for weathering the storm appropriates the LGBTQ movement's most recognizable symbol: the rainbow. The ad concludes with sunny skies greeting the multicultural "rainbow coalition" of straight citizens defending traditional marriage—along with liberty.[12]

A related conservative organization, the National Marriage Project (NMP) reinterprets the American exceptionalism that had so alarmed compilers of the 1908–1909 government report. The NMP finds US attitudes toward marriage and divorce still exceptional—but in a manner warranting self-congratulation rather than the concern voiced in the earlier study. According to the NMP's 2007 annual report, US citizens fall into three categories based on the degree to which they "embrace[] secular individualism."

Thirty-one percent are "Orthodox" and 17 percent "Progressives," leaving a buffer of 46 percent "Independents." Unlike in the 1908–1909 government study, the NMP's report a century later takes solace in international comparisons: "The Orthodox category [in the United States] is far larger than one finds in Western Europe and the other Anglo nations, and the Progressive category (i.e., secular individualist) is considerably smaller, and therein lies the major basis for American family exceptionalism."[13] In other words, because the United States has more "Orthodox" citizens with conservative attitudes toward marriage, the nation is implicitly (but unquestionably) morally superior to "Western Europe and other Anglo nations." (The superiority to non-Western, non-Anglo nations apparently needs no demonstration.) And so the NMP maintains the conclusion of the 1908–1909 government report—that US marital patterns are exceptional—but rewrites what appeared a century earlier as the decline of a nation into its triumph. In doing so, they also explicitly align the legacy of progressivism with anti-family trends, casting both from the authentically "American" category.

What is it about the mere prospect of changing marital norms that can elicit apocalyptic reactions and fervent assertions of America first? The same factors that render marriage an institution critical to maintaining the status quo also make marriage useful for challenging it. As the fundamentalist preacher I just quoted and Thorstein Veblen both understood, marriage is a microcosm of society, or more precisely of white middle class society. Marriage is, to quote Havelock Ellis one final time, the "miniature of life."[14] Attempts to revise marital norms, then, spark strong reactions precisely because they indicate that even greater social changes could follow. And depending on one's vantage point, such change might signify—as it did to the evangelical preacher, the conservatives lampooned by Veblen, defenders of DOMA, or members of the National Organization for Marriage and National Marriage Project—that the collapse of civilization is imminent. Or marital reform might mean, as it did to the Progressive era reformers, an ascent to more egalitarian relationships that would bring about, in turn, higher levels of consciousness.

Let us hope the latter ideal prevails.

Notes

PREFACE

1. James P. Lichtenberger, *Divorce, A Social Interpretation* (New York: McGraw-Hill, 1931), 249.

2. Charlotte Perkins Gilman quoted in Charles Walter Stetson, *Endure: The Diaries of Charles Walter Stetson*, ed. Mary Armfield Hill (Philadelphia: Temple University Press, 1985), 63; Mitchell quoted in Charlotte Perkins Gilman, *The Living of Charlotte Perkins Gilman* (Madison: University of Wisconsin Press, 1963), 96. Biographical information drawn from these sources and also Cynthia J. Davis, *Charlotte Perkins Gilman: A Biography* (Stanford: Stanford University Press, 2010) and Ann J. Lane, *To Herland and Beyond: The Life and Work of Charlotte Perkins Gilman* (New York: Pantheon, 1990).

3. Gilman, (*Living* 87–88).

4. Charlotte Perkins Gilman, *Women and Economics: A Study of the Relation between Women and Men* (New York: Prometheus Books, 1994), 220. Subsequent references to this text will be made parenthetically.

5. Quotation about Lucy Clews in Peter H. Hare, *A Woman's Quest for Science: Portrait of Anthropologist Elsie Clews Parsons* (Buffalo, NY: Prometheus, 1985), 27; Thorstein Veblen, *The Theory of the Leisure Class* (New York: Modern Library, 1931), 68; Elsie Clews Parsons, *The Old-Fashioned Woman: Primitive Fancies about the Sex* (New York: G.P. Putnam's Sons, 1913), 49. Biographical information drawn from Hare and Desley Deacon, *Elsie Clews Parsons, Inventing Modern Life* (Chicago: University of Chicago Press, 1997).

6. Parsons quoted in Deacon, *Elsie Clews Parsons*, 55; Deacon, *Elsie Clews Parsons*, 49; Elsie Clews Parsons, *The Family* (New York: G.P. Putnam's Sons, 1906), 349.

7. Herbert Parsons and Elsie Clews Parsons quoted in Deacon, *Elsie Clews Parsons*, 88, 89, 135; Parsons quoted in Hare, *A Woman's Quest*, 61.

8. Edith Wharton quoted in Hermione Lee, *Edith Wharton* (New York: Vintage Books, 2007), 389; Edith Wharton's Love Diary (which she actually called "The Life Apart" [*L'âme close*]) published in Kenneth M. Price and Phyllis McBride, "'The Life Apart': Text and Contexts of Edith Wharton's Love Diary," *American Literature* 66:4 (December 1994), 663–88.

Biographical information derived from these sources as well as R.W.B. Lewis, *Edith Wharton: A Biography* (New York: Harper and Row, 1975); Cynthia Griffin Wolff, *A Feast of Words: The Triumph of Edith Wharton* (New York: Oxford University Press, 1977); Gloria C. Erlich, *The Sexual*

Education of Edith Wharton (Berkeley: University of California Press, 1992); and Shari Benstock, *No Gifts from Chance: A Biography of Edith Wharton* (New York: Charles Scribner's Sons, 1994).

In *Edith Wharton's Brave New Politics* (Madison: University of Wisconsin Press, 1994), Dale M. Bauer provides a fine analysis of Wharton's reaction to changing ideas about marriage in her late fiction. See also Laura K. Johnson, "Edith Wharton and the Fiction of Marital Unity," *Modern Fiction Studies* 47:4 (2001), 947–76.

9. For instance, Wharton wrote in her Love Diary, ""I knew then, dearest dear, all that I had never known before—the interfusion of spirit & sense, the double nearness, the . . . mingled communion of touch & thought" (Price and McBride, 679).

10. Henry James quoted in Lewis, *Edith Wharton*, 52; Lewis, *Edith Wharton*, 53; Lucretia Jones quoted in Lewis, *Edith Wharton* 53; Edith Wharton quoted in Lewis, *Edith Wharton*, 54.

11. Lewis, *Edith Wharton*, 50; Edith Wharton, *The House of Mirth* (New York: Signet Classic, 1964), 8; Benstock, *No Gifts*, 252; Teddy Wharton's doctor quoted in Lee, *Edith Wharton*; Edith Wharton's friend (and co-author Ogden Codman) quoted in Lee, *Edith Wharton*, 386; Lee, *Edith Wharton*, 363.

12. Edith Wharton, *The Custom of the Country* (New York: Collier Books, 1941), 182–84; Ehrlich, *Sexual Education*, xii.

13. Havelock Ellis, *Eonism and Other Supplementary Studies*, Volume Two, Part 2, of *Studies in the Psychology of Sex* (New York: Random House, 1936), 523; Charlotte Perkins Gilman, *The Home: Its Work and Influence* (Urbana: University of Illinois Press, 1972), 312, 3, 4, 30, 101. Subsequent references to both of these texts will be made parenthetically.

14. For demonstrating that there is never any single or authoritative view of marriage, I am indebted to Phyllis Rose's brilliant *Parallel Lives: Five Victorian Marriages* (New York: Vintage, 1984).

15. Jean Strouse's concept of the many "semi-obscure" historical subjects, in between famous and unknown, is informative. Most in the semi-obscure category are, Strouse notes, women (Jean Strouse, "Semiprivate Lives" in *Studies in Biography*, ed. Daniel Aaron [Cambridge: Harvard University Press, 1978]), 114.

INTRODUCTION

1. "Sinclair Sorry He Wed," *San Francisco Examiner*, January 30, 1909, 1–2.

2. Mitchell Kennerly, quoted in Upton Sinclair, *The Brass Check*, eds. Robert W. McChesney and Ben Scott (Urbana: University of Illinois Press, 2003), 107.

3. According to Nancy F. Cott, English use of the term *feminism* was an import from the French *féminisme*, first used by suffragist Hubertine Auclert in the 1880s. Cott speculates that the first American use may have been in 1906 (Nancy F. Cott, *The Grounding of Modern Feminism* [New Haven: Yale University Press, 1987], 14). In Chapter 5 I discuss Neith Boyce and Hutchins Hapgood's use of the French term.

4. Ellen Fitzpatrick, *Endless Crusade: Women Social Scientists and Progressive Reform* (New York: Oxford University Press, 1990), 141, her emphasis.

5. Elsie Clews Parsons, "Penalizing Marriage and Child-Bearing," *Independent* 60 (January 18, 1906), 146–47. As did so many others, Parsons lost faith in progress around the time of America's entrance into World War I. See, for instance, "A Progressive God," *New Review* 4 (June 1917), 181–82.

6. Characterization of *Independent* drawn from Frank Luther Mott, *A History of American Magazines, 1741–1930*. Volume Two (Cambridge, MA: Harvard University Press, 1957), 368–77 (quotation at 377), accessed September 1, 2012, http://quod.lib.umich.edu .ezproxy.lib.uconn.edu/cgi/t/text/textidx?c=acls;cc=acls;q1=history%200f%20american%20 magazines;q2=ACLS%20Humanities%20E-Book;op2=and;rgn=full%20text;rgn1=full%20 text;rgn2=series;view=toc;idno=heb00678.0002.001; Parsons, "Penalizing," 146.

7. Barbara Sicherman, *Well-Read Lives: How Books Inspired a Generation of American Women* (Chapel Hill: University of North Carolina Press, 2010), quotations at 3; Hochman, "Readers," 601, 602.

8. Gordon Hutner, *What America Read: Taste, Class, and the Novel, 1920-1960* (Chapel Hill: University of North Carolina Press, 2009), 19; Sicherman, *Well-Read*, 5; Nancy Glazener, "The Novel in Postbellum Print Culture, *Cambridge History of the American Novel*, eds. Leonard Cassuto, Clare Virginia Eby, and Benjamin Reiss (Cambridge: Cambridge University Press, 2011), 349; Janice A. Radway, *Reading the Romance: Women, Patriarchy, and Popular Literature* (Chapel Hill: University of North Carolina Press, 1984); Barbara Hochman, *Getting at the Author: Reimagining Books and Reading in the Age of American Realism* (Amherst: University of Massachusetts Press, 2001), 6.

9. Hutner, *What America*, 4, 2. According to Barbara Hochman, by the end of the nineteenth century, scenes of reading had become "a staple in fiction" ("Readers and Reading Groups," *Cambridge History of the American Novel*, eds. Leonard Cassuto, Clare Virginia Eby, and Benjamin Reiss [Cambridge: Cambridge University Press, 2011], 607). My understanding of how changes in print culture impacted Progressive era writers has been shaped also by Richard Brodhead, "Literature and Culture," *Columbia Literary History of the United States*, eds. Emory Elliott, Martha Banta, Terence Martin, David Minter, Marjorie Perloff, and Daniel B. Shea (New York: Columbia University Press, 1988), 467-81; Richard Brodhead, *Cultures of Letters: Scenes of Reading and Writing in Nineteenth-Century America* (Chicago: University of Chicago Press, 1993) ; Charles Johanningsmeier, *Fiction and the American Literary Marketplace: The Role of Newspaper Syndicates, 1860-1900* (Cambridge: Cambridge University Press, 1997); Nancy Glazener, *Reading for Realism: The History of a U.S. Literary Institution, 1850-1910* (Durham: Duke University Press, 1997).

10. Hochman discusses the increasing interest in authors' private lives in *Getting at the Author*, 24.

11. Paul De Man, "Autobiography as De-facement," *Modern Language Notes*, 94 (December 1979), 920-21; Christopher Lasch, *The New Radicalism in America (1889-1963): The Intellectual as a Social Type* (New York: Knopf, 1965), 271.

12. Robert M. Crunden, *Ministers of Reform: The Progressives' Achievement in American Civilization, 1889-1920* (New York: Basic, 1982), ix; Christopher P. Wilson, *The Labor of Words: Literary Professionalism in the Progressive Era* (Athens: University of Georgia Press, 1985). Wilson also notes that literary naturalists such as Sinclair "were seminal 'makers' and disseminators" of progressive tenets (xv).

More recently, Michael Lundblad uses progressivism to argue that the idea of the "jungle" was used to "naturaliz[e] . . . heterosexuality" (see "Epistemology of the Jungle: Progressive-Era Sexuality and the Nature of the Beast," *American Literature* 81:4 [December 2009], 748).

13. Recent studies of the relationship between African American and white attitudes toward marriage in the Progressive era include Christina Simmons, *Making Marriage Modern: Women's Sexuality from the Progressive Era to World War II* (Oxford: Oxford University Press, 2009) and Nina Miller, *Making Love Modern: The Intimate Public Worlds of New York's Literary Women* (Oxford: Oxford University Press, 1999). Frances Smith Foster's anthology *Love and Marriage in Early African America* (Hanover: University Press of New England, 2008) draws together source documents such as sermons and songs illuminating African American marriage, while foundational analyses of African American women's writings about marriage can be found in Ann du Cille, *The Coupling Convention: Sex, Text, and tradition in Black Women's Fiction* (Oxford: Oxford University Press, 1993); Claudia Tate, *Domestic Allegories of Political Desire: The Black Heroine's Text at the Turn of the Century* (Oxford: Oxford University Press, 1992); and Tess Chakkalakal, *Novel Bondage: Slavery, Marriage, and Freedom in Nineteenth-Century America* (Urbana: University of Illinois Press, 2011).

In 1909, W.E.B. Du Bois edited *The Negro American Family* (reprint, New York: Negro Universities Press, 1969). For more recent historical studies, see Wilman A. Dunaway, *The*

African American Family in Slavery and Emancipation (Cambridge: Cambridge University Press, 2003); Herbert George Gutman, *The Black Family in Slavery and Freedom, 1750–1925* (New York: Pantheon, 1976); Jacqueline Jones, *Labor of Love, Labor of Sorrow: Black Women, Work, and the Family, from Slavery to the Present* (New York: Basic Books, 1985). See also Charlotte J. Rich, *Transcending the New Woman: Multiethnic Narratives in the Progressive Era* (Columbia: University of Missouri Press, 2008). Regarding the establishment of white ideals as norms, see Julian B. Carter, *The Heart of Whiteness: Normal Sexuality and Race in America, 1880–1940* (Durham: Duke University Press, 2007).

Many of the stories by Sui Sin Far, pen name of Edith Maude Eaton and one of the first US writers of Asian descent, focus on marriage, indicating that the Progressive era conversation extended well beyond the familiar black-white color line (see for instance *Mrs. Spring Fragrance*, ed. Hsuan L. Hsu [Buffalo, NY: Broadview, 2011]); insightful treatments of the marriage theme can be found in Jane Hwang Degenhardt, "Situating the Essential Alien: Sui Sin Far's Depiction of Chinese-White Marriage and the Exclusionary Logic of Citizenship, *Modern Fiction Studies* 54:4 (Winter 2008), 654–88; and Yu-Fang Cho, "Domesticating the Aliens Within: Sentimental Benevolence in Late-Nineteenth-Century California Magazines," *American Quarterly* 61:1 (March 2009), 113–36.

14. Stephanie Coontz, *The Social Origins of Private Life: A History of American Families 1600–1900* (New York: Verso, 1988), 252; Eli Zaretsky, *Capitalism, the Family, and Personal Life* (New York: Harper Colophon Books, 1976), 73; Michael Grossberg, *Governing the Hearth: Law and Family in Nineteenth-Century America* (Chapel Hill: University of North Carolina Press, 1985); Nancy F. Cott, *Public Vows: A History of Marriage and the Nation* (Cambridge: Harvard University Press, 2000); Norma Basch, *Framing American Divorce from the Revolutionary Generation to the Victorians* (Berkeley: University of California Press, 1999); Carter, *The Heart of Whiteness*.

See also Lawrence Stone, *The Family, Sex and Marriage in England 1500–1800* (Abridged Edition, New York: Harper & Row, 1977), arguing that the "affective individualism" characterizing the family beginning with the late seventeenth century causes the "further walling-off of the nuclear family" (quotation at 149). See also Donna J. Zenor, "Untying the Knot: The Course and Patterns of Divorce Reform," *Cornell Law Review* 57 (1972), 649–67; Stephanie Coontz, *The Way We Never Were: American Families and the Nostalgia Trap* (New York: Basic Books, 2000).

For a literary iteration of the marriage-and-nation theme, see William R. Handley, *Marriage, Violence, and the Nation in the American Literary West* (Cambridge: Cambridge University Press, 2002). In *The Anarchy of Empire in the Making of U.S. Culture* (Cambridge: Harvard University Press, 2002), particularly in discussing the 1890s vogue for historical romances, Amy Kaplan links nation—which she examines through the lens of empire-building—with marriage.

15. Havelock Ellis, *Eonism and Other Supplementary Studies*. Volume Two, Part 2, of *Studies in the Psychology of Sex* (New York: Random House, 1936), 523; Ellen Key, *Love and Marriage*, trans. Arthur G. Chater (New York: G.P. Putnam's Sons, 1911), 3.

16. Virginia Woolf, *The Captain's Death Bed and Other Essays*, quoted in Jennifer Haytock, *Edith Wharton and the Conversations of Literary Modernism* (New York: Palgrave Macmillan , 2008), 14.

17. Michael McGerr, *Fierce Discontent: The Rise and Fall of the Progressive Movement in America, 1870–1920* (New York: Free Press, 2003), xiv ff.

June Howard's *Publishing the Family* (Durham and London: Duke University Press, 2001) provides an eloquent demonstration of how historical change is not linear.

For discussion of the Greenwich Village bohemians as transforming—or retaining—middle-class sexual mores, see Ann Douglas, *Terrible Honesty: Mongrel Manhattan in the 1920s* (New York: Farrar, Straus, and Giroux, 1995); John D'Emilio and Estelle B. Freedman, *Intimate Matters: A History of Sexuality in America* (New York: Harper and Row, 1988), Chapter 10; Joanna

Levin, *Bohemia in America, 1858–1920* (Stanford: Stanford University Press, 2010); Kenneth Lynn, "The Rebels of Greenwich Village," *Perspectives in American History* 8 (1974), 335–77; Miller, *Making Love Modern*; Gerald L. Marriner, "A Victorian in the Modern World: The 'Liberated' Male's Adjustment to the New Woman and the New Morality," *South Atlantic Quarterly* 76 (1977), 190–203; Christina Simmons, *Making Marriage Modern: Women's Sexuality from the Progressive Era to World War II* (Oxford: Oxford University Press, 2009); Christina Simmons, "Women's Power in Sex Radical Challenges to Marriage in the Early-Twentieth-Century United States," *Feminist Studies* 29:1 (Spring 2003), 169–98; Christine Stansell, *American Moderns: Bohemian New York and the Creation of a New Century* (New York: Henry Holt, 2000); Ellen Kay Trimberger, "Feminism, Men, and Modern Love: Greenwich Village, 1900–1925," in *Powers of Desire: The Politics of Sexuality* (New York: Monthly Review Press, 1983), 131–52; and Ross Wetzsteon, *Republic of Dreams: Greenwich Village and the American Bohemia, 1910–1920* (New York: Simon & Schuster, 2002). For an illuminating contemporary account, see Floyd Dell's *Love in Greenwich Village* (1926; rpt., Freeport, New York: Books for Libraries, 1970). Dell largely repudiates bohemian love ideals in *Love in the Machine Age* (New York: Farrar and Rinehart, 1930).

In *Him/Her/Self: Sex Roles in Modern America* (New York: Harcourt Brace Jovanovich, 1975), 131, Peter G. Filene voices a now-standard interpretation when he says the "1920s marked the beginning of modernity" in terms of sexuality. Filene's path-breaking study was reissued in 1998 as *Him/Her/Self: Gender Identities in Modern America*. See also Paula S. Fass, *The Damned and the Beautiful: American Youth in the 1920's* (Oxford: Oxford University Press, 1977).

18. While I use *companionate marriage* in its more restricted sense, historians use the term in various ways. In the more restricted sense, companionate marriage emerged in the 1920s. In the words of Rebecca L. Davis, the ideal shifted "from a patriarchal, procreative institution into a relationship premised on equal sexual desires and mutual emotional fulfillment" ("'Not Marriage at All, but Simple Harlotry': The Companionate Marriage Controversy," *Journal of American History* 94:4 [March 2008], 1137–63). This iteration of companionate marriage is associated particularly with Ben B. Lindsey and Wainwright Evans's *The Revolt of Modern Youth* (New York: Boni and Liveright, 1925) and *The Companionate Marriage* (New York: Boni and Liveright, 1927). According to the latter, "*Companionate Marriage is legal marriage, with legalized Birth Control, and with the right to divorce by mutual consent for childless couples, usually without payment of alimony*" (as quoted in Lichtenberger, *Divorce*, 438). For recent discussions, see Simmons, *Making Marriage Modern*, especially Chapters 3 and 4; David R. Shumway, "Something Old, Something New: Romance and Marital Advice in the 1920s"; *An Emotional History of the United States*, eds. Peter N. Stearns and Jan Lewis (New York: New York University Press, 1998), 305–18.

However, historians also use *companionate marriage* to describe a much broader phenomenon. Thus in a comparative study that takes a long view, Roderick Phillips describes the responsibility for selecting a mate shifting to the individual, along with an increasing emphasis on emotional compatibility (*Putting Asunder: A History of Divorce in Western Society* [Cambridge: Cambridge University Press, 1988], 355). Stephanie Coontz discerns a similarly broad trend, as identified in her subtitle, *Marriage, A History: From Obedience to Marriage, or How Love Conquered Marriage* (New York: Viking, 2005). Stone (*Family*, Chapters 7–8) and Degler (*At Odds*) place the transition "from marriages based primarily on interest [e.g., wealth, rank] to those based on affection" in the eighteenth century (as characterized by Phillips, *Putting* 355). For other discussions of the eighteenth-century origins of this shift, see Linda Kerber, *Women of the Republic: Intellect and Ideology in Revolutionary America* (Chapel Hill: University of North Carolina Press, 1980), 175–77; Jay Fliegelman, *Prodigals and Pilgrims: The American Revolution against Patriarchal Authority, 1750–1800* (Cambridge: Cambridge University Press, 1982), Chapter 5; Mary Beth Norton, *Liberty's Daughters: The Revolutionary Experience of American Women, 1750–1800* (Boston: Little, Brown, 1980). Other historians, such as Glenda Riley (*Divorce: An American*

Tradition [Oxford: Oxford University Press, 1991], 55, 57) and Michael Grossberg (*Governing*), see the Victorians as promulgating companionate marriage.

Not everyone applauds this trend. Christina Simmons finds the companionate ideal having "achieved cultural hegemony by the 1930s" and perpetuating fears of homosexuality ("Companionate Marriage and the Lesbian Threat" [*Frontiers* IV:3 (Fall 1979), 54, while Cott argues that the new ideal made marriage even more obligatory for women, thus contributing to a tendency to pathologize women who did not marry (*Grounding* 156, 194). John C. Spurlock examines how the heightened expectations women had for "modern marriage" (with particular reference to the 1920s) led to pervasive unhappiness ("The Problem of Modern Married Love for Middle-Class Women," *An Emotional History of the United States*, eds. Peter N. Stearns and Jan Lewis [New York: New York University Press, 1998], 319-21).

For discussion of the "companionate family," see Steven Mintz and Susan Kellogg, *Domestic Revolutions: A Social History of American Family Life* (New York: The Free Press, 1988), Ch. 6.

19. Raymond Williams, *Marxism and Literature* (Oxford: Oxford University Press, 1977), 131-33.

20. Ibid., 133.

21. D'Emilio and Freedman, *Intimate Matters*.

Focusing on the social hygiene movement, John C. Burnham's "The Progressive Era Revolution in American Attitudes toward Sex" (*Journal of American History* 59:4 [March 1973] 885-908, quotation at 907) provides a narrower but similar view of the period's "fundamentally conservative" tendencies.

22. Ian Watt, *The Rise of the Novel: Studies in Defoe, Richardson and Fielding* (Berkeley: University California Press, 1957), particularly Chapter 5; Nancy Armstrong, *Desire and Domestic Fiction: A Political History of the Novel* (Oxford: Oxford University Press, 1987); Tony Tanner, *Adultery in the Novel: Contract and Transgression* (Baltimore: Johns Hopkins University Press, 1979), quotation at 15; Joseph Allen Boone, *Tradition Counter Tradition: Love and the Form of Fiction* (Chicago: University of Chicago Press, 1987), quotation at 10; David R. Shumway, *Modern Love: Romance, Intimacy, and the Marriage Crisis* (New York: New York University Press, 2003); D. A. Miller, *Narrative and Its Discontents: Problems of Closure in the Traditional Novel* (Princeton: Princeton University Press, 1981), ix.

Other influential accounts of marriage and the novel include Evelyn J. Hinz, "Hierogamy Versus Wedlock: Types of Marriage Plots and Their Relationship to Genres of Prose Fiction," *PMLA* 91:5 (October 1976), 900-13; Alfred Habegger, *Gender, Fantasy, and Realism in American Literature* (New York: Columbia University Press, 1982); Rachel Blau Du Plessis, *Writing beyond the Ending: Narrative Strategies of Twentieth-Century Women Writers* (Bloomington: Indiana University Press, 1985).

More specialized studies relevant to my argument include Kimberly A. Freeman, *Love American Style: Divorce and the American Novel* (New York: Routledge, 2003); Allen F. Stein, *After the Vows Were Spoken: Marriage in American Literary Realism* (Columbus: Ohio State University Press, 1984); James Harwood Barnett, *Divorce and the American Divorce Novel, 1858-1937: A Study in Literary Reflections of Social Influences* (New York, Russell & Russell, 1939); Brook Thomas, *American Literary Realism and the Failed Promise of Contract* (Berkeley: University of California Press, 1997); Debra Ann MacComb, *Tales of Liberation, Strategies of Containment: Divorce and the Representation of Womanhood in American Fiction, 1880-1920* (New York: Garland, 2000); and Margit Stange, *Personal Property: Wives, White Slavery, and the Market in Women* (Baltimore: Johns Hopkins University Press, 1998). As I was completing revisions of this book, Mark W. Van Wienen's *American Socialist Triptych: The Literary-Political Work of Charlotte Perkins Gilman, Upton Sinclair, and W.E.B. Du Bois* (Ann Arbor: University of Michigan Press, 2011) appeared, one chapter of which argues that the efforts of Gilman, Sinclair, Du Bois, and Hamlin Garland failed to put into practice radical forms of partnering in line with their socialist ideals. Van Wienen's most important contribution lies in the complexity and variation that he traces in socialism at the turn of the century.

23. Amy Kaplan, *The Social Construction of American Realism* (Chicago: University of Chicago Press, 1988); Walter Benn Michaels, *The Gold Standard and the Logic of Naturalism* (Berkeley: University of California Press, 1987); Hutner, *What America Read*, 6, 63. A recent iteration of this theme focusing specifically on the question of reform can be found in William M. Morgan, *Questionable Charity: Gender, Humanitarianism, and Complicity in U.S. Literary Realism* (Durham, NH: University of New Hampshire Press, 2004), 10, arguing that "realism's humanitarian impulse is complicit from beginning to end with the economic project of U.S. capitalism."

24. Amanda Claybaugh, *The Novel of Purpose: Literature and Social Reform in the Anglo-American World* (Ithaca: Cornell University Press, 2007), 2; Donna M. Campbell, *Resisting Regionalism: Gender and Naturalism in American Fiction, 1885–1915* (Athens: Ohio University Press, 1997); Jennifer L. Fleissner, *Women, Compulsion, Modernity: The Moment of American Naturalism* (Chicago: University of Chicago Press, 2004); Tom Lutz, *Cosmopolitan Vistas: American Regionalism and Literary Value* (Ithaca: Cornell University Press, 2004).

25. Boone, *Tradition*, 9.

26. Phyllis Rose, *Parallel Lives: Five Victorian Marriages* (New York: Vintage, 1984), 7; Boone, *Tradition*, 114.

The secondary literature on autobiography is voluminous. In addition to works cited elsewhere, I have found the following especially useful: Timothy Dow Adams, *Telling Lies in Modern American Autobiography* (Chapel Hill: University of North Carolina Press, 1990); Paul John Eakin, ed., *American Autobiography: Retrospect and Prospect* (Madison: University of Wisconsin Press, 1991); James Olney, ed., *Autobiography: Essays Theoretical and Critical* (Princeton: Princeton University Press 1980); James O'Rourke, *Sex, Lies, and Autobiography: The Ethics of Confession* (Charlottesville: University of Virginia Press, 2006); Roy Pascal, *Design and Truth in Autobiography* (Cambridge: Harvard University Press, 1966); Burton Pike, "Time in Autobiography," *Comparative Literature* 28:4 (Autumn 1976), 326–42; William C. Spengemann and L.R. Lundquist, "Autobiography and the American Myth," *American Quarterly* 17:3 (Autumn 1965), 501–19; and Albert E. Stone, *Autobiographical Occasions and Original Acts: Versions of American Identity from Henry Adams to Nate Shaw* (Philadelphia: University of Pennsylvania Press, 1982).

27. Mary S. Hartman, *The Household and the Making of History: A Subversive View of the Western Past* (Cambridge: Cambridge University Press, 2004), quotation at 4; Kelly Hager, *Dickens and the Rise of Divorce* (Burlington, VT: Ashgate, 2010).

In addition, Basch's *Framing American Divorce* demonstrates how the American Revolution helped legitimate divorce and in doing so liberalized attitudes toward marriage. In *The Wedding Complex* (Durham, NC: Duke University Press, 2002), xv, Elizabeth Freeman charts another sort of alternative history, showing how depictions of "excessive and/or failed weddings" in literature and film work against the stable norms associated with marriage.

28. Coontz, *Marriage, A History*, Part Three.

29. Antonio R. Damasio, *Descartes' Error: Emotion, Reason, and the Human Brain* (New York: Quill, 1994).

I draw my account of emotion from Martha C. Nussbaum, *Upheavals of Thought: The Intelligence of Emotions* (Cambridge: Cambridge University Press, 2001); Jon Elster, *Alchemies of the Mind: Rationality and the Emotions* (Cambridge: Cambridge University Press, 1999); Helena Wulff, *The Emotions: A Cultural Reader* (New York: Berg, 2007); Robert J. Sternberg and Karin Weis, eds., *The New Psychology of Love* (New Haven: Yale University Press, 2006); Carol Z. Stearns and Peter N. Stearns, eds. *Emotion and Social Change: Toward a New Psychohistory* (London: Holmes & Meier, 1988); Keith Oatley, Dacher Keltner, and Jennifer M. Jenkins, *Understanding Emotions*, 2nd edition (New York: Blackwell, 2006); Patrick Colm Hogan, *What Literature*

Teaches Us About Emotions (Cambridge: Cambridge University Press, 2011); and particularly Keith Oatley, *Best Laid Schemes: The Psychology of Emotions* (Cambridge: Cambridge University Press, 1992).

Literary scholars have also extensively explored emotion. Taking a cue from Harriet Beecher Stowe's famous conclusion to *Uncle Tom's Cabin* that the reader should "feel right," literary scholarship on emotion first examined sentimentalism. Two literary studies are particularly relevant to my interests. In *Wounded Hearts: Masculinity, Law, and Literature in American Culture* (Chapel Hill: University of North Carolina Press, 2005), Jennifer Travis examines how particular types of emotion get recoded as male in the late nineteenth and early twentieth centuries, and I will return to her insights in my chapter on the Sinclairs. In *Affecting Fictions: Mind, Body, and Emotion in American Literary Realism* (Cambridge: Harvard University Press, 2007), Jennifer F. Thrailkill boldly redefines realism. Loosening the association of realism and positivism, Thrailkill argues that in the late nineteenth century, emotion and science were not seen as dichotomous, making a case for what she calls "emotive realism" (21).

30. Oatley, *Best Laid*, 412; Elster, *Alchemies*, 286; Oatley, Keltner, and Jenkins, *Understanding*, 260.

31. Oatley, Keltner, and Jenkins, *Understanding*, 401; Hogan, *What Literature*, 287. See also Nussbaum, *Upheavals*; Oatley, *Best-Laid*; Elster, *Alchemies*. For a rigorous questioning of whether empathy generated by reading actually translates into action in the real world, see Suzanne Keen, *Empathy and the Novel* (Oxford: Oxford University Press, 2007). Keen also emphasizes that while empathy has an emotional component, it is also cognitive, and that "when texts invite readers to feel, . . . They also stimulate readers' thinking" (28). Emotion researchers often distinguish between empathy (which may encourage identification across racial, gendered, or other lines of difference) and sympathy (which may reinforce those differences).

32. Nussbaum, *Upheavals*; Oatley, *Best-Laid*.

Similarly, "structures of feeling," according to Raymond Williams, are decidedly social, manifesting particularly in new ways of interacting, communicating, making oneself known to others. In particular, Williams says, they involve "affective elements of consciousness and relationships: not feeling against thought, but thought as felt and feeling as thought" (*Marxism*, 132).

33. Oatley, *Best-Laid*, 131.

34. In *The Refuge of Affections: Family and American Reform Politics, 1900–1920* (New York: Columbia University Press, 2001), Eric Rauchway examines three "reform couples"—Mary and Charles Beard, Lucy Sprague and W.C. Mitchell, Dorothy Whitney and Willard Straight—tracking their "conscientious attempt[s] to apply the relations implicit in marriage and family to larger social relations" (13). McGerr argues that progressives transformed gender relations and ranked the individual as more important than the institution (*Fierce Discontent*, xiv and passim). Particularly in his chapter on Anna Strunsky Walling, Leon Fink in *Progressive Intellectuals and the Dilemma of Democratic Commitment* (Cambridge: Harvard University Press, 1997), examines how progressives sought to "weave love into the fabric of [their] work and political activity" (quotation at 147).

Although not his primary focus, William O'Neill claims the Progressive era "attack on marriage. . . . conditioned the public for the alterations in sexual standards that became manifest after the First World War" (William L. O'Neill, *Divorce in the Progressive Era* (New Haven: Yale University Press, 1967, xxxv ff). According to Roderick Phillips, "many progressives saw the family as so pivotal an institution that they believed that social change would begin with the transformation of familial relationships" (*Putting Asunder* 480). In *New Radical*, xiii, Christopher Lasch traces a "rebellion against the conventional family" originating in the Progressive era. For Lasch, the "new radicals" are distinguished from their predecessors in their interest in matters beyond the realm of conventional politics, and particularly in new ideas about sexuality (90).

35. Hofstadter quoted in Daniel T. Rodgers, "In Search of Progressivism," *Reviews in American History* 10:4 (December 1982), 117; Robert H. Wiebe, *The Search for Order, 1877–1920* (New York: Hill and Wang, 1967); Crunden, *Ministers*, x. Perhaps the sharpest critique of the term comes from Peter G. Filene, "An Obituary for 'The Progressive Movement,'" *American Quarterly* 22:1 (Spring 1970), 20–34.

36. According to Gabriel Kolko, for instance, the reformist agenda was a cover for fundamentally conservative politics. See *The Triumph of Conservatism: A Reinterpretation of American History, 1900–1916* (New York: Free Press of Glencoe, 1963).

37. Nancy Cohen, *The Reconstruction of American Liberalism, 1865–1914* (Chapel Hill: University of North Carolina Press, 2002), 226.

38. Nancy F. Cott, "What's in a Name? The Limits of 'Social Feminism; or, Expanding the Vocabulary of Women's History,'" *Journal of American History* 76:3 (December 1989), 825; Robyn M. Muncy, *Creating a Female Dominion in American Reform, 1890–1935* (New York: Oxford University Press, 1991); Nancy S. Dye, "Introduction," *Gender, Class, Race, and Reform in the Progressive Era*, eds. Noralee Frankel and Nancy S. Dye (Lexington: University Press of Kentucky, 1991), 4; Muncy, *Creating a Female Dominion*, 226.

For representative scholarship on the settlement movement, see (in addition to works cited in notes 39 and 40 to Chapter 1) Louise W. Knight, *Citizen: Jane Addams and the Struggle for Democracy* (Chicago: University of Chicago Press, 2005); Allen F. Davis, *American Heroine: The Life and Legend of Jane Addams* (New York, Oxford University Press, 1973); Victoria Bissell Brown, *The Education of Jane Addams* (Philadelphia: University of Pennsylvania Press, 2004); Shannon Jackson, *Lines of Activity: Performance, Historiography, Hull-House Domesticity* (Ann Arbor: University of Michigan Press, 2000); Eleanor J. Stebner, T*he Women of Hull House: A Study in Spirituality, Vocation, and Friendship* (Albany, NY: State University of New York Press, 1997).

On women working for progressive reform, see also Catherine Gilbert Murdock, *Domesticating Drink: Women, Men, and Alcohol in America, 1870–1940* (Baltimore: Johns Hopkins University Press, 1998); Elizabeth J. Clapp, *Mothers of All Children: Women Reformers and the Rise of Juvenile Courts in Progressive Era America* (University Park, PA: Pennsylvania State University Press, 1998); Lorine Swainston Goodwin, *The Pure Food, Drink, and Drug Crusaders, 1879–1914* (Jefferson, NC: McFarland, 1999); Alison M. Parker, *Purifying America: Women, Cultural Reform, and Pro-censorship Activism, 1873–1933* (Urbana: University of Illinois Press, 1997).

39. John Dewey, *The Public and Its Problems: An Essay in Political Inquiry* (Chicago: Gateway Books, 1946), 14. Jürgen Habermas issues his charge in *The Structural Transformation of the Public Sphere: An Inquiry into a Category of Bourgeois Society*, trans. Thomas Burger (Cambridge, MA: MIT Press, 1994). The literature on this subject is vast. A particularly influential critique of privatization can be found in Lauren Berlant, "Poor Eliza," *American Literature* 70 (September 1998), 635–68.

40. Robinson quoted in Henry F. May, *The End of American Innocence* (Oxford: Oxford University Press, 1959), 131; Martin J. Sklar, *The Corporate Reconstruction of American Capitalism, 1890–1916* (Cambridge: Cambridge University Press, 1988), 439. Examining the new political currents beginning in the 1890s on both sides of the Atlantic that were rising by the 1910s, Daniel T. Rodgers notes there was no single, agreed-upon term. *Democrat, reformer, liberal, radical, collectivist*—all were used, but Rodgers concludes the most useful remains *progressive* (*Atlantic Crossings: Social Politics in a Progressive Age* [Cambridge: Harvard University Press, 1998], 52). In another transatlantic study, Kloppenberg argues the term is useful in "captur[ing] the novelty and the amorphousness" of progressive ideology (*Uncertain Victory*, 299).

41. Nell Irvin Painter, *Standing at Armageddon: The United States, 1877–1910* (New York: W.W. Norton, 2008), xxxiv–xxxv. According to Kloppenberg, "the rhetoric, if not the ideas, of social democracy and progressivism has moved so successfully from the periphery to the center of

the political stage that the significance of these programs has been consigned by familiarity to contempt" (*Uncertain Victory*, 11).

42. Charles Hanson Towne, "Some Noted Contributors," *The Delineator*, November 1910 (LXXVI), 368.

CHAPTER ONE

1. This account of marriage draws from: Basch, *Framing*; Norma Basch, *In the Eyes of the Law: Women, Marriage, and Property in Nineteenth-Century New York* (Ithaca: Cornell University Press, 1982); Ann Braude, *Radical Spirits: Spiritualism and Women's Rights in Nineteenth-Century America* (Boston: Beacon Press, 1989); Coontz, *Marriage, A History*; Coontz, *Social Origins*; Coontz, *The Way We Never Were*; Cott, *Public Vows*; Degler, *At Odds*; Department of Commerce and Labor, US Bureau of the Census, *Marriage and Divorce*; Ariela R. Dubler, "Governing through Contract: Common Law Marriage in the Nineteenth Century," *Yale Law Journal* 107:6 (April 1998), 1885–1920; Lawrence M. Friedman, *Private Lives: Families, Individuals, and the Law* (Cambridge: Harvard University Press, 2004); Grossberg, *Governing*; Hartog, *Man and Wife in America*; George Elliott Howard, *A History of Matrimonial Institutions*, three volumes (Chicago: University of Chicago Press, 1904); Hartman, *Household*; Patricia Lucie, "Marriage and Law Reform in Nineteenth-Century America" in *Marriage and Property*, ed. Elizabeth M. Craik (Aberdeen, UK: Aberdeen University Press, 1991), 138–58; Steven Mintz and Susan Kellogg, *Domestic Revolutions: A Social History of American Family Life* (New York: The Free Press, 1988); Raymund Lee Muncy, *Sex and Marriage in Utopian Communities: Nineteenth-Century America* (Bloomington: Indiana University Press, 1973); Glenda S. Riley, *Divorce: An American Tradition* (Oxford: Oxford University Press, 1991); Stone, *Family, Sex and Marriage*; Seidman, *Romantic Longings*; Reva B. Siegel, "Home As Work: The First Woman's Rights Claims Concerning Wives' Household Labor, 1850–1880," *The Yale Law Journal* 103:5 (March 1994): 1073–217; Stone, *Family, Sex, and Marriage* Edward Westermarck, *A History of Human Marriage* (New York: Macmillan, 1891); Marilyn Yalom, *A History of the Wife* (New York: Harper Collins, 2001). Sources focused more on divorce are identified in note 22 to this chapter.

2. Luther quoted in Howard, *History*, I: 387–88; Stone, *Family, Sex, and Marriage*, 100–104; 165, 182.

In *Doctrine and Discipline of Divorce* (1643), John Milton sought to broaden the grounds for divorce; his belief that "contrariety of mind" justified divorce approaches modern ideas, although his considering the husband's rights as greater than the wife's does not (quoted in Nelson Manfred Blake, *The Road to Reno: A History of Divorce in the U.S.* [New York: Macmillan, 1962], 30).

3. Blackstone quoted in Lucie, "Marriage and Law Reform," 143; Hartog, *Man and Wife*, 107; Basch, *In the Eyes*, quotation at 55.

4. Anthony and Stanton quoted in Lucie, "Marriage and Law Reform," 151.

The legal concept of equity or fairness—ancillary to common law—emerged in the thirteenth century and gradually produced precedents that undercut marital unity, some of them improving wives' legal condition. In addition, the marriage settlement provided a way to circumvent common law, for instance by providing a means of keeping property out of the husband's hands (Basch, *In the Eyes* 20–21, 74–75). But such legal loopholes had limited utility as they were exercised only by the wealthy. See also Phillip Mallett, "Woman and Marriage in Victorian Society," *Marriage and Property*, ed. Elizabeth M. Craik (Aberdeen: Aberdeen University Press, 1991), 159–89.

5. Basch, *In the Eyes* 69. Basch explains that Reeve, while rejecting marital unity, arrived at equally patriarchal results, seeing the wife as inevitably the weaker party and thereby making "the results of coverture his premise" (*In the Eyes* 57–58, quotation at 58). Kent recognized

that the interests of husband and wife would not always be identical but still found divergence anomalous; he also believed that any incursion on the husband's power would undermine marriage. Basch critiques Kent's view of women and marriage for its "sentimentality and paternalism" (*In the Eyes* 63).

6. Cott, *Grounding* 186; Linda K. Kerber, *No Constitutional Right to Be Ladies: Women and the Obligations of Citizenship* (New York: Hill and Wang, 1998), xxiii–xxiv, 307.

7. Maine quoted in George R. Uba, "Status and Contract: The Divorce Dispute of the 'Eighties' and Howells' *A Modern Instance*," *Colby Library Quarterly* 19:2 (June 1983), 79. Brook Thomas brings together legal history about the "Age of Contract" with literary-historical discussion of the "Age of Realism," with many references to marriage, in *American Literary Realism*. For influential discussions of contract by Progressive era writers, see Havelock Ellis, *Sex in Relation to Society*, Volume Two, Part 3 of *Studies in the Psychology of Sex* (New York: Random House, 1936), 471–89; and Howard, *History of Matrimonial Institutions*, especially Volume One, Part 1, Chapter 4.

8. Cott, *Public Vows*, 101, 1.

9. Blackstone interpreted marriage as a contract, a premise that, Basch contends, has radical implications, since contracting individuals could theoretically set their own terms (*In the Eyes*, 48). Yet Blackstone forestalled those radical consequences, for he also maintained that once contracting parties marry, their marriage then becomes a status, at which point coverture curtails the legal agency of wives.

10. Grossberg, *Governing*, 19; Stanton quoted in Dubler, "Governing through Contract," 1909; Supreme Court Justice quoted in Riley, *Divorce*, 131.

Some reformers, such as novelist and feminist activist Mona Caird, argued for a distinctive type of contract marriage: a union that would last for a specified length of time (O'Neill, *Divorce*, 105).

11. Dubler, "Governing through Contract," 1886; Kent quoted in Grossberg, *Governing*, 70–71; Grossberg, *Governing*, 76.

Kent's defense of common law marriage was almost immediately challenged by Chief Justice Theophilus Parsons of the Massachusetts Supreme Judicial Court, who became the primary authority cited by those criticizing the validity of common law marriage.

12. Basch, *Framing*, 58.

Haddock v. Haddock was superseded in 1942 by *Williams et al. v. North Carolina* (Riley, *Divorce*, 141).

13. Robert Owen quoted in Muncy, *Sex and Marriage*, 55–56; Robert Dale Owen quoted in Riley, *Divorce*, 157.

14. Davis quoted in Braude, *Radical Spirits*, 119; Davis quoted in Basch, *Framing*, 83.

15. Phillips, *Putting Asunder*, 484.

16. Braude, *Radical Spirits*, 127.

17. The first round of the debate was reprinted in *Love, Marriage, and Divorce, and the Sovereignty of the Individual: A Discussion between Henry James, Horace Greeley, and Stephen Pearl Andrews* (Boston: B.R. Tucker, 1889); the second in Greeley's *Recollections of a Busy Life* (New York: J.B. Ford, 1868).

18. Victoria Woodhull, "Beecher-Tilton Scandal Case," *Woodhull & Clafin's Weekly* 5:7 (November 2, 1872), 8.

19. Quoted in Muncy, *Sex and Marriage*, 137; J.H. Beadle, *Polygamy or, the Mysteries and Crimes of Mormonism, Being a Full and Authentic History of this Strange Sect From its Origin to the Present Time With a Thrilling Account of the Inner Life and Teachings of the Mormons and an Exposé of the Secret Rites and Ceremonies of the Deluded followers of Brigham Young* (1882).

20. According to Grossberg, "the battle with the Mormons allowed the American legal system to arm itself with unusual power to enforce the nation's allegiance to monogamy" (*Governing* 125). See also Philip L. Barlow, *Mormons and the Bible: The Place of the Latter-Day Saints in Ameri-*

can Religion (Oxford: Oxford University Press, 1991); Nancy Bentley, "Marriage as Treason: Polygamy, Nation, and the Novel," *The Futures of American Studies*, eds. Donald Pease and Robyn Wiegman (Durham, NC: Duke University Press, 2002), 341-70; Kathryn M. Daynes, *More Wives Than One: Transformation of the Mormon Marriage System, 1840-1910* (Urbana: University of Illinois Press, 1991); Edwin Brown Firmage and Richard Collin Mangrum, *Zion in the Courts: A Legal History of the Church of Jesus Christ of Latter-day Saints, 1830-1900* (Urbana: University of Illinois Press, 1988); Carmon B. Hardy, *Solemn Covenant: The Mormon Polygamous Passage* (Urbana: University of Illinois Press, 1992); Rodney Stark, *The Rise of Mormonism*, ed. Reid L. Neilsen (New York: Columbia University Press, 2005); and Richard S. Van Wagoner, *Mormon Polygamy: A History* (Salt Lake City: Signature, 1989). In *Public Vows*, 72-75 and 111-124, Cott elaborates on the significance of the Mormon controversy.

21. Basch, *Framing*, 73, 77; "Declaration of Sentiments" quoted in Lucie, "Marriage and Law Reform," 148; Lucy Stone and Henry Blackwell, "Marriage Protest," accessed January 18, 2010; *http://womenshistory.about.com/library/etext/bl_marriage_stone_blackwell.htm?p=1*; Stanton quoted in Lucie, "Marriage and Law Reform," 151; John Stuart Mill, *The Subjection of Women* (London: Longmans, Green, Reader, and Dyer, 1869), 177, accessed January 18, 2010; http://books.google.com/books?id=LgwAAAAAYAAJ&printsec=frontcover&source=gbs_ge_summary_r&cad=0#v=onepage&q=moral%20regeneration&f=false.

22. In addition to titles mentioned in note 1 of this chapter, this account of divorce draws from Basch, *Framing*; Blake, *Road to Reno*; J. Herbie DiFonzo, *Beneath the Fault Line: The Popular and Legal Culture of Divorce in Twentieth-Century America* (Charlottesville: University Press of Virginia, 1997); Samuel W. Dike, "Some Fundamentals of the Divorce Question," *Special Issues of the National League for the Protection of the Family for 1909*, No. 1 (Boston: Fort Hill Press, 1909), 3-12 ; Lawrence M. Friedman, "Rites of Passage: Divorce Law in Historical Perspective," *Oregon Law Review* 63 (1984): 649-69; Lichtenberger, *Divorce*; Lucie, "Marriage and Law Reform," 138-58; K.N. Llewellyn, "Behind the Law of Divorce: I," *Columbia Law Review* XXXII:8 (December 1932), 1281-307; K.N. Llewellyn, "Behind the Law of Divorce: II" *Columbia Law Review* XXXIII: (1933), 250-94; Elaine Tyler May, *Great Expectations: Marriage and Divorce in Post-Victorian America* (Chicago: University of Chicago Press, 1980); O'Neill, *Divorce in the Progressive Era*; Phillips, *Putting Asunder*; Riley, *Divorce*; Zenor, "Untying the Knot."

23. Quoted in Riley, *Divorce*, 47.

24. Kelly Hager, *Dickens*, 37. Conversion to today's rate calculated according to measuring-worth.com, using RPI.

25. Early in the Republican period, Northern states began replacing legislative divorce with the still-familiar judicial divorce, a transition largely complete by the mid-nineteenth century. This change made divorce less expensive and thus far more pervasive.

26. For instance Maine's liberal 1849 omnibus law allowed for a divorce when the judge found it "reasonable and proper, conducive to domestic harmony, and consistent with the peace and morality of society" (quoted in Friedman, "Rights," 654). Indiana went further, in 1824 granting courts authority to grant a divorce for "any other cause" they deemed "proper" (quoted in Blake, *Road to Reno*, 119).

27. Basch, *Framing*, 21. Codification of marriage as a civil right, however, did not occur until the Supreme Court struck down Virginia's antimiscegenation statute in *Loving v. Virginia* (1967) (Zenor, "Untying the Knot," 650).

28. French visitor quoted in Riley, *Divorce*, 34; Riley, *Divorce*, 61; O'Neill, *Divorce*, 20; Basch, *Framing*, 35-42, quotation at 42; Riley, *Divorce*, 51-57; Degler, *At Odds*, 168, 174; O'Neill, *Divorce*, viii; Phillips, *Putting Asunder*, 494-95, 506, 514.

29. Carroll D. Wright, *A Report on Marriage and Divorce in the United States, 1867 to 1886*, (Washington, DC: Government Printing Office, 1889); Roosevelt quoted in Department of Commerce and Labor, US. Bureau of Census, "Introduction" to *Marriage and Divorce 1867-1906*, I:4; Wiebe, *Search for Order*.

Comments that Roosevelt had made to a group of ecclesiastics were included in the report's discursive section. Among them, TR explained that matters such as "the tariff and the currency are of literally no consequence whatsoever compared with the vital question of having the unit of our social life, the home, preserved." If spouses would only "fulfill their duties toward one another and toward their children as Christianity teaches them, " he continued, "then we may rest absolutely assured that the other problems will solve themselves." As if that were not enough, the president continued, "But if we have solved every other problem. . . . it shall profit us nothing if we have lost our own national soul" (quoted in *Marriage and Divorce 1867–1906*, I:4). TR's successor William Howard Taft continued the theme: "Our country rests upon its homes, and if we cannot keep our homes sacred and free from constant demoralizing breaking-up, we had better go out of the business of government altogether" (quoted in Carson, *Marriage Revolt*, 378).

30. Department of Commerce and Labor, US Bureau of Census, "Introduction" to *Marriage and Divorce 1867–1906*, I:11-12, 23-24; Riley, *Divorce*.

31. O'Neill, *Divorce*, 27; Elaine Tyler May, *Great Expectations*, 4. According to William O'Neill, the 1908–1909 report marks the height of the anti-divorce movement.

32. Dike, "Some Fundamentals," 5, 9, 10.

33. Pennypacker quoted in Lichtenberger, *Divorce*, 190.

Lichtenberger provides a good overview of the uniform divorce law movement (*Divorce* 188-97); for another contemporary account, see G.E. Howard, "Divorce and Public Welfare," *McClure's Magazine* XXXIV: 2 (December 1909), 237-38. See also Blake, *Road to Reno*, 130-46; Basch, *Framing* 89-90; Grossberg, *Governing*, 90-93; Riley, *Divorce*, 108-110; and O'Neill, *Divorce*, 48.

34. Herbert Croly, *The Promise of American Life* (New York: Capricorn Books, 1964), 346. That book includes its own curious, if indirect, call for marital reform. In the context of recommending that the state should attempt to prevent crime and insanity, Croly suggests a person might "inquire whether the institution of marriage . . . does not in its existing form have something to do with the prevalence and increase of insanity and crime; it might conceivably reach the conclusion that the enforced celibacy of hereditary criminals and incipient lunatics would make for individual and social improvement even more than would a maximum passenger fare on the railroads of two cents a mile" (345-46).

35. Walter Francis Willcox, "The Divorce Problem–A Study in Statistics," *Studies in History, Economics and Public Law*, eds. University Faculty of Political Science, Columbia College 1:1 (1891), 3, 72.

36. Hutchins Hapgood, "Divorce," newspaper article clipping (no date), Hapgood Family Papers (hereafter HFP), Box 26, Folder 708, Beinecke Library, Yale University.

Many historians have sided with the progressives in arguing that rising divorce rates correspond to higher expectations about marriage. See, for instance, Lawrence Stone, *Family, Sex, and Marriage*, 233; Elaine Tyler May, *Great Expectations*, 47; Glenda Riley, *Divorce*, 59; Roderick Phillips, *Putting Asunder*, 402; O'Neill, *Divorce*, 12. A seed of this idea appears in Westermarck's claim that rates of marriage had declined in the modern era because the increased expectations make it more difficult to find an acceptable partner (*History of Human Marriage*, 150).

37. Herbert Spencer, *Principles of Sociology*, in three volumes (New York: D. Appleton, 1898), I:615-16; I:621-22).

On the professionalization of social science, see Mary O. Furner, *Advocacy and Objectivity: A Crisis in the Professionalization of American Social Science, 1865–1905* (Lexington: University Press of Kentucky, 1975); Robert C. Bannister, *Sociology and Scientism: The American Quest for Objectivity, 1880–1940* (Chapel Hill: University of North Carolina Press, 1987); and Thomas L. Haskell, *The Emergence of Professional Social Science: The American Social Science Association and the Nineteenth Century Crisis of Authority*; Dorothy Ross, *The Origins of American Social Science* (Cambridge: Cambridge University Press, 1991). On professionalization more generally in this period see Burton J. Bledstein, *The Culture of Professionalism: The Middle Class and the Development of*

Higher Education in America (New York: Norton, 1976); Bruce A. Kimball, *The "True Professional Ideal" in America: A History* (Cambridge: Blackwell, 1992); and, regarding the professionalization of novelists in this period, see Wilson, *The Labor of Words*.

According to William O'Neill, Howard's *History* opened the door for objective discussion of divorce. To illustrate the quick diffusion of Howard's liberal ideas, O'Neill cites a 1915 textbook by Willystine Goodsell, *History of the Family* (*Divorce* 178, 182). See also Riley, *Divorce*, 121–23, regarding how social scientists managed to change the discussion on American divorce.

38. William Graham Sumner, "The Family and Social Change," *Papers and Proceedings of the American Sociological Society*, American Social Science Publications 3–4 (1908–1909), 15; Rabbi Krauskopf, "Is Freer Divorce an Evil?" *Papers and Proceedings of the American Sociological Society*, 176; George Elliott Howard, "Is Freer Divorce an Evil?" *Papers and Proceedings of the American Sociological Society*, 155.

39. Allen F. Davis, *Spearheads for Reform: The Social Settlements and the Progressive Movement* (Oxford: Oxford University Press, 1967), xii; Jane Addams, *Twenty Years at Hull House* (New York: Signet, 1960), 98; Muncy, *Creating a Female Dominion*, xvi.

40. Ernest Poole quoted in Davis, *Spearheads*, 32; Muncy, *Creating*, 16; Jane Addams poem quoted in Victoria Bissell Brown, *The Education of Jane Addams* (Philadelphia: University of Pennsylvania Press, 2004), 259; Brown, *Education*, 257; Mia Carson, *Settlement Folk: Social Thought and the American Settlement Movement 1885–1930* (Chicago: University of Chicago Press, 1990), 54; Robin K. Berson, *Jane Addams: A Biography* (Westport, CT: Greenwood Press, 2004), 32, accessed through ABC-CLIO e-book collection, August 19, 2012, http://ebooks.abc-lio.com .ezproxy.lib.uconn.edu/reader.aspx?isbn=9780313084935&id=GR2354-128#128; Brown, *Education*, 259.

41. Kathryn Kish Sklar, *Florence Kelly and the Nation's Work: The Rise of Women's Political Cultures, 1830–1900* (New Haven: Yale University Press, 1995), quotation at 186.

42. Peter Gabriel Filene, *Him/Her/Self: Sex Roles in Modern America* (New York: HBJ, 1975), 86; Lester Frank Ward, *Pure Sociology: A Treatise on the Origin and Spontaneous Development of Society* (New York: Macmillan, 1907), 296, 313, 314.

My account here also draws from: Gail Bederman, *Manliness and Civilization: A Cultural History of Gender and Race in the United States, 1880–1917* (Chicago: University of Chicago Press, 1995); Carter, *The Heart of Whiteness*; Joe Dubbert, "Progressivism and the Masculinity Crisis," *The American Man*, eds. Elizabeth H. Pleck and Joseph Pleck (Englewood Cliffs, NJ: Prentice-Hall, 1989); Kaplan, *Anarchy of Empire*; Peter N. Stearns, *Be a Man! Males in Modern Society*, Second Edition (London: Holmes & Meier, 1990); Anthony E. Rotundo, *American Manhood: Transformations in Masculinity from the Revolution to the Modern Era* (New York: Basic Books, 1993).

See also Grossberg regarding the 1840s "crisis of the family" (*Governing*, 10); Filene regarding the "crisis" of masculinity in the Progressive era (*Him/Her/Self* 85 ff, 107 ff); Seideman, *Romantic Longings*, regarding the early twentieth century; Julian Carter, *Heart of Whiteness*, Chapter 2, regarding the 1920s and 1930s; and Shumway, *Modern Love*, tracing the "crisis" to the end of the twentieth century. Coontz, *Way We Never Were*, 257, 283, discusses how the whole notion of "crisis" gets recycled throughout American history. T.J. Jackson Lears's *No Place of Grace: Antimodernism and the Transformation of American Culture, 1880–1920* (New York: Pantheon, 1981), especially Chapter 3, establishes invaluable contexts for understanding the turn-of-the-century "crisis" of masculinity.

Secondary literature on the New Woman is voluminous. See, for instance: Elizabeth Ammons, "The New Woman as Cultural Symbol and Social Reality: Six Women Writers' Perspectives," in *1915, the Cultural Moment*, eds. Heller and Rudnick (New Brunswick, NJ: Rutgers University Press, 1991), 82–97; Cecilia Tichi, "Women Writers and the New Woman," *Columbia Literary History of the United States*, eds. Emory Elliott et. al. (New York: Columbia University

Press), 589–606; Cott, *Grounding*; Jean V. Matthews, *The Rise of the New Woman: The Woman's Movement in America, 1875–1930* (Chicago: Ivan R. Dee, 2003); Martha H. Patterson, *Beyond the Gibson Girl: Reimagining the American New Woman, 1895–1915* (Urbana: University of Illinois Press, 2005); Carroll Smith-Rosenberg, *Disorderly Conduct: Visions of Gender in Victorian America* (New York: Knopf, 1985); Lois Rudnick, "The New Woman," in Heller and Rudnick, 69–81; Christine Stansell, *American Moderns: Bohemian New York and the Creation of a New Century* (New York: Henry Holt, 2000); Ellen Kay Trimberger, "The New Woman and the New Sexuality: Conflict and Contradiction in the Writings and Lives of Mabel Dodge and Neith Boyce," in Heller and Rudnick, 98–115. For a still useful overview of literary themes regarding the New Woman, see Carolyn Forrey, "The New Woman Revisited," *Women's Studies* 2:1 (1974), 37–56.

43. Howard, "Is Freer Divorce an Evil?," 157.

44. Anna A. Rogers, *Why American Marriages Fail and Other Papers* (Boston: Houghton Mifflin, 1909), 11, 17; Robert Herrick, *Together* (New York: Macmillan, 1925), 513, 391.

45. Dewey quoted in Kloppenberg, *Uncertain Victory*, 351; Kloppenberg, *Uncertain Victory*, 395.

Of the figures considered in this study, Charlotte Perkins Gilman particularly illustrates the progressive quarrel with possessive individualism. Croly's *Promise of American Life* also provides a good example: "Under a system of collective responsibility the process of social improvement is absolutely identified with that of individual improvement." But the "economic individualism of our existing national system" undermines true individualism. Rejecting the merely "quantitative" and money-driven idea of individualism as false and limiting, Croly links progress with a higher type of individualism. And so the "question" for democracy becomes, "How can it contribute to the increase of American individuality?" (408–12).

On the relationship between the era's mounting individualism and anarchism (with some reference to Havelock Ellis and Edward Carpenter), see David Weir, *Anarchy and Culture: The Aesthetic Politics of Modernism* (Amherst: University of Massachusetts Press, 1997), especially Chapter 5, "Aesthetics: From Politics to Culture," 158–200.

46. Spencer, *Principles* I, 610, 758; Ellis, *Eonism*, 508; David Graham Phillips, *Susan Lenox* (New York: Popular Library, 1978), 637; Muncy, *Sex and Marriage*, 10–13.

47. Dike, "Some Fundamentals," 8; Margaret Deland, "The Change in the Feminine Ideal," *Atlantic Monthly* 105 (March 1910), 292, 295, 296.

48. O'Neill, *Divorce*, 73.

CHAPTER TWO

1. Frank Norris, *McTeague* (New York: Penguin, 1982), 165.

2. See *Papers and Proceedings of the American Sociological Society*, American Social Science Publications 3–4 (1908–1909), 16–29, and 150–160, respectively.

3. *Loving Frank* centers on the affair of Frank Lloyd Wright and Mamah Borthwick Cheney, a translator for Ellen Key. In Horan's account, although Cheney eventually becomes disillusioned, initially Key provides the sheltered housewife both a rationale for her affair and, more importantly, a sense of purpose as a worker. Interestingly, at one point when Cheney and Wright have tired of reading scandal-mongering news accounts about their relationship, Meta Fuller Sinclair's affair with Harry Kemp—which I address in the next chapter—"'knocked us off the front page,'" in the words of the Wright character (Nancy Horan, *Loving Frank* [New York: Random House, 2008], 244).

4. Brome, *Havelock Ellis*, 170; Edith Ellis quoted in Havelock Ellis, *My Life* (Boston: Houghton Mifflin, 1939), 481.

5. Gilman, *Women*, 220.

6. Gilman, *Home*, 4; Gilman, *Women*, 215; Carl Degler, *In Search of Human Nature: The Decline*

and Revival of Darwinism in American Social Thought (Oxford: Oxford University Press, 1991), 112; Key, *Love*, 11; Charlotte Perkins Gilman, "The Passing of Matrimony," *Harper's Bazaar* 40:6 (June 1906), 496.

See also Richard Hofstadter, *Social Darwinism and American Thought* (Boston: Beacon Press, 1983) and Robert C. Bannister, *Social Darwinism: Science and Myth in Anglo-American Social Thought* (Philadelphia: Temple University Press, 1979).

7. Gilman, *Women*, 93; Parsons, *Family*, 345; Key, *Love*, 24; Howard, *History* III, 235.

8. Gilman, *Home*, 82, 89; Charlotte Perkins Gilman, *Human Work* (Lanham and New York: Alta Mira Press, 2005), 185; 258.

Charlotte Perkins Gilman's *The Living of Charlotte Perkins Gilman* (Madison: University of Wisconsin Press, 1990), 275, identifies *Human Work* as Gilman's "greatest" book in terms of its ideas, but also the "poorest" in terms of its writing.

9. Bederman, *Manliness*, 122, 135, cites Addams and the number of American editions.

10. Gilman, *Home*, 22; Gilman, *Women*, 23, 22, 38, 71, 5.

11. Marx and Engels castigated the bourgeois family for maintaining "prostitution both public and private" (as quoted in Stephanie Forward, "Attitudes to Marriage and Prostitution in the Writings of Olive Schreiner, Mona Caird, Sarah Grand and George Egerton," *Women's History Review* 8:1 [1999], 54).

On the significance of the prostitute for Gilman, see Judith A. Allen, "Reconfiguring Vice: Charlotte Perkins Gilman, Prostitution, and Frontier Sexual Contracts," in *Charlotte Perkins Gilman: Optimist Reformer*, eds. Jill Rudd and Val Gough (Iowa City: University of Iowa Press, 1999): 173–99. For an overview of literary representations, see Laura Hapke, *Girls Who Went Wrong: Prostitutes in American Fiction, 1885–1917* (Bowling Green, OH: Bowling Green State University Popular Press, 1989).

Like Gilman and Schreiner, British writer Mona Caird criticized the "twin-system of marriage and prostitution," both allowing "the purchase of womanhood" (Caird quoted Phillip Mallett, "Woman and Marriage in Victorian Society," *Marriage and Property*, ed. Elizabeth M. Craik [Aberdeen, UK: Aberdeen University Press, 1991], 180. For the British context, see Bradford Keyes Mudge, *The Whore's Story: Women, Pornography, and the British Novel, 1684–1830* (New York: Oxford University Press, 2000), and Deborah Epstein Nord, *Walking the Victorian Streets: Women, Representation, and the City* (Ithaca, NY: Cornell University Press, 1995).

Prostitution in the period has been extensively studied. For starters, see Marc Connelly, *The Response to Prostitution in the Progressive Era* (Chapel Hill: University of North Carolina Press, 1980); Barbara Meil Hobson, *Uneasy Virtue: The Politics of Prostitution and the American Reform Tradition* (New York: Basic Books, 1987); Ruth Rosen, *The Lost Sisterhood: Prostitutes in America, 1900–1915* (Johns Hopkins University Press, 1982).

12. Gilman, *Women*, 109, 110, 63–64.

13. Ibid., 35, 37, 73; see also Gilman, *Home* 22–30.

14. Characterization of *Woman and Labour* cited in Laurence Lerner, "Olive Schreiner and the Feminists," *Olive Schreiner and After: Essays on South African Literature in Honour of Guy Butler*, ed. D. Maclennon (Cape Town: David Philip Publishers, 1983), 68; Davis, *Charlotte Perkins Gilman*, 78; Olive Schreiner, *Woman and Labour* (accessed as Project Gutenberg e-book, through University of Connecticut Net Library, June 3, 2009), 20.

After marrying, Schreiner's husband was known as Samuel Cronwright-Schreiner.

15. In *Sexual Anarchy: Gender and Culture at the Fin de Siècle* (New York: Viking, 1990), 48, Elaine Showalter describes *Woman and Labour* as "among the first efforts to work out the relationship between feminism and capitalism."

16. Schreiner, *Woman*, 22, 23, 17.

17. Ibid., 30, 38. On Schreiner's complex feelings about prostitutes, see Forward, "Attitudes,"

58–63; and Christine Barsby, "Olive Schreiner: Towards a Redefinition of Culture," *Pretexts* 1:1 (1989 Winter): 23–24.

Gilman discusses female parasitism throughout *Women and Economics* and again in her 1931 "Parasitism and Civilized Vice," in *Woman's Coming of Age*, eds. Samuel D. Schmalhausen and V.F. Calverton (New York: Liveright, 1931), 110–126. In *No Man's Land: The Place of the Woman Writer in the Twentieth Century*, Volume 2, *Sexchanges* (New Haven: Yale University Press, 1989), 71, Sandra M. Gilbert and Susan Gubar note that this essay "reads like a meditation on Schreiner's *Woman and Labour*."

18. Schreiner, *Woman*, 41, 49.

19. Ibid., 34, 50.

20. Ibid., 25; Carolyn Burdett, *Olive Schreiner and the Progress of Feminism: Evolution, Gender, Empire* (New York: Palgrave Macmillan, 2001), 67.

21. Veblen comments briefly on the "instinct of workmanship" in *Leisure Class*; see especially 93. For a fuller exposition, see Thorstein Veblen, *The Instinct of Workmanship and the State of the Industrial Arts* (New York: Norton, 1941) and Thorstein Veblen, "The Instinct of Workmanship and the Irksomeness of Labor," rpt. in *Essays in Our Changing Order*, ed. Leon Adrzroon (New York: Augustus M. Kelley, 1964), 78–96.

22. Veblen, *Leisure Class*, 179, 354, 356.

23. I discuss the complexities of Veblen's attitudes toward privacy, with particular reference to his own first marriage, in "Boundaries Lost: Thorstein Veblen, *The Higher Learning in America*, and the Conspicuous Spouse," *Prospects* 26 (2001), 251–93. For discussion of Veblen's cautious feminism, see also Clare Virginia Eby, "Veblen's Anti-Anti-Feminism," *Intellectual Legacies in Modern Economics: The Legacy of Thorstein Veblen*, ed. Rick Tilman (Surrey, UK: Edward Elgar, 2003), 360–84.

24. Veblen, *Leisure*, 53, 23, 83. Veblen elaborates on the gendered origins of ownership in "The Barbarian Status of Women," *Essays in Our Changing Order*, ed. Leon Ardzrooni (New York: Viking, 1934).

25. Veblen, *Leisure*, 353, 356, 357.

26. Elsie Clews Parsons, "Privacy in Love Affairs," *The Masses*, July 1915, 12.

27. Parsons, "Privacy in Love Affairs," 12; Morton G. White, *Social Thought in America: The Revolt against Formalism* (New York: Viking, 1949).

28. Arthur James Todd, "George Elliott Howard, 1849–1928." *American Journal of Sociology* 34:4 (January 1929), 693, 696. My biographical sketch of Howard derives also from the American Sociological Association's "George Elliott Howard," http://www2.asanet.org/governance/Howard.html, accessed March 31, 2008.

29. Howard, *History of Matrimonial* III:224; I:388.

30. Ibid., I:331; III:223–24.

31. Ibid., II:127; III:226; III:220; III:182; III:226; III:227. Degler, *In Search of Human Nature*, 13. For an example of Howard's reach outside the academy, see George Elliott Howard, "Divorce and Public Welfare," *McClure's Magazine* XXXIV: 2 (December 1909), 232–42.

32. Howard, *History* II:127; III:183.

33. Ellis, *Sex in Relation*, 316–17. In *Intimate Matters*, D'Emilio and Freedman describe the American influence of *Studies in the Psychology of Sex*, which "assaulted almost every aspect of the nineteenth-century sexual heritage" (224). Rita Fellski sums up how Freud came to eclipse Ellis: "the Freudian revolution" established "a seemingly impenetrable barrier" that made sexology hard to understand ("Introduction" to *Sexology in Culture: Labeling Bodies and Desires*, eds. Lucy Bland and Laura Doan [Chicago: University of Chicago Press, 1998], 1).

Focusing on Edith Ellis, Jo-Ann Wallace persuasively identifies a literary-historical reason for the eclipse of this generation of writers who "made little distinction between literary and polemical writing." Because their enthusiasm for reform causes made them embarrassing to the more famous writers identified with high modernism, the contribution of the Ellises and others have been neglected (Jo-Ann Wallace, "The Case of Edith Ellis," in *Modernist Sexualities*, eds. Hugh Stevens and Caroline Howlett [Manchester, UK: University of Manchester Press, 2000], quotation at 15).

Perhaps most critical, Sheila Jeffreys in *The Spinster and Her Enemies* (London: Pandora Press, 1985), 128, charges Ellis with an "onslaught upon feminism with all the authority of 'science.'" Further negative interpretations can be found in Carroll Smith-Rosenberg, *Disorderly Conduct: Visions of Gender in Victorian America* (New York: Oxford University Press, 1985), especially 275–80; Lucy Bland, *Banishing the Beast: Sexuality and the Early Feminists* (New York: New Press, 1995); Margaret Jackson, *The Real Facts of Life: Feminism and the Politics of Sexuality c. 1850–1940* (Bristol, PA: Taylor & Francis, 1994), 111–126; Lillian Faderman, *Surpassing the Love of Men: Romantic Friendship and Love between Women from the Renaissance to the Present* (New York: Morrow, 1981), 241–48.

Merl Storr provides a useful overview of lesbian and gay scholars' reactions to sexology in "Transformations: Subjects, Categories and Cures in Krafft-Ebing's Sexology," *Sexology in Culture: Labeling Bodies and Desires*, ed. Lucy Bland and Laura Doan (Chicago: University of Chicago Press, 1998). In that same volume, Lesley A. Hall argues that modern feminists' assumption of a fundamental divide between feminism and sexology would have been incomprehensible to feminists at the time ("Feminist Reconfigurations of Heterosexuality in the 1920s," in *Sexology in Culture*, eds. Bland and Doan, 135, 136).

34. Havelock Ellis, *My Life*, 154, 149; Ellis, *Sex in Relation*, 483, 194; Ellis, *Eonism*, 515.

35. Ellis, *Sex in Relation*, 129, 427. "I have always instinctively desired to spiritualise the things that have been counted low and material," Ellis explains in *My Life*, for "where others have seen all things secular, I have seen all things sacred" (433).

36. Key, *Love and Marriage*, 51; Floyd Dell, *Women as World Builders: Studies in Modern Feminism* (1913; Westport, CT: Hyperion, 1976), 83; Norman Hapgood quoted in Cott, *Grounding*, 46.

37. Key, *Love and Marriage*, 16–17, 15; William E. Carson, *The Marriage Revolt: A Study of Marriage and Divorce* (New York: Hearst's International Library, 1915), 85–86.

38. Deacon, *Elsie Clews Parsons*, 61, 65, 157; Hare, *A Woman's Quest*, 13; Parsons, *Family*, 349; *New York Herald* quoted in Deacon, *Elsie Clews Parsons*, 68, 69; Deacon, *Elsie Clews Parsons*, 90; Mencken quoted in Deacon, *Elsie Clews Parsons*, 449, n. 31.

39. Mrs. Havelock Ellis [Edith Mary Oldham (Lees) Ellis], "A Novitiate for Marriage," rpt. in *New Horizon*, 13; see also Edith Ellis, "Love of To-Morrow," rpt. in *New Horizon*, 1–9.

According to her husband, as a child Edith Ellis attended a convent school and wanted to convert to Catholicism and become a nun, to the horror of her agnostic father. Edith quickly gave up the ambition but "retained an affection for nuns, and . . . always regarded the Roman Catholic Church as the only possible form of Christianity" (Havelock Ellis, *My Life*, 256–57).

40. Elsie Clews Parsons, "Sex Morality and the Taboo of Direct Reference," *Independent* 61 (August 16, 1906), 392.

41. Edith Ellis, "Love of To-Morrow," 1.

42. Beverly Thiele, "Coming-of-Age: Edward Carpenter on Sex and Reproduction," *Edward Carpenter and Late Victorian Radicalism*, ed. Toni Brown (New York: Routledge 100–101); Chushichi Tsuzuki, *Edward Carpenter 1844–1929: Prophet of Human Fellowship* (Cambridge, UK: Cambridge University Press, 1980), 82, 58; Carpenter, *Love's*, 123, 124, 125.

43. Samuel D. Warren and Louis D. Brandeis, "The Right to Privacy," *Harvard Law Review* IV: 5 (December 15, 1890), 195, 196; Parsons, "Right to Privacy." Warren and Brandeis share with the marriage reformers other fundamental views, including a faith in progressive evolution and belief that a "spiritual" (but not religious) realm provides a more valid basis for ethical claims than does the pervasive emphasis on "property."

44. Carpenter, *Love's*, 106; Ellis, *Sex in Relation*, 480.

Bohemian sex radicals, inspired by many of the books discussed in this chapter, arrived at very different interpretations by emphasizing the *voluntary* part while overlooking the *monogamy*.

45. Key, *Love and Marriage*, 7, 13.

46. Gilman, *Women*, 300–301.

47. Havelock Ellis, *Eonism*, 522; Havelock Ellis, *My Life*, 305; Edith Ellis, "Semi-Detached Marriage," rpt. in *New Horizon*, 23–31; Edith Ellis, "Havelock Ellis," *The Bookman* 47:5 (July 1918), 561 (accessed online).

Complete economic independence proved elusive, according to Havelock, because Edith's power of earning lagged behind his own. He discusses the discrepancy between theory and practice in *My Life*, especially 261–63.

48. Westermarck, *History*, Chapters IV–VI; Howard, *History* I: 222–23.

49. Ellis, *Eonism*, 523; Carpenter, *Love's*, 89; Ellis, *Eonism*, 528.

50. Carpenter, *Love's*, 103–104; Key, *Love and Marriage*, 325; Carpenter, *Love's*, 103–104.

51. Edith Ellis, "Novitiate," 21; Edith Ellis, "Semi-Detached," 30; Key, *Love and Marriage*, 36; Carpenter, *Love's*, 103. As I discuss in the epilogue, notwithstanding the Ellises' ambiguous theories, in practice they both openly had extramarital affairs.

52. Schreiner, *Woman*, 8, 9; Key, *Love and Marriage*, 34, Parsons, *Family*, 348–49; Carpenter, *Love's*, 117, 95, 93; Gilman, *Women*, 25; Ellis, *Sex in Relation*, 421; Gilman, "Passing," 497; Ellis, *Eonism* 486.

53. Dan Savage quoted in Mark Oppenheimer, "Married, With Infidelities," *New York Times Magazine*, 3 July 2011, MM22; accessed on August 17, 2011, through www.nytimes .com, http://www.nytimes.com/2011/07/03/magazine/infidelity-will-keep-us-together .html?pagewanted=7&sq=dan savage&st=cse&scp=2; Ross Douthat, "More Perfect Unions," *New York Times*, July 3, 2011, A19; accessed on August 17, 2011, through www.nytimes.com: http://www.nytimes.com/2011/07/04/opinion/04douthat.html?_r=1&emc=eta1.

54. Department of Commerce and Labor, *Marriage and Divorce 1867–1906*, I:11, 23; McGerr, *Fierce Discontent*, 92, describes Howard as the preeminent authority on divorce.

55. Carpenter, *Love's*, 105.

56. Parsons, *Family*, 143.

57. Key, *Love and Marriage*, 294, 299.

58. Howard, *History* III: 219, 252.

59. Havelock Ellis, *The Sexual Impulse in Women*, Volume One, Part 2 of *Studies in the Psychology of Sex* (New York: Random House, 1936), 193–94 and ff; Carpenter, *Love's*, 17, 23; Edith Ellis, "Love of To-Morrow," 2; Upton Sinclair, *American Outpost: A Book of Reminiscence* (Pasadena, CA: by the author, 1932), 39.

60. Michel Foucault, *The History of Sexuality*, Volume One: An Introduction, translated by Robert Hurley (New York: Vintage Books, 1990), 69, 17; Kevin White, "The New Man and Early Twentieth-Century Emotional Culture in the United States," *An Emotional History of the United States*, ed. Peter N. Stearns and Jean Lewis (New York: New York University Press, 1998), 334.

Peter Gay's *The Bourgeois Experience: Victoria to Freud* (New York: Oxford University Press, 1984–1998) has been crucial in countering the myth of Victorian repression. See also Ellen K. Rothman, *Hands and Hearts: A History of Courtship in America* (New York: Basic Books, 1984); Steven Seidman, *Romantic Longings: Love in America, 1830–1980* (New York: Routledge, 1991). Coontz argues that the Victorian emphasis on romantic love, with marriage the central event in a person's life, had the unintended effect of "revolutionizing marital ideals and behaviors" (*Marriage, A History*, 177). Degler admits a "new ideology of sexual behavior" emerged by 1850 that played down women's sexuality and urged restraint, but he contends there is no evidence it changed anyone's sexual practice (*At Odds: Women and the Family in America from the Revolu-*

tion to the Present [Oxford: Oxford University Press, 1980], 253). And while Helen Lefkowitz Horowitz demonstrates the coexistence of four competing "frameworks" for understanding sex in nineteenth-century America—one of them the "sexual enthusiasts"—her study also confirms that the official position on sex and marriage became increasingly conservative after the middle of the century (*Rereading Sex: Battles over Sexual Knowledge and Suppression in Nineteenth-Century America* [New York: Random House, 2002]).

61. Parsons, "Sex Morality," 391, 392.

62. Reviewers quoted in Brome, *Havelock Ellis*, 147; Foucault, *History*, 39; Margaret Sanger's *Autobiography* quoted in Jeffrey Weeks, "Havelock Ellis and the Politics of Sex Reform," in Sheila Rowbotham and Jeffrey Weeks, *Socialism and the New Life: The Personal and Sexual Politics of Edward Carpenter and Havelock Ellis* (London: Pluto Press,1977), 182.

The most balanced treatment of sexology that I have encountered is *Sexology in Culture: Labeling Bodies and Desires*, eds. Lucy Bland and Laura Doan (Chicago: University of Chicago Press, 1998). Also insightful but focusing on a single volume of the *Studies* is Ivan Crozier, "Philosophy in the English Boudoir: Havelock Ellis, *Love and Pain*, and Sexological Discourses on Algophilia," *Journal of the History of Sexuality* 13:3 (July 2004), 275-305. For a recent critical view of normalizing trends in attitudes toward sexuality, see Carter, *Wages of Whiteness*. Wendy Kline notes a new concept of normality, which she discusses within the context of intelligence testing in *Building a Better Race: Gender, Sexuality, and Eugenics from the Turn of the century to the Baby Boom* (Berkeley: University of California Press, 2001).

63. Havelock Ellis, Preface to First Edition, *Studies in the Psychology of Sex*, Volume One, Part 2, vii; Foucault, *History*, 38.

64. Havelock Ellis, *Analysis of the Sexual Impulse*, Volume One, Part 2, of *Studies in the Psychology of Sex* (New York: Random House, 1936), 277. Ellis does describe inverts (homosexuals) as abnormal in *Sexual Inversion*. However, as Jo-Ann Wallace argues, he also describes inverts as *natural* or congenital, and thus his theory "dictates liberal tolerance" ("The Case of Edith Ellis," 30). For an argument that homosexuals and lesbians were not "defined and contained by inversion theory against their will" but rather that the theory was "developed by inverts themselves," see Chris White, "'She Was Not Really Man at All': The Lesbian Practice and Politics of Edith Ellis," in *What Lesbians Do in Books*, eds. Elaine Hobby and Chris White (London: Women's Press, 1991), 83.

65. Foucault, *History*, 63. On tumescence and detumescence, see Ellis, *The Mechanism of Detumescence*, Volume Two, Part 2 of *Studies in the Psychology of Sex* (New York: Random House, 1936).

66. Havelock Ellis, *The Sexual Impulse in Women*, Volume One, Part 2, of *Studies in the Psychology of Sex* (New York: Random House, 1936), 205.

67. Ellis, *Sexual Impulse*, 239. In his analysis of marital advice books, Peter Laipson argues that the new emphasis meant "middle-class women gained the possibility of pleasure but at the cost of sexual autonomy; middle-class men maintained the promise of authority but at the expense of a sometimes paralyzing expectation of sexual performance" ("'Kiss Without Shame, For She Desires It': Sexual Foreplay in American Marital Advice Literature, 1900-1925," *Journal of Social History* 29.3 [1996], 509).

68. Key, *Love and Marriage*, 91, 84, 82.

69. Schreiner, *Woman*, 9; Ellis, *Sex in Relation*, 214; Ellis, *Eonism* 522; Ellis, *Sex in Relation*, 588-601. Account of Parsons drawn from Deacon, *Elsie Clews Parsons*, 159.

When it comes to sex, Gilman seems to be the odd woman out. She argued that couples should have sex only at the instigation of the wife, and in "The New Mothers of a New World," *The Forerunner* 4 (June 1913), 145-49, that sex should be rare when the intent was not reproduction.

70. Ellis, preface to first edition, *Studies in the Psychology of Sex*, Volume One, Part 2, vii.

71. Diana Fuss, *Essentially Speaking: Feminism, Nature, and Difference* (New York: Routledge, 1989), 1; Ellis, preface to first edition, *Studies in the Psychology of Sex*, Volume One, Part 2, vii; Havelock Ellis, *Love and Pain*, Volume One, Part 2, of *Studies in the Psychology of Sex* (New York: Random House, 1936), 103; Ellis, *Sex in Relation*, 4; Weeks, "Havelock Ellis," 170.

Socialism provides an important context for thinking through the marriage reformers' understanding of gender difference. Engels, for one, considered the sexual division of labor natural, reflecting fixed characteristics determined by gender (Sheila Rowbotham, "Edward Carpenter: Prophet of the New Life," in Rowbotham and Weeks, *Socialism and the New Life*, 110).

In *The Modernization of Sex: Havelock Ellis, Alfred Kinsey, William Masters and Virginia Johnson* (New York: Harper and Row), Paul Robinson discusses Ellis's "lingering Victorianism" (17), and similar criticisms have been made about Carpenter, for instance by Rowbotham ("Edward Carpenter," 111, 112).

72. Key, *Love and Marriage*, 182; Key, *Woman Movement*, 56, her emphasis.

In Ellen Key's *The Woman Movement* (trans. Mamah Bouton Borthwick [New York: G.P. Putnam's Sons, 1912], 79), she acknowledges "'Sapphic' woman" but claims not to have known any.

73. Helen Zimmern, "Ellen Key: Sweden's Foremost Woman, and Her Vogue in Germany," *Putnam's Monthly* 3 (January 1908), 436; "The Conflict between 'Human' and 'Female' Feminism," *Current Opinion* 54 (April 1913), 291.

A writer for the same journal concluded that "Progression, with Charlotte Gilman, means a humanizing process; with Ellen Key a maternalizing one" (*Current Opinion* 54 [February 1913], 138). On the differences between Gilman and Key, see Key, *The Woman Movement*, especially 176–80; Charlotte Perkins Gilman, "On Ellen Key and the Woman Movement," *Forerunner* 4 (February 1913), 3835–38; Charlotte Perkins Gilman, "Education for Motherhood," *Forerunner* 4 (October 1913); Cott, *Grounding*, 48–49; Jane P. Senn, "The Feminism of Ellen Key and Charlotte Perkins Gilman: A Comparative Study. " MA thesis, University of Wisconsin–Eau Claire, 1975.

Gilman declared herself in "full agreement" with most of *Love and Marriage*; it was only upon reading Key's far more conservative *Woman Movement* that Gilman recognized sharp differences (Gilman, "On Ellen Key," 35). Even then, Gilman and Key continued to agree about women's moral superiority and the importance of motherhood—only defining motherhood in slightly different terms. Their most significant differences prior to *The Woman Movement* seem to me to involve Key's more liberal attitude toward female sexuality; and Gilman's more collectivist, Key's more individualist philosophy.

74. Key, *Love and Marriage*, 177, 205, 263.

On Key's views of motherhood see also Cheri Register, "Motherhood at Center: Ellen Key's Social Vision," *Women's Studies International Forum* 5:6 (1982), 599–610; and Dina Lowy, "Love and Marriage: Ellen Key and Hiratsuka Raicho Explore Alternatives," *Women's Studies* 33 (2004), 361–80. Two fine shorter treatments can be found in Cott, *Grounding*, 46–49; and Mary Jo Buhle, *Women and American Socialism, 1879–1920* (Urbana: University of Illinois Press, 1981).

75. Dell, *Women as World Builders*, 78, 83; Cott, *Grounding*, 47–48.

76. Ellis, *Eonism*,492; Gilman, *Women*, 306.

77. Schreiner, *Woman*, 56, 109; Veblen, *Leisure*, 361.

In "Veblen's Attack on Culture," *Prisms*, trans. Samuel and Shierry Weber (Cambridge: MIT Press, 1981), Theodor W. Adorno notes how this nostalgic idea of the woman's "pre-glacial" standing conjoins positivism with a Rousseauesque "ideal state" (88).

78. Tsuzuki, *Edward Carpenter*, 103, 196; Carpenter, *Love's*, 97.

George Bernard Shaw contemptuously called Carpenter the "Noble savage" (quoted by Keith Nield, "Edward Carpenter: The Uses of Utopia," in *Edward Carpenter and Late Victorian Radicalism*, ed. Brown, 18).

79. Spencer, *Principles* I: 765; Catherine A. Lutz, "Emotion, Thought, and Estrangement:

Emotion as a Cultural Category," reprinted in *The Emotions: A Cultural Reader* (Oxford: Berg, 2007), 25; Battan, "'Rights' of Husbands," 167; T.J. Jackson Lears, *No Place of Grace: Antimodernism and the Transformation of American Culture, 1880-1920* (New York: Pantheon, 1981), quotation at 7; Glazener, *Reading for Realism*, 159.

On Carpenter's anarchism, see Allan Antliff, *Anarchist Modernism: Art, Politics, and the First American Avant-Garde* (Chicago: University of Chicago Press, 2001), 45-46. On the literary, artistic, and cultural implications of anarchism, see David Weir, *Anarchy and Culture: The Aesthetic Politics of Modernism* (Amherst: University of Massachusetts Press, 1997).

80. Ellis, *Sex in Relation* 417; Parsons, "Marriage and Parenthood—A Distinction," 514, 515.

81. See, for instance, Bederman, *Manliness*; Kline, *Building a Better Race*; Molly Ladd-Taylor, "Eugenics, Sterilisation and Modern Marriage in the USA: The Strange Career of Paul Popenoe," *Gender and History* 13:2 (August 2001), 298-327; Alexandra Minna Stern, *Eugenic Nation: Faults and Frontiers of Better Breeding in Modern American* (Berkeley: University of California Press, 2005); Edward J. Larson, *Sex, Race, and Science: Eugenics in the Deep South* (Baltimore: Johns Hopkins University Press, 1995). On Olive Schreiner and eugenics, see Carolyn Burdett's fascinating argument that *Women in Labour* represents a sustained "challenge" to the eugenics of her one-time close friend Karl Pearson (*Olive Schreiner and the Progress of Feminism: Evolution, Gender, Empire* [New York: Palgrave Macmillan, 2001], 62-77; quotation at 64).

82. Key, *Love and Marriage*, 150.

83. Galton quotation from *Essays in Eugenics* (1909), quoted in Daniel J. Kevles, *In the Name of Eugenics: Genetics and the Uses of Human Heredity* (New York: Knopf, 1985), 12.

84. Roosevelt quoted in Donald K. Pickens, *Eugenics and the Progressives* (Nashville: Vanderbilt University Press, 1968), 125; Pickens, *Eugenics*, 124. My overview derives also from Kevles, *In the Name of Eugenics*.

Traditionally, historians have seen enthusiasm for eugenics in the United States waning by around 1930, but more recent scholarship illustrates its persistence in different forms throughout the twentieth century and indeed throughout the developing world. See, for instance, in addition to sources cited in note 75, Frank Dikötter, "Race Culture: Recent Perspectives on the History of Eugenics," *American Historical Review* 103:2 (April 1998): 467-478; Ian Robert Dowbiggin, *Keeping America Sane: Psychiatry and Eugenics in the United States and Canada, 1880-1940* (Ithaca, NY: Cornell University Press, 1997); Troy Duster, *Backdoor to Eugenics* (New York: Routledge, 1990); Stephen Jay Gould, *The Mismeasure of Man*. (New York: Norton, 1981); Haller, *Eugenics: Hereditarian Attitudes in American Thought* (New Brunswick, NJ: Rutgers University Press, 1984); Hasian, *The Rhetoric of Eugenics in Anglo-American Thought* (Athens, GA: The University of Georgia Humanities Center Series on Science and the Humanities, 1996); Laura L. Lovett, *Conceiving the Future: Pronatalism, Reproduction, and the Family in the United States, 1890-1938* (Chapel Hill: University of North Carolina Press, 2007); Dorothy Nelkin and M. Susan Lindee, *The DNA Mystique: The Gene as a Cultural Icon* (New York: W.H. Freeman, 1995); Nancy Ordover, *American Eugenics: Race, Queer Anatomy, and the Science of Nationalism* (Minneapolis: University of Minnesota Press, 2003); Diane Paul, *Controlling Human Heredity, 1865 to the Present* (New Jersey: Humanities Press, 1995); Martin Pernick, *The Black Stork: Eugenics and the Death of "Defective" Babies in American Medicine and Motion Pictures Since 1915* (New York: Oxford University Press, 1996); Joan Rothschild, *The Dream of the Perfect Child* (Bloomington: Indiana University Press, 2005); Nancy Leys Stepan, *"The Hour of Eugenics": Race, Gender and Nation in Latin America* (Ithaca: Cornell University Press, 1991).

85. Ladd-Taylor, "Eugenics," 299; Dikötter, "Race Culture," 467.

Sociologist Edward Ross coined the term "race suicide" to describe the decline in the Anglo-Saxon birthrate while nonwhites reproduced at a higher rate.

86. Edward Bellamy, *Looking Backward* (New York: Penguin, 1982), 187, 191.

87. Charlotte Perkins Gilman, "What May We Expect of Eugenics," *Physical Culture* 31

(March 1914), 220; Key, *Love and Marriage*, 145, 146; Havelock Ellis, *The Task of Social Hygiene* (Boston: Houghton Mifflin, 1912), 59.

On Gilman's views of motherhood, see Sandra M. Gilbert and Susan Gubar, "'Fecundate! Discriminate!' Charlotte Perkins Gilman and the Theologizing of Maternity," *Charlotte Perkins Gilman: Optimist Reformer*, eds. Jill Rudd and Val Gough (Iowa City: University of Iowa Press, 1999), 200-15. Regarding Gilman's racial views, see Susan K. Lanser's pioneering "Feminist Criticism, 'The Yellow Wallpaper,' and the Politics of Color," *Charlotte Perkins Gilman, 'The Yellow Wallpaper,'* eds. Thomas L. Erskine and Connie L. Richards (New Brunswick: Rutgers University Press, 1993), 225-56, (originally published in *Feminist Studies* 15:3 [Fall 1989],415-41); Lisa Ganobcsik-Williams, "The Intellectualism of Charlotte Perkins Gilman: Evolutionary Perspectives on Race, Ethnicity, and Class, *Charlotte Perkins Gilman: Optimist Reformer*, eds. Rudd and Gough, 16-41; Tracy Fessenden, "Race, Religion, and the New Woman in America: The Case of Charlotte Perkins Gilman," *Furman Studies* 37 (June 1995): 15-28.

Regarding sexual selection in the period more broadly, see Bert Bender, *Evolution and the "Sex Problem": American Narratives During the Eclipse of Darwinism* (Kent, Ohio: Kent State University Press, 2004) and Bert Bender, *The Descent of Love: Darwin and the Theory of Sexual Selection in American Fiction, 1871-1926* (Philadelphia: University of Pennsylvania Press, 1996).

See Kline, *Building a Better Race*, Chapter 1, regarding eugenics-based arguments about which women are fit mothers.

88. On "mainline" eugenics see Kevles, *In the Name*, 88 and passim.

89. Ellis, *Sex in Relation*, 591 (and Ellis also invokes the phrase "race suicide," citing Scott Nearing, in *Task*, 193-94); Ellis, *Task*, 173, Parsons, *Old-Fashioned*, 90; Ellis, *Task*, 190; Ellis, *Sex in Relation*, 586.

Contemporaneous with the *Studies*, Ellis's *The Task of Social Hygiene* concentrates on eugenics.

90. Kevles, *In the Name*, 99-100; Pickens, *Eugenics*, 88; Ellis, *Sex in Relation*, 623; Ellis, *Task*, 273; Ellis, *Sex in Relation*, 623; Ellis, *Task*, 292.

91. Ellis, *Eonism*, 530-31; Howard, *History* I, 222-23; Schreiner, *Woman*, 50; Ellis, *Eonism*, 507.

92. Key, *Love and Marriage*, 3.

93. Naeem Murr, personal communication.

CHAPTER THREE

1. Upton Sinclair, *American Outpost: A Book of Reminiscence* (Pasadena, California: by the author, 1932), 230; Sinclair, *Brass Check*, 102.

2. William Brevda, one of few scholars to draw on it, calls Meta's manuscript an "aborted . . . novel" ("Love's Coming-of-Age: The Upton Sinclair-Harry Kemp Divorce Scandal, *North Dakota Review* 51:2 [Spring 1983], 66). I see it very differently: while not a continuous narrative, Meta's manuscript does provide a coherent account—and more importantly, an alternative one. Some segments are titled "Corydon and Thrysis"; others, "Thrysis and Corydon." I use the former attribution since placing the wife's name first seems more in keeping with Meta's agenda. The manuscripts cannot be precisely dated, but by 1910 Meta was talking about writing a novel and there is evidence that she was working on it by 1911.

3. According to Leon Harris, "Sinclair urged Meta to write the most important passages about Corydon" (*Upton Sinclair: American Rebel* [New York: Thomas Y. Crowell, 1975], 121). In a letter to Meta's mother, Sinclair claims that Meta revised the entire text of *Love's Pilgrimage* (Upton Sinclair to Mrs. [Mary] Fuller, October 15, 1913, Sinclair Manuscripts VI [hereafter Sinclair MSS VI], Lilly Library, Indiana University).

4. Sinclair to John Stone, October 12, 1964, Folder 1912-1965, Stone MSS.

5. Meta Fuller Sinclair [Stone] to Alfred Kuttner, no date, Folder Stone, Mrs. Meta (Fuller) to Kuttner, Alfred B. I, Stone MSS; Stone, Mrs. Meta (Fuller), to Kuttner, Alfred B. I, no date

but headed "Arden Delaware," Folder n.d. Stone, Mrs. Meta (Fuller) to Kuttner, Alfred B. I, Stone MSS.

Here and elsewhere, I have silently corrected inconsequential errors in unpublished documents, such as "vols" instead of "volumes" here or the failure to underline the title of a book.

6. Rauchway, *Refuge*, 9.

7. Sinclair extends the saga of "Thrysis" and "Corydon" into two autobiographies: *American Outpost* and *The Autobiography of Upton Sinclair* (New York: Harcourt, Brace, & World, 1962). The names also appear in letters.

8. Gilman, *The Living*, 26.

Walter Lippman believed Sinclair used radical ideas "to barricade himself more elaborately against the world whose contamination he dreaded," and in that dubious way, achieved "fabulous victories over creatures of his own imagination" ("Upton Sinclair," *The Saturday Review of Literature* IV:32 [March 3. 1928], 648).

In addition to the biographies of Sinclair by Leon Harris, Anthony Arthur, and Kevin Mattson, a good source of information on Helicon Hall is Lawrence Kaplan's "A Utopia During the Progressive Era: The Helicon Home Colony, 1906-1907," *American Studies* 25:2 (Fall 1984), 59-73. Kaplan sees the colony as "confront[ing] the Victorian world at its center; and in this respect it represented the Progressive challenge in miniature" (60).

In *Upton Sinclair and the Other American Century* (New York: John Wiley & Sons, 1906), Kevin Mattson provides the best account of the significance of the EPIC campaign, arguing that while Sinclair lost the election, his campaign helped shift the country, including FDR, to the left.

9. "Sinclair Sorry He Wed," *San Francisco Examiner*, January 30, 1909, 1-2.

10. Upton Sinclair, *Love's Pilgrimage* (London: Mitchell Kennerly, 1911), 141-42, 538. Subsequent references will be made parenthetically.

11. Lester Frank Ward, "Our Better Halves," *Forum*, November 1888, 275; Schreiner, *Woman*, 9; Carson, *Marriage Revolt*, 41.

12. Ellis, *Sex in Relation*, 539.

13. On masculinity in the Progressive era, see Gail Bederman's pioneering *Manliness and Civilization*. For analysis of the role of gender in American realism and naturalism, see Campbell, *Resisting Regionalism*; Fleissner, *Women, Compulsion, Modernity*; Rachel Bowlby, *Just Looking: Consumer Culture in Dreiser, Gissing, and Zola* (New York: Methuen, 1985); Naomi Schor, *Breaking the Chain: Women, Theory, and French Realist Fiction* (New York: Columbia University Press, 1985). On Sinclair and gender, see also Ingrid Kerkhoff , "Wives, Blue Blood Ladies, and Rebel Girls: A Closer Look at Upton Sinclair's Females," *Upton Sinclair: Literature and Social Reform*, ed. Dieter Herms (Frankfurt: Peter Lang, 1990), 176-94; Scott Derrick, "'What a Beating Feels Like': Authorship, Dissolution, and Masculinity in Sinclair's *The Jungle*," *Studies in American Fiction* 23:1 (Spring 1995), 85-101. Mark W. Van Wienen looks at the Sinclair marriage (and *Love's Pilgrimage*) from the vantage point of Upton Sinclair's difficulties in blending socialism and feminism (*American Socialist Triptych*, 108-13).

Biographers have linked Sinclair's commitment to reform to his psychosexual makeup. For Harris, at the time of Sinclair's marriage, he was even more strongly motivated by sex than by "his yearning for justice" (*Upton Sinclair*, 42); while for Mattson, Sinclair's attraction to socialism around 1904-1905 reflects how "this dream of a better world allowed him to escape the domestic hell of his marriage" (*Upton Sinclair*, 59).

14. Meta Fuller Sinclair [Stone], Folder Thrysis and Corydon V, Stone MSS; Leon Fink, *Progressive Intellectuals*, 3.

Sinclair's conception of the reformer also corresponds with Crunden's profile of the typical American progressive in *Ministers of Reform*. Crunden briefly discusses Sinclair as a "doctrinaire moralist" (94). For Christopher Lasch, also, progressivism functions as a replacement for the waning of traditional theology (*New Radicalism*, 11).

15. Sinclair quoted in Dell, *Upton Sinclair: A Study in Social Protest* [New York: George H. Doran, 1927], 63; Upton Sinclair, *American Outpost: A Book of Reminiscence* (Pasadena, California: by the author, 1932), 39.

It seems likely that while Sinclair saw some of Thrysis's limitations at the time he wrote *Love's Pilgrimage*, he did not have much critical distance. In *Mammonart* he records an argument with Jack London who objected to the sexual "asceticism" of *Love's Pilgrimage*. Sinclair recalls, "I am not sure how clearly I myself saw at that time the peculiar working of sex-idealism" (Upton Sinclair, *Mammonart* [Pasadena, CA: by the author, 1925], 365). In a 1913 letter, London said he found "Sinclair's "sex-poise, or sex-attitude" to be "alien" (Sinclair, *My Lifetime in Letters* [Columbia: University of Missouri Press, 1960], 27-28). Sinclair's friend Frederick van Eeden, the Dutch novelist and psychoanalyst who helped him get a divorce in Holland, also told him Thrysis had "defects which you [Sinclair] do not seem to consider as defects" (Sinclair, *My Lifetime*, 115-16). Floyd Dell, however, felt Sinclair constructed his hero's naiveté and neuroses deliberately, intending to show his development in the second volume, "Love's Progress" (*Upton Sinclair*, 129).

16. Meta Fuller Sinclair [Stone], "Folder Thrysis and Corydon III, Stone MSS.

17. Meta Fuller Sinclair [Stone], Their Wedding Night," Folder Thrysis and Corydon III, Stone MSS.

18. Meta Fuller Sinclair [Stone], Folder Thrysis and Corydon III, Stone MSS.

19. Meta Fuller Sinclair [Stone], Folder Thrysis and Corydon IV, Stone MSS.

20. Meta Fuller Sinclair [Stone], Folder Thrysis and Corydon IV, Stone MSS; Sinclair, *American Outpost*, 64. "There are dangers in 'Puritanism,'" Sinclair writes, "and there are compensations" such as "great intensity and power of concentration" (*American Outpost*, 66).

21. Harry Kemp, *Tramping on Life: An Autobiographical Narrative* (New York: Boni and Liveright, 1922), 417; Havelock Ellis letter printed in Sinclair, *My Lifetime*, 125-26.

22. According to Anthony Arthur, Meta was subsequently treated by Ellis (Anthony Arthur, *Radical Innocent: Upton Sinclair* [New York: Random House, 2006], 63).

23. Havelock Ellis, *The Sexual Impulse in Women*, Volume One, Part 2, of *Studies in the Psychology of Sex* (New York: Random House, 1936), 219, 189, 193.

24. Ellis, *Sexual Impulse*, 239.

25. Ellis, *Sex in Relation*, 178, 167, 179; Ellis, *Analysis of the Sexual Impulse*, 27; Ellis, *Mechanism*, 142; Ellis, *Sex in Relation*, 170, 173.

26. Ellis, *Sex in Relation*, 213, 214, 201.

27. Meta Fuller Sinclair [Stone], Folder Thrysis and Corydon IV, Stone MSS.

28. Basch, *Framing*, 59; Harris, *Upton Sinclair*, 134.

Sinclair's first suit in New York was declined because testimony exceeded what was legally permissible; the second, because the judge decided the husband was partly responsible for his wife's conduct (Arthur, *Radical Innocent* 134).

29. Blake, *Road to Reno*, 7; Howard, "Divorce and Public Welfare," 240.

30. Hartog, *Man and Wife*, 66, 73.

31. Lawrence M. Friedman and Robert V. Percival, "Who Sues for Divorce? From Fault through Fiction to Freedom," *Journal of Legal Studies* 5:1 (January 1976), 67; Riley, *Divorce*, 161.

32. Arthur, *Radical Innocent*, 156. My characterization of Sinclair's insistence on suing Meta for divorce is based on an undated letter he wrote her which appears in the Stone manuscripts. Unfortunately, due to the ineptitude of the literary agency representing Sinclair's heirs, I am not able to quote the actual letter.

In a letter to her former husband six years after the separation, Meta wrote, "I made the great mistake of my life by not fighting you in 1911" (Meta Fuller [Sinclair] Keene [Stone] to Upton Sinclair, May 25, 1917, Folder 1912-1965, Stone MSS).

33. Sinclair later explained that "because Meta was almost out of her mind, and I did not

know what to do with [their son] David, I started Helicon Hall" (Sinclair quoted in Howard H. Quint, "Upton Sinclair's Quest for Artistic Independence—1909," *American Literature* 27 [May 1957], 195). As Kevin Mattson puts it, founding Helicon Hall "allowed Sinclair to mistake the remaking of his private life for social transformation" (*Upton Sinclair*, 69).

34. Meta believed the relationship flopped because, in giving herself freely rather than making Kuttner chase her, she "failed to play the sex game" (Meta Fuller Sinclair [Stone] to "My dear André" [Alfred Kuttner], no date, Stone MSS). She also wrote her son David many years later, "Alfred didn't know how to be a lover, . . . because he didn't love" and that he was "somewhat homosexual" (Meta Fuller [Stone] to David Sinclair, February 18, 1942, Folder 1912–1965, Stone MSS).

35. William Brevda, *Harry Kemp, The Last Bohemian* (Lewisburg, PA: Bucknell University Press, 1986), 42.

Biographers disagree about the timing and extent of the Sinclairs' adultery, particularly Meta's. There were certainly other men, most notably John Armistead Collier (whom Anthony Arthur calls "a brilliant but periodically insane theology student from Memphis"), but I find no reliable evidence that she took a lover before Kuttner (Arthur, *Radical Innocent*, 98).

Harry Kemp publicly announced that Sinclair had proposed to two women before divorcing Meta ("U. Sinclair 'Too Conventional,'" *Boston Journal* December 28, 1911, 5). That claim is corroborated by a letter Kemp wrote to his one-time mentor who had disappointingly assumed the role of outraged spouse. Kemp reminds Sinclair that he showed no interest in Meta in Battle Creek, that Sinclair had himself pursued other women while still married to Meta, proposed to three while still married, and actually insisted that Kemp take Meta away with him (Harry Kemp to Upton Sinclair, December 29, 1911, July-December 1911 folder, Sinclair MSS I, Lilly Library).

Sinclair's own correspondence is also incriminating. In an undated letter from 1910 he wrote an unidentified woman, admitting it odd to have asked her to marry him after knowing her around four days. Letters from September 1911—right after Sinclair had publicly announced his intent to divorce Meta—make clear that he had been romantically involved with Craig and that they had colluded to orchestrate the New York divorce trial.

36. Meta Fuller Sinclair [Stone], Folder Thrysis and Corydon V, Stone MSS.

In "Love's Progress," Sinclair writes about Thrysis's affair with the Anna Noyes figure, including what is probably the most sexually explicit writing he has ever penned (see Book VII, "The Delectable Mountains," Sinclair MSS IV).

37. Meta Fuller Sinclair [Stone], Folder Thrysis and Corydon IV, Stone MSS.

38. Meta Fuller Sinclair [Stone], Folder Thrysis and Corydon IV, Stone MSS; Meta Stone to David Sinclair [no date], N.D. Stone MSS L-X Folder, Stone MSS.

Harry Kemp confirms Meta's account in "Poet Kemp Tells How Mrs. Sinclair Entered His Life," *New York Globe*, December 27, 1911.

39. Meta Fuller Sinclair [Stone], Folder Thrysis and Corydon IV, Stone MSS.

40. Meta Fuller Sinclair [Stone], Folder Thrysis and Corydon IV, Stone MSS; Meta Fuller Sinclair [Stone], Folder Thrysis and Corydon II, Stone MSS; Meta Fuller Sinclair [Stone], Folder Thrysis and Corydon IV, Stone MSS.

41. Meta Fuller Sinclair [Stone], Folder Thrysis and Corydon IV, Stone MSS; Meta Fuller Sinclair [Stone] to Alfred Kuttner, no date, Folder n. d. L-Z, Stone MSS; Meta Fuller Sinclair [Stone] to Alfred B. Kuttner, Sunday morning, April 18 [1910?], Stone to Kuttner, Alfred B. I Folder; Meta Fuller Sinclair [Stone] to Alfred Kuttner, September 30, [no year]; Stone MSS; Meta Fuller Sinclair to Alfred B. Kuttner, March 29, 1911, 1911 Folder, Stone MSS.

42. Sicherman, *Well-Read Lives*, 54; Edith Ellis and *Punch* cartoon both quoted in Ann Heilman, *New Woman Fiction: Women Writing First-Wave Feminism* (St. Martins, 2000), 56–57, 2. See also Ann L. Ardis, *New Woman, New Novels: Feminism and Early Modernism* (Rutgers, 1990), 3;

Sally Ledger, *The New Woman: Fiction and Feminism at the Fin de Siècle* (Manchester: Manchester University Press, 1997), 3.

43. Meta Fuller Sinclair [Stone], "Uncertainty" (the same poem appears elsewhere titled "Quest"); Meta Fuller Sinclair [Stone], "Rivers," all in Poems Folder, Stone MSS.

44. Meta Fuller Sinclair [Stone], Thrysis and Corydon V folder, Stone MSS; Meta Fuller Sinclair [Stone], Thrysis and Corydon XIII folder, Stone MSS.

45. Sinclair, *Brass Check*, 112.

46. Johanningsmeier, *Fiction and the American Literary Marketplace*, 18, 25.

47. "Terse Telegrams," *Belleville* (Illinois) *News-Democrat*, October 19, 1907, 6; "Upton Sinclair Denies Reports," *New York Times*, November 7 1907, 6; "Sinclair Sorry He Wed / Says Ceremony Is Farce," *San Francisco Examiner*, January 30 1909, 1–2; Sinclair, *Brass Check*, 90–92; "Sorry He Married / Upton Sinclair Mighty Lugubrious about Matrimony," *Morning Olympian* [Olympia, Washington] January 31, 1909, 1.

48. "Sinclair Freaky, Papa-in-Law Says," *Morning Oregonian*, November 11, 1911, 3; "Kansas Poet and Wife of Radical Author, Who Say They Took Husband at His Word" (*Globe*, clipping stamped with date December 27, 1911, no page number given, Printed material folder, Stone MSS).

49. "Harry Kemp Named Co-Respondent by Sinclair," *Idaho Daily Statesman*, August 29, 1911, 1; [untitled], *Grand Forks* (North Dakota) *Herald*, September 2. 1911, 4; "Sinclair's Plight," *Morning Oregonian* January 10, 1912, 8; [untitled] *Life*, September 7, 1911; *Bookman*, November 1911, 219, 220–21.

50. "Favors a Divorce for Upton Sinclair," *New York Times*, November 30, 1911.

51. "Upton Sinclair Enters His Suit," *Baltimore American*, August 29, 1911, 9; "Sinclair Divorces Wife, But They're Friends," *New York Times*, August 29, 1911, 1.

52. Will Irwin, "Power of the Press," 8; Will Irwin, "What is News?" 30; Will Irwin, "Power of the Press," 8, Irwin, What is News?" 30, all reprinted in the *American Newspaper. [rpt.] Series First Appearing in Collier's January–July 1911*, with comments by Clifford F. Weigle and David G. Clark (Ames, IA: Iowa State University Press).

In an illuminating prehistory to my account, Part 3 of Basch's *Framing* focuses on Victorian sensational divorce trials covered in the news and pamphlets, in which she finds "extraordinary sympathy" for the wives (144). For a very different analysis of how the press worked to disseminate progressivism, see David Paul Nord, *Communities of Journalism: A History of American Newspaper and Their Readers* (Urbana: University of Illinois Press, 2001).

53. "Not a Nice Story," *Hartford Courant* August, 29, 1911, 8; "Sinclairs Friendly in Divorce Talk," *Hartford Courant*, August 29, 1911, 10.

54. "Kansas Poet and Wife of Radical Author," *New York Globe*, clipping stamped with date December 27, 1911, printed material folder, Stone MSS; "Mrs. Sinclair Explains Her Creed," *Bellingham Herald*, September 7, 1911, 6.

55. "These Are Affinity Poems," *The Daily Oklahoman* September 17, 1911, 7.

The *New York Journal* gave Kemp and Meta a different sort of immortality by using them in a "Dingbat" comic strip, playing bulldog and hound, respectively, with Sinclair a pug (Brevda, *Harry Kemp*, 63).

56. "Mrs. Sinclair Explains Her Creed," *Bellingham Herald*, September 7, 1911, 6; "The Friend, the Wife, the Husband in the Sinclair 'Dramatic Triangle,'" *Idaho Daily Statesman*, September 6, 1911, 3; "No Free Love in Creed Avowed by Mrs. Sinclair," clipping, no title or date given, printed material folder, Stone MSS; "Mrs. Sinclair Calls Women Jelly Fish," *New York American* clipping stamped with date August 1911, printed material folder, Stone MSS; "Try a Marriage; If a Failure Try Again," *Idaho Daily Statesman*, September 6, 1911, 3; "Upton Sinclair Enters His Suit," *Baltimore American* August 29, 1911, 9; "Sinclair Sues, Names Kemp," *Kansas City Star*, August 28, 1911, 3; "Mrs. Sinclair Braves Opinion," clipping stamped "from Chicago"

with date December 1, 1911, printed material folder, Stone MSS; "Approves Mrs. Sinclair," *New York Times*, September 14, 1911.

Meta pasted the *Idaho Daily Statesman* clipping into one of her typescripts, writing in by hand, "These remarks are almost verbatim as I gave them" (Meta Fuller Sinclair [Stone], Thrysis and Corydon V folder, Stone MSS).

57. Frank Luther Mott, *American Journalism, A History: 1690-1960* (New York: Macmillan 1962), 598.

58. Alice Fahs, *Out on Assignment: Newspaper Women and the making of Modern Public Space* (Chapel Hill: University of North Carolina Press, 2011), Alice Fahs, *Out on Assignment: Newspaper Women and the Making of Modern Public Space* (Chapel Hill: University of North Carolina Press, 2011), quotation at 7.

59. John D. Stevens, "Social Utility of Sensational News: Murder and Divorce in the 1920s," *Journalism Quarterly*, 57, 58.

60. Kemp, *Tramping*, 373, 316.
One of Kemp's poems to Meta commemorates when,

> . . . for the first time we'd the spasm
> And gush of mutual orgasm

(Harry Kemp, "Dear Little cunning cuddly Naa," [April 1? 1913] Stone MSS). Kemp and Meta thought the nicknames "Naa" and "Kaa" suggested cavemen and women, and thus captured their passion. They referred to Upton Sinclair as "Baa" and Mary Craig Kimbrough as "Blaa."

61. Kemp, *Tramping*, 382, 404, 423, 352, 391, 402, 396. As Brevda puts it, "Kemp's affair with Meta Sinclair put into practice what Upton Sinclair had been preaching (and sometimes practicing) for years" ("Love's Coming of Age," 68).

62. Frank Luther Mott, *A History of American Magazines, 1741-1930*. Volume IV (Cambridge, MA: Harvard University Press, 1957), 55, 499, accessed electronically January 10, 2012: http://hdl.handle.net/2027/heb.00678.0004.001.

63. Meta Fuller Sinclair, "A Plea for Freer Divorce," *The World To-day; A Monthly Record of Human Progress* 21 (October 1911), 1202, 1203, 1204, 1205, 1202, 1204. The other publication of hers is the "affinity poem" referenced above and published in the *Daily Oklahoman*.

64. Upton Sinclair, "Marriage and Divorce," *The World To-day; A Monthly Record of Human Progress* 21 (October 1911), 1199, 1198, 1201, 1200.

65. Warren and Brandeis, "Right to Privacy," 195, 199-200.

66. Sinclair, *Brass Check*, 429; Arthur, *Radical Innocent*, 182.

67. Mott, *American Journalism*, 593; Marion Tuttle Marzolf, *Civilizing Voices: American Press Criticism 1880-1950* (New York: Longman, 1991), 18; Mott, *American Journalism*, 559; Marzolf, *Civilizing Voices*, 72.

In addition to Mott and Marzolf, this brief history of the press draws also from Robert Miraldi, *Muckraking and Objectivity: Journalism's Colliding Traditions* (New York: Greenwood Press, 1990); Will Irwin, *The American Newspaper*; Nord, *Communities of Journalism*; and Johanningsmeier, *Fiction and the American Literary Marketplace*.

68. Marzolf, *Civilizing Voices*, 76.

69. Sinclair, *Brass Check*, 10, 18-19.

70. Ibid., 105, 106.

71. Ibid., 102.

72. Ibid., 114, 283, 332.

73. Dean Eric Allen cited in Marzolf, *Civilizing Voices*, 78; McChesney and Scott, Introduction to *Brass Check*, xi-xii, quotation at xii.

The ever-opinionated H.L. Mencken described Sinclair's proposals in *The Brass Check* as "simple, clear, bold, and idiotic" (quoted in Harris, *Upton Sinclair*, 180).

74. Characterization of New Journalism drawn from John Hollowell, *Fact and Fiction:*

The New Journalism and the Nonfiction Novel (Chapel Hill: University of North Carolina Press, 1977), 22.

Anthony Arthur says that Sinclair's modus operandi is to personalize all disputes (*Radical Innocent*, 212). Noting the "substantial autobiographical oversimplification," Christopher P. Wilson says that Sinclair "lived in and out of his fiction," which served "as a realm of self-envisionment and projection" (*Labor* 119, 123, 121). For discussion of Sinclair's career-long investment in autobiography, see also Renate von Bardeleben, "Upton Sinclair and the Art of Autobiography," *Upton Sinclair: Literature and Social Reform*, ed. Dieter Herms (Frankfurt: Peter Lang, 1990), 114–130.

75. Sinclair, *Brass Check*, 15–16, 387, 436, 437, 287; Loren Glass, *Authors Inc.: Literary Celebrity in the Modern United States, 1880–1980* (New York: New York University Press, 2004), 18.

76. Jennifer Travis, *Wounded Hearts: Masculinity, Law, and Literature in American Culture* (Chapel Hill: University of North Carolina Press, 2005), quotation at 10.

77. Upton Sinclair, "Happy Marriage: How Can It Be Assured?" *Physical Culture* 29 (February 1913), 302, 301; Upton Sinclair, "The Real Marriage–What It Is," 130, 131, 133.

Sinclair's novels *Sylvia* (1913) and *Sylvia's Marriage* (1919), about sexually transmitted diseases, derive from stories Craig told him. According to Arthur, Sinclair projected onto his character Lanny Budd his own view that there were two types of women: the unsatisfied artists (like Meta) and those "'mother-soul[s]'" who sacrificed their own personalities in the service of their husbands (like Craig). After Craig's death, Sinclair married May Willis—after having proposed to several women, including one, by mail, whom he had never met (Anthony Arthur, *Radical Innocent: Upton Sinclair* [New York: Random House, 2006], 317–18).

78. Upton Sinclair, *The Book of Life: Mind and Body* (Girard, KS: Haldeman-Julius, 1921), I:40.

79. Sinclair, *Book of Life*, I:53; II:65; II:56; II:51; II:77; II:90; II:58–59.

80. Harris, *Upton Sinclair*, 36; Dell, *Upton Sinclair*, 156.

81. Meta Fuller Sinclair [Stone], Folder Thrysis and Corydon IV, Stone MSS.

82. Theodore Dreiser to Sara O. White, February 1, 1898, Dreiser MSS II, Manuscripts Department, Lilly Library, Indiana University, Bloomington, Indiana (hereafter Dreiser MSS II).

CHAPTER FOUR

1. Arthur Henry quoted in Richard Lingeman, *Theodore Dreiser: At the Gates of the City* (New York: G.P. Putnam's Sons, 1986), 223; Lingeman, *Theodore Dreiser*, 309; Theodore Dreiser, *Newspaper Days*. University of Pennsylvania Dreiser Edition, ed. T.D. Nostwich (Philadelphia: University of Pennsylvania Press, 1991), 470.

2. Arthur Henry, *An Island Cabin* (New York: McClure, Phillips, & Co., 1902), 178. The book was first serialized in the *New York Post*. Accessed October 10, 2011: http://books.google.com/books?id=CIYpAQAAIAAJ&printsec=frontcover&dq=island+cabin&hl=en&ei=ZAQeTrqOB-bzogH_tdXZBw&sa=X&oi=book_result&ct=result&resnum=1&ved=0CCkQ6AEwAA#v=onepage&q&f=false

3. Henry, *Island Cabin*, 180, 192, 196, 192, 193, 206.

4. Ibid., 195.

5. Dreiser quoted in Thomas P. Riggio's introduction to Theodore Dreiser's *American Diaries 1902–1926*, eds. Thomas P. Riggio, James L.W. West, III, and Neda Westlake, (Philadelphia: University of Pennsylvania Press, 1983),11. Many courtship letters have been published in Theodore Dreiser, *Letters to Women*, Volume Two of *New Letters*, ed. Thomas P. Riggio, (Urbana: University of Illinois Press, 2009).

6. Dreiser, *American Diaries, 1902–1926*, 165, 92. The first diary entry dates from 1902 and the second from 1917, marking very different stages in the marriage.

7. Riggio, introduction to *Letters to Women*, xxvii.

Most of Dreiser's works were extensively edited and at times bowdlerized by third parties before their publication; the Dreiser Edition (previously known as the Pennsylvania Edition) is an ongoing effort to publish his works as he originally wrote them.

8. H.L. Mencken to Theodore Dreiser, March 25 [1915], in *Dreiser-Mencken Letters: The Correspondence of Theodore Dreiser and H. L. Mencken, 1907–1945*, ed. Thomas P. Riggio, Volume One (Philadelphia: University of Pennsylvania Press, 1986) 191; Floyd Dell, *Homecoming: An Autobiography* (New York: Holt & Rinehart, 1933), 239–40.

9. Elia W. Peattie, "Mr. Dreiser Chooses a Tom-Cat for a Hero," 1915; rpt. in *Theodore Dreiser: The Critical Reception*, ed. Jack Salzman (New York: David Lewis, 1972), 242–44; unidentified reviewer quoted in Louis J. Oldani, "A Study of Theodore Dreiser's *The 'Genius*,'" dissertation, University of Pennsylvania, 1972, 145.

10. Donald Pizer, *The Novels of Theodore Dreiser: A Critical Study* (Minneapolis: University of Minnesota Press, 1976), 144.

Dreiser's interest in marriage is part of a larger pattern identified by Riggio: the novelist often "raised to the level of philosophical discourse issues in which he had a personal stake" (*American Diaries*, 20).

11. Theodore Dreiser, *The Genius*, Dreiser Edition, ed. Clare Virginia Eby (Urbana: University of Illinois Press, 2008), 851, 581.

This chapter focuses primarily on the 1911 edition and secondarily on a comparison of the two editions. Subsequent citations will be made parenthetically to the 1911 *The Genius* unless designated as from the 1915 *"Genius"* (noted parenthetically as *"Genius"*). References in the text to *The "Genius"* (New York: Boni and Liveright, 1915) will refer *only* to the 1915 edition—for instance, comments about reviews of the novel.

12. Ellen Moers, *Two Dreisers* (New York: Viking Press, 1969).

13. Hutchins Hapgood, *A Victorian in the Modern World* (New York: Harcourt, Brace, 1939), 588.

14. Thomas Riggio, "Another Two Dreisers: The Artist as 'Genius,'" *Studies in the Novel* 9 (1977), 128.

Eugene's sexual vitiation would have been diagnosed as neurasthenia. According to the preeminent authority, George M. Beard in *Sexual Neurasthenia [Nervous Exhaustion]: Its Hygiene, Causes, Symptoms, and Treatment, With a Chapter on Diet for the Nervous*, ed. A.D. Rockwell (New York: E.B. Treat, 1884), 105–106, "exhaustion of the sexual organs, through excess or masturbation, brings on at first indifference to the opposite sex, then positive fear or dread of normal intercourse." In addition, "the unhappiest marriages are those where there is the greatest indulgence."

15. Edith Ellis, "Novitiate," 14, 13, 19; Edith Ellis, "Love of To-Morrow," 1; Edith Ellis, "Eugenics and the Mystical Outlook," rpt. in *New Horizon*, 44; Havelock Ellis, *Eonism*, 523.

16. Carpenter, *Love's*, 24; Schreiner quoted in Mallett, "Woman and Marriage," 182; Key, *Love and Marriage*, 50, 356; Carter, *Heart of Whiteness*, 24; Peter N. Stearns, *American Cool: Constructing a Twentieth-Century Emotional Style* (New York: New York University Press, 1994), 37.

17. Ellis, *Eonism*, 515.

18. Key, *Love and Marriage*, 294.

19. Parsons, *The Family*, 349 ; Stansell, *American Moderns*, 28.

For extended discussion of this topic, see Barbara Sicherman, *Well-Read Lives: How Books Inspired a Generation of American Women* (Chapel Hill: University of North Carolina Press, 2010).

20. Theodore Dreiser to Sara Osborne White [February 1,1898], Dreiser MSS II; Theodore Dreiser to Sara Osborne White, July 10,1896, *Letters to Women*, 17; Dreiser, *Newspaper Days*, 394.

21. Swanberg, *Dreiser*, 175, 124.

Jerome Loving observes in *The Last Titan: A Life of Theodore Dreiser* (Berkeley: University of California Press), 192, 193, that for years Sara was Dreiser's "emotional and domestic anchor," in part because she "mothered Dreiser the way his own mother had."

22. Theodore Dreiser to Sara Osborne White, c. December 26, 1897, Dreiser MSS II; Theo-

dore Dreiser to Sara Osborne White, July 10, 1896, *Letters to Women*, 16; Theodore Dreiser to Sara Osborne White, October 4, 1896, Dreiser MSS II.

23. Theodore Dreiser, "Deeper than Man-Made Laws," rpt. in *Theodore Dreiser: Uncollected Prose*, ed. Donald Pizer (Detroit: Wayne State University Press, 1977), 191.

24. Clare Virginia Eby, "Dreiser and Women." *The Cambridge Companion to Theodore Dreiser*, eds. Leonard Cassuto and Clare Virginia Eby (Cambridge: Cambridge University Press, 2004), 142–59. For further discussion of Dreiser's portrayal of women and sexuality in the 1911 *The Genius*, see Clare Virginia Eby, "Intellectual and Cultural Background to *The Genius*: The 1911 Version to Print," *The Genius* by Theodore Dreiser, 765–68.

For negative appraisals of Dreiser's portrayal of and relationships with women, see Irene Gammel, *Sexualizing Power in Naturalism: Theodore Dreiser and Frederick Philip Grove* (Calgary, CN: University of Calgary Press, 1994); Shelley Fisher Fishkin, "Dreiser and the Discourse of Gender," *Theodore Dreiser: Beyond Naturalism*, ed. Miriam Gogol (New York: New York University Press, 1995), 1–30; Priscilla Perkins, "Self-Generation in a Post-Eugenic Utopia: Dreiser's Conception of the 'Matronized' Genius," *American Literary Realism* 32:1 (Fall 1999), 12–32; and especially Susan Wolstenholme, "Brother Theodore, Hell on Women." *American Novelists Revisited: Essays in Feminist Criticism*, ed. Fritz Fleischmann (Boston: G.K. Hall, 1982), 243–64.

25. Ellis, *The Sexual Impulse in Women*, 189, 192, 247.

26. Dreiser's story "Married," which reworks the early years of the Witla marriage, includes a variant of this idea of the wife as an emotional genius (Theodore Dreiser, "Married," *Free and Other Stories* [New York: Boni & Liveright, 1918], 345–47).

27. Nussbaum, *Upheavals*, 328; Elster, *Alchemies*, 312.

28. Source: measuringworth.com, using CPI.

29. Jude Davies, "Historical Commentary" to Theodore Dreiser, *Political Writings*, ed. Jude Davies (Urbana: University of Illinois Press, 2011), 10; Towne, "Some Noted Contributors," 368; Dreiser quoted in Davies, *Political Writings*, 9.

30. Theodore Dreiser to Fremont Rider, January 24, 1911, in *Letters of Theodore Dreiser: A Selection*, ed. Robert H. Elias (Philadelphia: University of Pennsylvania Press, 1959), Volume. One, 110.

31. Theodore Dreiser, "Greenwich Village," unpublished MS, Theodore Dreiser Papers, Annenberg Rare Book and Manuscript Library, University of Pennsylvania (hereafter TD Papers). On the dating of *The Genius* and Dreiser's reluctance to publish it, see Clare Virginia Eby, "The Composition of *The Genius*: The 1911 Version to Print," *The Genius* by Theodore Dreiser, 753.

32. Dreiser, *Newspaper Days*, 170, 240–41.

33. H.L. Mencken, *My Life as Author and Editor*, ed. Jonathan Yardley (New York: Knopf, 1993), 152.

34. Floyd Dell, *Love in Greenwich Village*, 240–41, 243, 248.

35. Theodore Dreiser, "Esther Norn," *A Gallery of Women*, Volume Two (New York: Horace Liveright, 1929), 761; Hapgood, *Victorian*, 202.

36. Trimberger, "Feminism, Men, and Modern Love," 132; Judith Schwarz, *Radical Feminists of Heterodoxy: Greenwich Village 1912–1940* (Lebanon, NH: New Victoria Publishers, 1984), 64; Florence Guy Woolson, "Marriage Customs and Taboos among the Early Heterodities," reprinted in Schwarz, *Radical Feminists*, 96.

On the feminist embrace of varietism, see also Margaret S. Marsh, "The Anarchist–Feminist Response to the 'Woman Question' in Late Nineteenth-Century America," *American Quarterly* 30:4 (Autumn 1978), 533–47.

37. Emma Goldman, "The Traffic in Women," rpt. in *Red Emma Speaks*, ed. Alix Kate Shulman (New York: Random House, 1972), 145; Emma Goldman, "Marriage and Divorce," rpt. in *Red Emma Speaks*, 158, 159.

38. Emma Goldman, "What I Believe," rpt. in *Red Emma Speaks*, 36; Goldman, "Marriage

and Divorce," 165; Emma Goldman, "The Tragedy of Woman's Emancipation," rpt. in *Red Emma Speaks*, 142; Goldman "Marriage and Divorce," 165; Emma Goldman, "Jealousy: Causes and a Possible Cure," rpt. in *Red Emma Speaks*, 169.

Regarding Goldman's differentiating between varietism and promiscuity—and particularly how her lover Ben Reitman's promiscuity sharpened Goldman's distinction—see Candace Serena Falk, *Love, Anarchy, and Emma Goldman*, Revised Edition (New Brunswick, NJ: Rutgers University Press, 1990), esp. Chapter 4.

39. Goldman, "Jealousy," 171. Stansell, *American Moderns*, 84, discusses Goldman's "Varietist or Monogamist" lecture.

40. Edward Westermarck, *The History of Human Marriage* (London: Macmillan, 1891), 15, 505; Spencer quoted in Westermarck, 509. Dreiser famously maintained that when he read Herbert Spencer's *First Principles*, it "quite blew me to bits intellectually" (*Newspaper Days*, 610).

41. Dreiser, *Newspaper Days*, 292–93.

In a nonfictional piece that analyzes the problems with marriage (rather than dramatizing them as he does in *The Genius*), Dreiser makes a similar point: "Marriage and Divorce," *Hey Rub A Dub Dub! A Book of the Mystery and Wonder and Terror of Life* (New York: Boni and Liveright, 1920), 215, 216.

42. On the discrepancy between theory and practice in male proponents of varietism, see Stansell, *American Moderns*; Trimberger, "Feminism"; Marriner, "A Victorian in the Modern World,"; and Simmons, "Women's Power in Sex Radical Challenges to Marriage."

43. Sara Dreiser quoted in Loving, *Last Titan*, 390; Thomas P. Riggio, "Dreiser and Kirah Markham: The Play's the Thing," *Studies in American Naturalism* 1:1 and 2 (Summer & Winter 2006), 122; Mencken, *My Life*, 141, 140.

44. Kirah Markham to TD, March 29, 1916, Kirah Markham to TD, May 9, 1916, both in Box 70, Folder 3970, TD Papers. Dreiser fictionalizes Kirah as Stephanie Platow in *The Titan*.

45. Kirah Markham to TD May 16, 1916, Box 70, Folder 3970, TD Papers.

In a 1913 letter to Kirah, Dreiser criticized the "exaggerated Bohemianism and the rapid intimacy" he associated with Dell (see *Letters to Women*, 64).

Dreiser's letters to Kirah from this same time provide mesmerizing reading; most have been published recently in *Letters to Women*. These letters confirm the two faces of Dreiser. On one hand, he dreams of lifelong monogamy with the perfect woman (April 27, 1913, 71) and declares he "was never cut out to be a bachelor nor even a promiscuous liver. . . . I'd like to settle down somewhere with you and just live in a simple, homey way" (February 24, 1915, 99). On the other, he refuses "having my movements controlled by a domestic arrangement" (May 30, 1916, 110). Riggio sees the disaffection as "largely . . . a result of Dreiser's unwillingness to enter into what he was coming to see as a conventional 'marital' relationship" (*Letters to Women*, 108).

In personal communication, Thomas Riggio has informed me that Kirah's standing up to Dreiser was a "bluff." No one knows more about Dreiser than Riggio, yet Kirah's bluffing does not alter my conclusions about Dreiser.

46. An 1896 piece Dreiser wrote for the music magazine he edited, *Ev'ry Month*, provides a different register of his distance from bohemia. Making fun of the popularity of bohemian novels, Dreiser identifies the formula: "first get your Bohemian plot, lay your scenes in well-known cafes, like Delmonico's and Pfaff's, 'ring in' an artist's studio or . . . a girl raised from the slums into high life, and presto! there you are, deep in a Bohemian story" ("Edward Al" [Theodore Dreiser], "The Literary Shower," *Ev'ry Month* February 1896, rpt. in *Theodore Dreiser's Ev'ry Month*, ed. Nancy Warner Barrineau [Athens, GA: University of Georgia Press, 1996], 49).

47. Key, *Love*, 76–77; Edith Ellis, "Love of To-Morrow," 9, 5, 9; Edith Ellis, "Marriage and Divorce," rpt. in *New Horizon*, 33.

48. The Scavenger, "The Dionysian Dreiser," rpt. in *Theodore Dreiser*, ed. Salzman, 209-10; "A Genius and Also a Cur," (ibid., 215); "A Riot of Eroticism," (ibid., 224); Randolph Bourne, "Desire as Hero," (ibid., 235).

49. Dell, *Homecoming* 278; Goldman, *Living My Life*, Volume One, (New York: Da Capo Press, 197), 219; Goldman, "Victims of Morality," rpt. in Goldman, *Red Emma Speaks*, 127.

50. H.L. Mencken, "The Dreiser Bugaboo," rpt. in *Dreiser-Mencken Letters*, Volume Two, 772, 773; "A Protest against the Suppression of Theodore Dreiser's *The 'Genius,'*" rpt. in *Dreiser-Mencken Letters*, Volume Two, 803; Folder 8072: *The "Genius,"* documents pertaining to its suppression, TD Papers; Richard Lingeman, *Theodore Dreiser: An American Journey, 1908-1945* (New York: G.P. Putnam's Sons, 1990), 137. For Mencken's critical review of *The "Genius,"* see "A Literary Behemoth" rpt. in *Letters* II: 754-59.

51. Mencken quoted in Oldani, "Study," 300; Oldani, "Study," 247; H.L. Mencken, "The Dreiser Bugaboo," rpt. in *Dreiser-Mencken Letters* 2: 773-74. Mencken repeatedly discusses his fear of Villagers jumping on the *"Genius"* bandwagon as a publicity stunt in *My Life*, 159, passim.

52. Dreiser, *Newspaper Days*, 324, 329, 325.

53. Joseph Katz, "Dummy: *The 'Genius,'* by Theodore Dreiser, *Proof* 1 [1971], 330; Sinclair Lewis, "The American Fear of Literature," rpt. in *The Man from Main Street*, ed. Harry E. Maule and Melville H. Cane (New York: Pocket Books, 1953), 7-8; Dorothy Dudley, *Forgotten Frontiers: Dreiser and the Land of the Free* (New York: Harrison Smith and Rat Haas, 1932), 367.

CHAPTER FIVE

1. Neith Boyce, "The Bachelor Girl," Paper 3, *Vogue* 11:24 (June 16, 1898), viii; Neith Boyce, "The Bachelor Girl," Paper 1, *Vogue* 11:18 (May 5, 1898), 294; Neith Boyce, "The Bachelor Girl," Paper 8, *Vogue* 12:1 (September 22, 1898), 190. Characterization of *Vogue* from Mott, *History of American Magazines*, Volume Five, 756-58; accessed electronically August 1, 2011, http://hdl .handle.net/2027/heb.00678.0004.001.

See Fahs, *Out on Assignment*, 133-62, on the popularizing of the Bachelor Girl by newspaper women in the late 1880s and 1890s. Fahs, who emphasizes the alternative domestic space inhabited by the Bachelor Girl, identifies the figure as "part of a larger critique of marriage at the turn of the century." Fahs quotes from an anonymous 1893 article positing that because the Bachelor Girl sees marriage through the eyes of other women, she "finds by some strange legal hocus-pocus the marriage ceremony transforms in a twinkling an independent, judicious woman into a legal nonentity" (quotations at 142).

2. Anonymous reviewer quoted in DeBoer-Langworthy's introduction to *The Modern World of Neith Boyce* (Albuquerque: University of New Mexico Press, 2003), 14; Hapgood, *Victorian*, 148. On women's newspaper work, see Fahs, *Out on Assignment*.

3. Lincoln Steffens, *The Autobiography of Lincoln Steffens* (New York: Harcourt, Brace, 1931), 314; Neith Boyce, "Autobiography," in *The Modern World of Neith Boyce*, ed. De Boer-Langworthy, 174; De Boer-Langworthy, "Introduction," 13.

De Boer-Langworthy provides the fullest source of biographical information in *The Modern World of Neith Boyce*. I draw biographical information also from Ellen Kay Trimberger, ed. *Intimate Warriors: Portraits of a Modern Marriage, 1899-1944. Selected Works by Neith Boyce and Hutchins Hapgood.* (New York: The Feminist Press, 1991); Trimberger, "Feminism, Men, and Modern Love"; Stansell, *American Moderns*, Hapgood, *Victorian*; Hutchins Hapgood, *The Story of a Lover* (New York: Boni & Liveright, 1919); Michael D. Marcaccio, *The Hapgoods: Three Earnest Brothers* (Charlottesville: University of Virginia Press, 1977); and Hapgood Family Papers, Yale Collection of American Literature, Beinecke Rare Book and Manuscript Library (hereafter HFP).

4. Hapgood, *Victorian*, 159; Boyce, "Autobiography"; Hutchins Hapgood, *Story of a Lover* (New York: Boni and Liveright, 1919), 116.

5. Carol Z. Stearns and Peter N. Stearns, eds., in the introduction to *Emotions and Social Change: Toward a New Psychohistory* (New York: Holmes and Meier, 1988), 7.

6. For instance, Boyce "sacrificed the independence she had struggled for as a writer when she got married, consciously immolating herself on the altar of Love" (Barbara Ozieblo, ed., in the introduction to *The Provincetown Players: A Choice of the Shorter Works* [Sheffield, UK: Sheffield Academic Press, 1994], 17). All the extended and most of the incidental commentary on the couple assume some variant of this position. See, for instance, Stansell, *American Moderns*, 261; DeBoer-Longworthy, *Modern World*; Simmons, *Making Marriage Modern*; Ellen Kay Trimberger, "The New Woman and the New Sexuality: Conflict and Contradiction in the Writings and Lives of Mabel Dodge and Neith Boyce," in *1915, the Cultural Moment*, ed. Heller and Rudnick, 98-111; and Levin, *Bohemia in America*, 369-71. Wetzsteon sees Hapgood and Boyce as negotiating a new form of marriage which was saved by conflict, but mischaracterizes Hapgood as unable to understand Boyce's need to write (*Republic of Dreams* 181-92). In the introduction to *Intimate Warriors*, Trimberger provides a more nuanced interpretation, but the volume as a whole has perpetuated the concentration on adultery because of the correspondence she selected to print. The only exception to this trend of which I am aware is Marcaccio, who describes Hapgood as "a monogamist who experimented, [but] he loved only Neith" (*Hapgoods*, 159).

7. On "varietism," including its philosophical basis, see also Chapter 4.

The connections branching out from a single one of Hapgood's Village intimacies illustrate the complex allegiances within this subculture. Hapgood had an affair with actress Mary Pyne, who died young of tuberculosis. Pyne was married to Harry Kemp, the one-time protégée of Upton Sinclair and whose affair with Sinclair's wife Meta led to their breakup (see Chapter 3). In Theodore Dreiser's sketch "Esther Norn," which is based on Pyne, he depicts Kemp as part genius, part clown, but mostly charlatan, and Hapgood as a Svengali. Hapgood, in turn, never forgave Dreiser for suggesting in "Esther Norn" that Hapgood's *Story of a Lover* was inspired by his relationship with Pyne, not Boyce. To Hapgood, this misattribution constituted Dreiser's "special ignominy" (*Victorian*, 430)—and Hapgood had plenty of other complaints, most dramatically voiced in his well-publicized charges of Dreiser's anti-Semitism.

The second inaugural production of the Provincetown Players was Susan Glaspell and George Cram Cook's *Suppressed Desires*, a comic look at the impact of psychoanalysis on a marriage. The Players, rechristened as the Playwright's Theatre in New York, performed ninety-three plays, including one by Dreiser and another by Kemp. Hapgood described the Players as "men and women who were really more free in all ways than many elements of Greenwich Village—free from violence and prejudice, either radical or conservative." Hapgood also identified the Players' beliefs in terms very similar to my definition of progressive reform—specifically that in expressing the truths of their own lives, "a step might be taken in the solution of our bigger social problems" (*Victorian*, 393).

Of the various genres in which Boyce wrote, her drama has received the most attention, although even then she gets overshadowed by more familiar Provincetown luminaries. Brenda Murphy provides the most extended treatment of Boyce's drama in *The Provincetown Players and the Culture of Modernity* (Cambridge, UK: Cambridge University Press, 2005). See also Ozieblo, "Introduction"; Cheryl Black, *The Women of Provincetown, 1915-1922* (Tuscaloosa, AL: University of Alabama Press, 2002); Kornelia Tancheva, "'I Do Not Participate in Liberations': Female Dramatic and Theatrical Modernism in the 1910s and 1920s," *Unmanning Modernism: Gendered Re-Readings*, eds. Elizabeth Jane Harrison and Shirley Peterson (Knoxville, TN: University of Tennessee Press, 1997), 153-67; Nicholas F. Radel, "Provincetown Plays: Women Writers and O'Neill's American Intertext," *Essays in Theatre* (9:1), 31-41; Arnold Goldman, "The Culture of the Provincetown Players," *Journal of American Studies* 12:3 (December 1978): 291-310.

8. Hutchins Hapgood, *The Story of a Lover* (New York: Boni and Liveright, 1919), 137, 138. Subsequent references will be made parenthetically.

9. Miller, *Making Love Modern*, 38; Floyd Dell quoted in Miller, *Making Love Modern*, 23;

Neith Boyce, *The Bond* (New York: Duffield & Co., 1908), 190, 191, 398. Subsequent references will be made parenthetically.

10. Shari Benstock in the afterword to *Intimate Warriors*, ed. Trimberger, 241.

11. Fink, *Progressive Intellectuals*, 147.

For discussion about entwining work and heterosexual romance as the goal of feminists from the 1890s through the 1910s, see Stansell, *American Moderns*, and Benstock, Afterword, 253.

12. Hutchins Hapgood to Neith Boyce (hereafter HH to NB), HFP, Box 11, Folder 347, "Sunday morning" [1897 or 8?]; HH to NB, HFP, Box 11, Folder 352, Thursday p.m. [1899]; HH to NB, HFP Box 11, Folder 353, Monday night [1899]; NB to HH, HFP, undated [catalogued as 1898 but more likely 1899], Box 18, Folder 488.

13. Hutchins Hapgood, "Learning and Marriage," unsigned news article, no date or citation information given, HFP, Box 27, Folder 740 (the article was likely written in response to Thomas's widely cited statement in May 1904); Hapgood quoted in Marcaccio, *Hapgoods*, 154.

14. Neith Boyce, *Harry* (New York: Thomas Seltzer, 1923), 44; Boyce, "Autobiography," 169; Neith Boyce, "The Bachelor Girl," *Vogue* 11:29 (May 19, 1898), 322; Neith Boyce, "The Bachelor Girl," *Vogue* 12:1 (July 7, 1898), 6; Neith Boyce, *Winter's Night*, in *Fifty More Contemporary One-Act Plays*, ed. Frank Shay (New York: D. Appleton and Co., 1928), 79–85.

15. For example, in *The Eternal* Spring (New York: Fox, Duffield & Co., 1906), a young female pianist is pursued by an older man; in *The Forerunner* (New York: Fox, Duffield & Co., 1903), a wife separates from her husband, hoping to resume the singing he forced her to abandon (and to pursue an ill-advised affair). "The Artist" features a young woman who marries an egoistic sculptor in order to subsidize his work in Rome (typescript, HFP, Box 40, Folder 1196). "The Careful Lover" has for its narrator an art critic who takes up with a Midwestern couple living in Paris (typescript, HFP, Box 40, Folder 1207). And in "Man Proposes," an attorney seeking a traditionally feminine wife ends up falling in love with an unconventional woman when he sees her practice a dance for vaudeville (HFP, Box 41, Folder 1281).

16. Edith Ellis, "Semi-Detached Marriage"; Havelock Ellis discusses his wife's view that separation enhances marital intimacy in *My Life*, 305.

17. In *Hapgoods*, Marcaccio categorizes Hapgood's urban writings in two phases: initially ghetto and bowery subjects and then, in the prewar period, shifting to more politicized portrayals of "labor, radicals, and Greenwich Village" (141). In *Slumming in New York: From the Waterfront to Mythic Harlem* (Urbana: University of Illinois Press, 2007), 2, Robert M. Dowling analyzes Hapgood's urban ethnographies as "outsider narratives" that undermine the patronizing tone of such works as Jacob Riis's *How the Other Half Lives* (1890).

18. Key, *Love and Marriage*, 153, 151.

19. DeBoer-Longworthy, 7; Key, *Love and Marriage*, 152.

20. Boyce, "Autobiography," 177, 195.

21. Neith Boyce, *Proud Lady* (New York: Knopf, 1923), 133, 291–92.

"Ambrotype" also differentiates between the (lesser) form and (greater) substance of marriage. This story centers on an elderly and once-beautiful woman who lived and died for a dubious "principle." As a young woman, she had refused the hand of the man she loved (and who loved her) because he was already engaged. The other woman does not give the man up, and so all three sacrifice, to use the terms of *Proud Lady*, the "substance" of marriage to its "form" (Neith Boyce, "Ambrotype," HFP, Box 39, Folder 1192).

22. In *Story of a Lover*, Hapgood contrasts "her conventional disapproval of my acts" with "her deeper infidelity of thought and feeling" (193). In a letter to his wife, Hapgood describes himself as a "spiritual monogamist" (HH to NB, "Later, Saturday night" [1915], HFP, Box 13, Folder 377).

23. Carpenter, *Love's*, 102, 104.

24. Oatley, *Best-Laid*, 67.

25. Ellis, *Eonism*, 522.

26. Hapgood, *Victorian*, 381; Hapgood, *Story*, 190.

27. Hapgood, *Victorian*, 410.

Bentley (1870-1957) received a PhD in sociology from Johns Hopkins. He later collaborated with John Dewey and introduced the idea of interest groups, most notably through his book *The Process of Government* (1908) (De Boer-Langworthy, 18; Trimberger, 237; Sidney Ratner, "Arthur F. Bentley, 1870-1957," *Journal of Philosophy* 55:14 [July 3, 1958], 73-78).

28. Boyce, *Harry*, 67.

Hapgood described himself as an anarchist, although he was not an overtly political figure. As Marcaccio explains, what Hapgood meant was "not anarchism, but restlessness, individualism, and an inability to subsume himself to a group's or a party's outlook." Rather than politics, Marcaccio explains, Hapgood was interested in what he considered "deeper things," such as philosophy and the spirit (148, 153). Brenda Murphy, who usefully discusses the relationship of Hapgood's anarchism to modernism, adds that many self-described anarchists in his day, unlike later iterations, believed in gradual change (*Provincetown Players*, 31-34). In *Anarchist Modernism: Art, Politics, and the First American Avant-Garde* (Chicago: University of Chicago Press, 2001), especially 30-38 and 41-43, Allan Antliff discusses the influence of Hapgood's anarchistic art writings on the development of American modernism. Hapgood's *An Anarchist Woman* (New York: Duffield & Company, 1909) sheds light on its author's interest in anarchism, distinguishing between anarchism in Europe ("mainly political") and in America ("mainly sexual"), 46. In the later memoir *Victorian*, Hapgood redefines himself as a liberal (203; cf. 278).

29. Hapgood, *Victorian*, 70.

In 1914, Boyce published a brief article in *Life* titled "Feminism." The article has little to do with women's rights—but it does synthesize key points in the progressive critique of marriage. Boyce laments what modern man has lost: his "gaudy dress" and "glancing plumage" has been taken from him and given to his wife (Gilman); having lost his "conspicuous leisure," man now must work to support his wife (Veblen); but "Woman is beginning to realize her loss, more consciously than Man," and is crying out, "'Give us back our work!'" (Schreiner).

See the introduction, note 3, on the dating of the term *feminism*.

30. HH to NB, Saturday, February 16, [1907], HFP, Box 12, Folder; NB to HH, HFP, Wed. [1907], HFP, Box 19, Folder 501. The couple (particularly Boyce) was negligent about dating their letters. Hers cited here has mistakenly been catalogued as January 1907, but it clearly responds to Hapgood's, which he dated February 16, 1907.

31. HH to NB, HFP, Box 12, Folder 366 [undated, but internal evidence suggests around 15 February 15, 1907]).

32. HH to NB, HFP, Box 12 Folder 367, February, 28, 1907; NB to HH, HFP, Wed [1907], Box 19, Folder 501.

33. Lincoln Steffens quoted in Miriam Hapgood DeWitt, *Taos: A Memory* (Albuquerque: University of New Mexico Press, 1992), 19; Dewitt, *Taos*, xiv; Hutchins Hapgood, "The Suffrage and Pretty Girls," unsigned article, clipping in HFP, undated and without title of journal, Box 27, Folder 802; Hutchins Hapgood, "The New Bohemia," HFP, Box 28, Folder 864.

In *Bohemia in America*, Joanna Levin dates the latter manuscript as 1913. It seems fair to say that Hapgood's views about feminism grew more conservative as he aged, much as Dell's *Love in the Machine Age* retracts his earlier feminist views.

For additional pro-suffrage writings, see also his account of Marie Jenney Howe, "a good example of the woman who is 'new' without losing the charm of the 'old'" ("A Woman Suffrage Politician," signed article, undated and without title of journal, clipping in HFP, Box 28, Folder 825); "Mrs. Pankhurst and Fanaticism," signed article, undated and without title of journal, clipping in HPF, Box 27, Folder 755.

34. Hapgood, "The New Bohemia."

35. See, for instance, Stansell, *American Moderns*, 275; Trimberger, "Introduction," 11-13; Trimberger, "New Woman," 104-108; and Miller, *Making Marriage Modern*, 47-50.

36. Trimberger admits "Neith's and Hutchins's deviations from norms of gendered personality—her autonomy and his emotional openness," but concludes that notwithstanding their "androgynous personalities, their writings document the tenacity of gender norms" (Introduction to *Intimate Warriors* 17-18).

37. Carpenter, *Love's*, 94.

38. Jessica Benjamin, *Shadow of the Other: Intersubjectivity and Gender in Psychoanalysis* (New York: Routledge, 1998), xiii, xviii.

39. Benjamin, *Shadow*, 79.

40. Oatley, *Best-Laid*, 253.

41. Stansell, *American Moderns*, 306.

42. HH to NB, June 22, 1919, HFP, Box 13 Folder 381; HH to NB, November 19, 1929, HFP, Box 13 Folder 389.

43. Edith Ellis, "Havelock Ellis," *The Bookman, A Review of Books and Life* 47:5 (July 1918), 564; Havelock Ellis, *Sex in Relation*, 539; Hutchins Hapgood, "Mother's Love," signed news article, clipping in HFP, Box 27, Folder 756 [no date or source given].

44. Hapgood, *Victorian*, 410.

Hapgood's reference in 1915 to "our book" seems to have *Story* (written but as yet unpublished) in mind (NB to HH, HFP, Box 19, Folder 506 Tuesday [1915]). Many years later Boyce referred to *A Victorian in the Modern World*, which he had dictated to her, as "my (*our*) book)" [sic] (NB to HH, HFP Box 13, Folder 394, 20 September 1939).

45. Boyce quoted in Benstock, 248.

46. Benjamin, *Shadow*, 24.

47. NB to HH, Monday [1912], HFP, Box 19, Folder 505.

48. Neith Boyce and Hutchins Hapgood, *Enemies*, in *Intimate Warriors*, ed. Trimberger 190, 193.

49. Ibid., 192, 191, 194, 195.

50. Hutchins Hapgood, "Love," signed news article in clipping file, undated, HFP, Box 27, Folder 745.

51. HH to NB, March 21, 1911, HFP, Box 12, Folder 372.

52. Ellis, *Eonism*, 528; Ellis, *Sex in Relation*, 491, 492; Ellis, *Eonism*, 528, 529.

53. Hapgood, *Victorian*, 430.

54. Carpenter, *Love's*, 92, 102-103.

55. NB to HH, Sunday [Fall 1905], HFP, Box 19, Folder 498.

56. See *Intimate Warriors*, ed. Trimberger, 227-28. Boyce explains that Hapgood's infidelities from early in their marriage caused her to withdraw emotionally and that his "long-continued secret relations" particularly hurt her. She proposes a "*real marriage*" based on "absolute mutual fidelity in every way, physical, spiritual—everything else" as the only way for them to be truly happy. Yet even in this letter, Boyce admits the contingency of her request: "This is my side of it—I know your side too—my failings toward you—and that's why I've never *blamed* you—why I really have no resentment."

57. Thursday [1915], HFP, Box 13 Folder 376; Neith Boyce to Mabel Dodge Luhan, Monday, no date, HFP, BOX 6, Folder 156; Neith Boyce to "Dearest Mabel," Thursday, no date, HFP, BOX 6, Folder 156; Neith Boyce to Mabel Dodge Luhan, Monday, no date, HFP, Box 6, Folder 156.

58. Charles [Hapgood] to "Dear Mother" [Neith Boyce], HFP, Box 6, Folder 156.

59. Trimberger finds the play "clarify[ing] Neith's position" on adultery (22), and, in "New Woman," provides an extended comparison of Boyce and Dodge. Miriam Hapgood DeWitt confirms that *Constancy* draws on Boyce's marriage as well as Dodge's relationship with Reed (*Taos*, viii).

60. Neith Boyce, *Constancy: A Dialogue. The Provincetown Players: A Choice of the Shorter Works*, ed. Barbara Ozieblo (Sheffield, UK: Sheffield Academic Press, 1994), 59, 61.

61. Hutchins Hapgood to Arthur F. Bentley, June 25, 1894, HFP, Box 1, Folder 14.

62. NB to HH, December 20, [1929], HFP, Box 20, Folder 513; HH to NB, January 7, 1930, HFP, Box 13, Folder 390.

63. Ellis, *Eonism*, 521.

EPILOGUE

1. Robert J. Sternberg, "A Duplex Theory of Love." *The New Psychology of Love*, eds. Robert J. Sternberg and Karin Weis (New Haven: Yale University Press, 2006), 190–94, quotation at 190. For an earlier and fuller account, see Robert J. Sternberg, *Love Is a Story* (New York: Oxford University Press, 1998).

2. Sternberg, "Duplex," 192, 194.

3. Many historians and commentators trace parallels between the Progressive era and current events. Among them, McGerr makes an especially compelling case in *Fierce Discontent*.

4. Thiele, "Coming-of-Age," 109. I draw this publication history from Brown, Thiele, and Chushichi Tsuzuki, *Edward Carpenter*, 128–34.

5. Havelock Ellis, *My Life*, 349; Edith Ellis, "Semi-Detached Marriage," rpt. in *The New Horizon in Love and Life* (London: A. and C. Black, 1921); Weeks, "Havelock Ellis," 163; Shaw quoted in Vincent Brome, *Havelock Ellis: Philosopher of Sex* [Boston: Routledge & Paul, 1979], 101. For accounts of the English publication history and trial of *Sexual Inversion*, see Ellis, *My Life*, 347–73 and Brome, *Havelock Ellis*, 101–105.

6. Ellis, *My Life*, 319, 458. Jo-Ann Wallace, who is writing a biography of Edith Ellis, ably contextualizes her life and writing in "The Case of Edith Ellis." Wallace explains that for Edith, marriage to Havelock was "a foundational and defining relationship," and that, as "for many social reformers of her time, 'evolved' marriage provided both a model and a vehicle for social change" for her (quotations at 26). For a critical appraisal of Havelock's constructions of his wife, see White, "She Was Not Really Man at All."

7. Margot Canaday, *The Straight State: Sexuality and Citizenship in Twentieth-Century America* (Princeton: Princeton University Press, 2009). The cases are *Hollingsworth v. Perry* and *United States v. Windsor.*

The thirteen states currently recognizing gay marriage are Maine, Maryland, Connecticut, New Hampshire, Vermont, Iowa, Massachusetts, New York, California, Delaware, Minnesota, Rhode Island, and Washington (in addition to the District of Columbia and three Native American tribes).

8. Cott, *Public Vows*, 115.

9. I have more to say about the earlier model of "fault" divorce—or as it is legally called, adversarial divorce—in the chapter on the Sinclairs.

10. Fundamentalist preacher quoted in Coontz, *Marriage, A History*, 273; Thorstein Veblen, *The Theory of the Leisure Class* (New York: Modern Library, 1931), 202–03.

11. US Department of Commerce and Labor, Bureau of the Census Special Reports, *Marriage and Divorce 1867–1906* (Part I, 1909, Part II, 1908), I:16, 19. Roderick Phillips notes that conservatives often use the language of natural disaster to describe the divorce rate, frequently called "a flood, a rising tide, an avalanche" (*Putting Asunder*, xii).

12. See *http://www.youtube.com/watch?v=4AzLrn5JVIo*. The ad has been repeatedly parodied, especially effectively by Wake Up World: see http://www.shootthemessengernyc.com/index.php?/wakeupworld/a_storm_is_gathering/

13. David Popenpoe, "The Future of Marriage in America," in *The State of Our Unions. The Social Health of Marriage in America: The Future of Marriage in America* (National Marriage Project, 2007), http://www.stateofourunions.org/pdfs/SOOU2007.pdf. The 2010 edition of *The State of Our Unions* features the scare-mongering subtitle "When Marriage Disappears."

14. Ellis, *Eonism*, 523.

As Stephanie Coontz puts it, "Americans have tended to discover a crisis in family structure and standards whenever they are in the midst of major changes in socioeconomic structure and standards." Coontz, *Way We Never Were*, 257. Cf. Degler: "No social changes seem so threatening as those that take place within the family because the family has s been for so long the ultimate sanctuary of men and women" (*At Odds*, 1994).

Index

UNIVERSITY OF WINCHESTER
LIBRARY

UNIVERSITY OF WINCHESTER
LIBRARY